AESTHETICS AND THE POETIC IMAGE OF RABINDRANATH TAGORE

AESTHETICS AND THE POETIC IMAGE OF RABINDRANATH TAGORE

Dr. ASIT KUMAR DATTA
M.A. (Beng. Eng.) Ph.D.,
Sir Asutosh Mukherjee Gold Medalist

ABHIJEET PUBLICATIONS
DELHI 110094

ABHIJEET PUBLICATIONS
2/46 Tukhmeerpur Extension
Delhi 110 094
Phone: 22960492, 65698474
e-mail: abhijeet_singh@vsnl.net
abhijeet_singh@indiatimes.com
abhijeetpublication@gmail.com

AESTHETIC AND THE POETIC IMAGE OF
RABINDRANATH TAGORE

First Published 2007

ISBN 978-81-89886-21-9

PRINTED IN INDIA

Published by J.K. Singh for Abhijeet Publications, Delhi 110094, Lasertypeset by Gaurav Graphics, Delhi and Printed at Himanshu Printers, Delhi.

Foreword

Poetry takes its stand on the poetical paintings carved out by the literary artists and consequently, much emphasis has been laid on poetical image, which forms the foundation of literary art. It is for this reason that Western theoreticians try to adjudicate beauty of specimen of poetic art by analysing political paintings. The characteristic features of a successful poetical painting accordingly have been laid down by Western Aesthets, who have considered all along the painting as the basic feature of poetry. Indian theoreticians all along have been emphasising emotive content as the soul of poetic creation and apparently it seems that poetical painting is not so important in their eyes. Unfortunately, when this conclusion is drawn attention is not paid to the total theory of literary criticism projected by Indian theoreticians, particularly the theory relating to the importance of literary embellishments, which are incorporated in the structure of poetry to present a complete and unified picture of the whole theme. When all the theories projected by Indian theoreticians are taken into account in order to have a complete idea of the principles of literary criticism floated by Indian theoreticians, this becomes clear that the external texture of poetry is not unimportant to them; rather it is as important as the inner content, represented by the emotional mood. Indian literary theoreticians have not only emphasised the necessity of incorporating literary embellishments in poetry, but also have asserted that a balance is to be maintained between the charmingness of sound and the charmingness of sense, so that each will compete with one another, but none will be allowed to surpass another in point of strikingness. This concept of maintenance of balance between the charmingness of expression and the charmingness of content is expressed by the peculiar term 'Vakrokti', recognised by Kuntaka as one of the essential elements of poetry.

Thus, Indian literary theory takes a holistic view of poetry and floats the theory that the poetry is to be considered as a whole. Indian literary theory, as a matter of fact, is the first to initiate the orgasmic theory of poetry, according to which Poetry is a living organism and consequently, no part of the poetry is capable of being separated from the total structure and this is so because the different elements of poetry are not combined together first and thereafter emotive content is implanted in it; rather the emotive content in its endeavour to express itself brings into being the expression and the content, the literary embellishment and the meter, the style and the techniques, as a result of which a total indivisible poetical painting is created. Though the suggestive emotive content is implanted in it; rather the emotive content in its endeavour to express itself brings into being the expression and the content, the literary embellishment and the metre, the style and the technique, as a result of which a total invidisible poetical painting is created. Though the suggestive emotive content is emphasised times without number a the soul of poetry and critics are advised to adjudicate beauty of poetry by analysing the emotive content, equal emphasis is placed on literary embellishment and style. Though a specimen of poetic art, abounding in verbal figures, which flatters the ears is described by theoreticians as an imitation of poetry only, literary artists expend considerable energy in writing such poems in order to show their dexterity in literary craftsmanship. This indicates the double stand taken by Indian literary theory; which on the one hand profound emphasis is attached to the symbolic content, on the other hand literary craftsmanship is encouraged by the society compelling literary theoreticians to recognise poetry abounding in verbal figures as a variety of poetry. Both Indian and western theories have tried to spell out the characteristic features of a successful poetical painting, and according to both the success of the poetic image depends on its freshness and universality, as also on its competence to reflect the universe in its small compass. Indian literary theory goes a step further and asserts that a successful poetical painting is required to reflect the Infinite, so that the entire poetical exercise can conduct the man to the gateway of the Infinite. According to Indian philosophers all artistic exercises undertaken by the man are to lead him to the Infinite, which is conceived of as a conglomeration of beauty and bliss, goodness and sublimity.

All this analysis shows the difficulty in analysing poetical paintings and in adjudicating the value of the poetical image. This analysis is capable of being done by a scholar, which is initiated into the hieroglyphics of both Indian and Western Aesthetics and is mature enough to make comparative analysis of the paintings carved out by different literary artists. The problem is complicated further by the fact that the philosophy of the literary artist influences the construction of poetical paintings, to a great extent, and consequently, a thorough acquaintance with the philosophy of the particular literary artist is required to make an analysis of the paintings carved out by him. As the attitude of literary artists differ and as the philosophies professed by them differ from each other the technique of carving out poetical paintings also differ.

It is because of this difficulty involved in making analysis of poetical paintings that as yet no attempt has been made by any scholar to evaluate poetical paintings carved out by Tagore, who is regarded as one of the finest specimen of Indian literary talent. Though Tagore accepts the tenets of the Upanishads as his guiding principle and believes in the existing benign order of the universe, with the passage of time his philosophy also changes, and these changes are effected to a great extent, when he sees the agencies of Imperialism inventing new mechanisms of tyranny to oppress the downtrodden and the weaker section of the society. It is because of this that though describing in poems written in earlier years he conceives of the man as the 'child of immortality' in perfect consonance with the Upanishadic philosophy and welcomes the God in both his aspects—in constructive as also in destructive forms, in poems composed in his later years he feels uneasiness at the existing order of the universe and longs for a creation in which oppression and tyranny, exploitation and frustration will disappear and a new order will be created enabling the man to march ahead on his road to fulfilment.

It is a matter of great joy that Dr. Asit Kumar Datta has laid his hands upon the task of analysing the poetic paintings of Tagore by applying both Indian and Western yardsticks of literary evaluation. This analysis of the poetical paintings of Tagore has started with presentation of the philosophy of Tagore also. It has already been pointed out that Tagore does not project one philosophy; his literary creations rather contain projections of different philosophies, because like the great Vyasa he is a literary monster projecting different theories at different periods. Dr. Asit Kumar Datta has tried to locate the impact of Marxist philosophy on Tagore and in this respect he has differed from the traditional view that the mind of Tagore had been influenced mainly by the speculations of the Upanishads. He approaches the poetry of Tagore from this angle, and naturally becomes successful in locating certain truths, not identified before. If research is considered as a process initiated to locate new truths and identify new relations among existing truths then the documents produced by Dr. Asit Kumar Datta is capable of being regarded as one of the finest products of research, which can be considered as a guide book for all research scholars trying to work on Tagore at a later date. Dr. Asit Kumar Datta has demonstrated throughout his work his profound penetration into the secrets of Western and Indian aesthetics and his command over the techniques of analysing the fabric of poetical painting by applying scientific methodology. This document is going to be considered as a lasting contribution to Tagore studies, encouraging scholars of future times to do work in the line analysis of poetic paintings shown by Datta and I am sure it will remove a long-felt want.

I congratulate Dr. Asit Kumar Datta and welcome his book to the arena of Tagore Studies.

RAMARANJAN MUKHERJI

Prelude

It is of bare necessity to explain once again the domain of the subject matter in totality as the same has been propounded and pin-pointed by no other personality than Dr. Ramaranjan Mukherjee, the doyen of Aesthetics and poetics of the orient and the occident.

The fundamental aspects dealt in the treatise "Aesthetics and Poetic Image of Rabindranath Tagore" are out and out related to embellishment and poetical painting, the ornamental coinage, whatever be the substantive creative material of the poet's thinking, philosophy dominated by the social superstructure in context of The Indian Renaissance.

The poems that are illumined as poetry are the living image, having the words, the meaning and the juxtaposition of them, and the individual entity, its creativity that creates the lilt of the poem, by the means of which readers feel the poet's sensitivity, aesthetic experience and his poetic ecstasy.

Here is our amenable acknowledgement that we have gone through the aesthetical documents and references of eastern and western profounders that have been stated in the notes and references of the treatise. We are greatly indebted to Dr. Ramaranjan Mukherjee who has taught me to step in into the world of aesthetics and its allied school of thoughts, and Dr. Debranjan Mukhopadhyay has opened up a broadway before me to begin to study the literature of Rabindranath.

Besides, we have tried to go through the works of Rabindranath and take all help from the literary history of the authority based on the works of Rabindranath. A lot thanks should be imparted to the press and all the specialist attached with its activities.

We must admit the role of Sri Subrata Nayek who has taken all round responsibility to make my effort illumined. We cannot thank him as he has got the quality to be member of our family.

The Author

Introductory Preface

Introductory notes on the modus operandi of the revelation of poetry and its relation to the poetic image.

The study of poetic image and its principles, rudiments and fundamentals, their use, their vesture and new application on the poetry of Rabindranath, are thc main purport of our treatise.

The following items of literary analysis have been taken with much details and consummate propriety, which is very similar to French 'explication de texte'.

(1) Explanation of difficult speech of the poem of Rabindranath has been dealt with much emphasis on different and pertinent interpretation.

(2) Workmanship follows, implying originally, arrangement and presentation. The technique to be examined includes ability to select, to improve topics by ornament, to convince through schemes of thought and words, to arouse feelings and to observe proprieties. These are also utilized in our treatise vividly.

(3) The comparison with the work of other writers, their mode of expression, their technique of using rhyme, simile, metaphor has been made laying much emphasis on the distinction of Rabindranath.

(4) Above all, every item of explicability, mode of

revelation, and modus operandi of demonstration have been shown in one poetic cornet i.e. poetic image. The poet's sensibility, his experiences, his style, mode of expression all become crystalised in the poetic image, which we have seen from the very dawn of Rabindranath's poetic career down to the fag end of his life, that is marked with new outlook, pangs, and novel interpretation of life.

The exploration and the manifestation of poetic image contains the following factors.

(1) Word choice—linguistically termed as 'Lexis' includes borrowings, coinages, poeticisms, colloquialisms, compounding epithets both decorative and functional and the relative use of different parts of speech.

(2) Movement termed in linguistic metries signifies prosodic patterns and their modulations by means such as unjambement and rhythm; rhyme; and the distribution of stresses; accent and sound-texture (phonemics) including the sequence of vowels and consonants.

(3) Grammatical structure named in linguistics as Morphemics, Phrasis, syntagmata and Transformational Grammar includes phrasal and clausal syntax, word order, subordination and elaboration.

(4) Meaning—in linguistics termed as semantics—consists of levels of understanding and their relation to context, the force of metaphor, simile, personification and metonymy; the use of symbols and iconography; the currency of poetic ideas.

(5) Rhetorical devices linguistically termed as 'stylists' contains gnomic utṭerance, epigram, parallelism, repetition, climax, antithesis, contrast, hyperbole, oxymoron.

2

Now, we shall clearly state the bearing, and impact of word-choice on the poetic image. "The associations that in time acquire with states of feeling are sources of poetic ideas, abstract and concrete. The special significant names active through poetry depends on relations with other words, such as verbs and adjectives."

This association, this sort of relation creates and prepares the scope for poetic image. How does this thing happen? It may be said that all these factors create and depict a consummate portrait, wherein adjectives are among the most revealing elements of a poet's vocabulary, telltale pointers to his fertility, propriety and discipline, verbs active ideas, and provide the sinews of poetic utterances.

Movement or Metrics is the very term that incorporates a wide range of prosodic effects, that is to say, it bears the stamp of sound, pause, tempo, rhythm, and accent. Feet or units of measurement are groups of syllables ordered to express meanings simultaneously with a controlled stream of sounds; one function of sound is to stimulate emotional response in the reader. Four basic feet in English Poetry are the Iamb, Anapaest, Trochee and Daetyl. To these should be added the spondee and pyrrhic, two feet in which length is a determined factor in English. In Bengali Literature "Poyer", "Trepades", "Kalavrtta", "Swaravrtta" control the sound system and attract the response and emotion of the reader. Good poetry has a good metries, intonation, sound, accent, rhyme and intonation. In the poem "Harmony" Rabindranath cannot allow the loose, nimble metre to the compactness, the consummateness and perfectness of poetic image. The poem clearly conveys a new outlook, novel idea and completely unconventional thought to the readers, who imbibe the poet's sensibility, his experience, his outlook, the consciousness of the age-all expressed and demonstrated not in isolated or detached manner, rather everything painted in a single and spectacular canvass.

The poetic image becomes spectacular, vividly expressed, and the readers respond to its appeal and feelings, that are conveyed through the poet's peculiar and distinguished mode of expression. And the poetic image is palpably grasped; it has colour, flavour, hue and character. These aspects depend mainly and universally on the grammatical structure. Many writers regard syntax as the basic of the poet's art. The following dictum has a pertinent bearing on the purport of our view-point. "In poetic language, which keeps as close as possible to the experiential flow, the meaning of a word is in each instance determined partly by the specific context of words, rhythms, images, mythological allusions, etc. in which it occurs. Shakespeare is a gold mine of examples: his ability to control meanings contextually is unsurpassed.

The recognition of an evocative quality is co-present everywhere in genuine poetry along with whatever specific denotations the poem may carry suggests a further distinctions between the literal and poetic uses of language, i.e. between monosign and plursign. It may be stated thus: the monosign is purely referential, the plurisign is to some degree what it means, what it refers to, its refined, is something distinct from itself. This is proved and illustrated by the familier fact that a monosign is exactly translatable.... The plurisign, on the other hand, while never entirely lacking in referential function, is at the same time semantically reflexive in the sense that it is a part of what it means. That is to say, the plurisign, the poetic symbol is not merely employed but enjoyed; its value is not entirely instrumental but largely aesthetic-intrinsic."

A poetic statement differs from a literal statement not, as Dr Richards thinks, in that the one has a merely subjective, the other an objective references, at least this is an unnecessary and generally irrelevant difference—but in their manner of asserting. There are differences of what may be called assertive weight. A literal statement asserts heavily : it can do so because its terms are solid. A poetic statement on other hand, consisting as it does in a conjunction or association of plurisigns has no such solid foundation, and affirms with varying degrees of lightness.

It is poetry because of its varying degrees of lightness, of its peculiar expressebility, mode of articulation, association with compactness, consummetness and perfectness. We have seen through the different chapters a 'cover-term' for a variety of poetic phenomena, embellished with metaphors, symbols associated ideas, different and divergent rhythm, metres congenial to impart some hue on the poetic atmosphere.

3

Inspite of all these variations, divergences and ingredients, one palpable and spectacular thing, one luminous object becomes obvious and pointed that readers and connoisseurs see a picture or aesthetic cornet when they for the first time read through a poem. It is not the syntax, not the association of ideas, not aesthetic experience, peculiar mode of expression, varying degrees of lightness that first strike the readers, or their grandeur, majestic way of expression that attracts the lilt of the readers, inherent song; but a sum-total experiences, a consummate presentation, consummate expression crystalised in the poetic image. The readers see things, objects that have no real entity, but they are similitude of things, that appears as fresh and tender, bright as the real and the practical one.

We through the different chapters such as poetic image and universalisation, symbolization want to make the impression effective and evocative that all qualities and qualification of good poetry are fundamental and rudimental, because they have a pertinent and consistent bearing on the poetic image. The poetic experience, his mode of thinking, his socio-economic apprehension, the impact of the said condition are all contents in the container of the poetic image.

Through the six Chapters we have observed meticulous details of the poetic image in the poetry of Rabindranath. In the meticulous and consummate descriptive sketch of the poetic image of Rabindranath we have touched all the factors and items such as his experience, his reaction on socio-economic condition, his keen perceptibility, his acute sensibility, his peculiar mode of expression, that differs from that of the proceeding poets. Everything, that is focused in the poem is presented and produced in the beautiful, perfect poetic image. We have studied his poetic image, classified it, expressed or put it in different and divergent assortment, imbibed its colour, fragrance and seen its multi-coloured waves. From the very dawn of his poetic career down to the last poem, wherein, Rabindranath states to have failed to be acquainted with her (Jibandebata) who engulfs him with varied net-work of deception. Rabindranath had been creating so many, so varied, so multiformed poetic images, everyone of which is distinguished, marked bright in peculiarity of expression, imagination, evocativeness and perfectness, that can never be dreamt of even by a master or poet laureate.

In the first three Chapters wẹ have seen poetry from its different and divergent aspects stressing mainly on the importance and propriety of poetic radical feature are put into for analytical estimate of the image and the principles and guidelines that are drawn from the general discussion and analysis of poetry; and its ingredients, its component aspects have been applied to have a consummate picture of the poetic image of the poetry of Rabindranath Tagore.

In the fourth chapter detailed and descriptive acquaintance of poetic image of Rabindranath has been given.

In the fifth chapter a comparative study between the poetic image of Rabindranath and that of Western and Eastern poets has been made with a view to observe and visualize the depth and originality of the image created by Rabindranath.

The sixth chapter is considered as adorning or embellishing new phase, new outlook. We have shown first the rudiments and principles of literary criticism and secondly, a critical and analytical estimate of the poetic image with a consistent conclusion that the former and the latter interpretation and explanation are to a great extent similar and at the same time identical. They have got different mode of thinking, way of analysing. But what is common to both of them is their analysis, interpretational estimate, mode of conveying the matter to the readers and connoisseurs. The critic grasps the very imaginative process of the poet. He fully understands the experience, on basis of which the critic prepares his outlook and conveys the same to the readers. He is sympathetic reader and interpreter. He is a bad critic who always finds fault with the writings of the poet. He cannot appreciate the poetic reality and his aesthetic sense, rather he wants to dissect it; he wants to look into the core of heart and finds nothing but pool of blood and chunk of flesh. But true and sympathetic critic observes his experience and treats it with much sympathy. He finds his keen sensibility, his reaction on the socio-economic condition through the poetic truth.

The analytical and critical Estimate of the poetic image denotes the same experience. It gives the total picture of the poem, the poet wants to depict through the image. Estimate of the poetic image is identical with the literary criticism because both the estimator and the critic observe the poetic experience, his mode of expression, his matter, his modus operandi, his peculiar outlook. All the qualities and ingredients are focused through the poetic image. If we analyse the poetic image we see all the qualities of the critic present in the estimate of the same.

Above all, their path of traversing is not the same. The vision of the critic is far-fetched and broad-based, but the estimate of the poetic image is limited, pointed and circumscribed. The critic may opine his own view. He has ample scope and independence. But in the spheres of poetic image it has limitation, lack of opportunity.

Lastly, we owe our heartfelt obeisance and allegiance to our predecessors and to them who have already produced a good and systematic treatise on this subject. We have inserted their names with respect in the select notes and references.

This work may be considered as the pertinent responsiveness to our heartfelt desire to compose a treatise on the poetic image of the poetry of Rabindranath; when we go through systematic work of this genre on Shakespeare and other writers, we feel ashamed of its want in our literature, specially in the poetry of Rabindranath. We cannot claim our work of its having systematic bearing and covering all the items of mature treatise; but would it be the fact that it has satisfied some sympathetic readers, our labour and tiresome work on this subject should be endowed with success and pleasant fructification.

Asit Kumar Datta

Contents

Dedication

The Man Who
Ushers New Civilization

1

Introduction

"Poetry is the communication through which words of certain experiences can be communicated in no other ways".[1]

That is to say, the poet wants to portray his experiences, his sensibilities that he has experienced, and that he has imbibed in his walks of life; so poetry is the focusing medium, the canvas of the poet's imagination and creative sensibility.

The ancient Alankrika defines thus: the poet, by means of his creative genius, creates a combination of words and meaning of the divine and delight-making element relating to inner and outer world, in the minds of the literary and sympathetic readers. This combination of words and meaning along with other ingredients makes the stock-in trade of Poetry.

It may be said in this way also that the poet creates an unique combination of words and meaning or association of the words and meanings, which conveys the poetic delight, poet's expression and aesthetic manifestation of poetic ecstasy. This is identical with Valmilki's poetic outburst or ejaculation of ecstasy, "Padabodhwoksharamatantri-laya samanwita". The ingredients of Poetry are formulated. The music of poetry is based on the harmony of the metre, consistence of words, time and tune.

Bhamaha defines as "Sabdarthau Sathitau Kavyam" poetry is the sum-total combination of words and their meaning. We may take the advice of P.V. Kane, the doyen of Indian poetics. 'True poetry is distinguished at least by three things, viz., by a certain peculiar diction, by its subject-matter and by the spirit in which it approaches the handling of its themes.'[2]

This definition is correct to its true sense. But Prof. Kane has failed to pinpoint the mode how the readers feel and sympathise with poetic experience and ecstasy with which the poet was long engrossed.

That is to say, that Prof. Kane is not so vocal about the existence of image in poetry, which is, we deem, the only medium of poetic expression, and which plays the vital role in manifestation of the meaning and communication of the purport of the poem. Croce in his famous book 'Theory on Aesthetic' harps the same tune with us in the following dictum.

"How can we really possess an intention of the geometrical begird we possess so accurate an image of it as to be able to trace it immediately upon paper or on the black-board?"

So, we see that the distinction of the poet lies in his creation of novel and audacious images. C.D. Leuis in his book "The Poetic Image" has rightly designated the image 'as the Soul of Poetry' as his (Poet's) main object. He states, 'In the present age the poet . . . seems to propose to himself as his main object and as that is the main characteristics of his art, new and striking images. We observe that, with the change of the age trends come and go, diction takes new course, metrical fashion changes; and that was taken as deeply based and unaltered goes out of recognition. But the principal use of metaphor remains the life principle of poetry, the poet's chief test and glory. As for example, the trends of the classical age differs from that of Romantic age. The form, fashion, metre have attained a great change in Romantic age; but which remains in the same luminance is the new and striking images. An analysis of the following poem makes this point more clear.

"As from fresh pasters and the dewy field
(when loaded cribs their evening banquet yield)

The lowing herds return; around them throng
With leaps and finds their late-imprisoned young
Rush to their mother with unruly joy
And echoing hills return in the tender cry."

As from fresh pasters and the dewy field (when loaded cribs their evening banquet yield) The lowing herds return; around them through with leaps and finds their late-imprisoned young rush to their mother with unruly joy and echoing hills return in the tender cry.

What is striking in the said lines is the image of the fresh pastures, 'the dewy field' loaded cribe (echoing hills and the tender cry.) If this simile were to be rendered literally, it would run thus : as calves seeing the droves of cows returning at night when they are filled with their pasturage, run skipping out to meet them, the stalls no longer detain them, but running round their dens they fill the plain with their lowings. The similitude becomes ridiculous if this were to be introduced into modern poetry. But what strikes us most is its striking images, the epigram and emotional coinage. Herbort Read is of the same opinion that 'I think, we should always be prepared to judge a poet—by the force and originality of his metaphors. Aristotle has the same money in his stock-in-trade, "The greatest thing by far is to have command of metaphor. This alone cannot be imparted by another, it is the mark of genius." So, it is of firm opinion that it is through the poetical image that the poet transplants his unmatched experience into the mind of the reader who is delighted to see his own vividly expressed in the passions of the artist.[4]

Now we may define poetry in the following dilation:

Poetry is the cluster of images or poetry is the image itself—the only broadway of expressing emotion and the aesthetic experience of the poet, containing in itself "a chain of events, set of objects, a situation and overall thought, feeling, expression, action and character, which are controlled by the superb imagination of the artists, that respects the similitude of things and brings into a being a perfect and complete image."

To speak the truth more clearly, 'Poetry is the brilliant expression of the poetic feeling, which is more or less shared by all the world, and it is through the poetical image that the poet transplants his unmatched experience into the mind of the reader, who is delighted to see his own passions in the passion of the artist. Poetic feeling expressed is to a greater extent with the poetic experience. The poet experiences some sort of feeling being acquainted with the object, the source of his experience, and takes the raw material to mould and invest with new colour and form of his imagination. The experience which comes to the poet as a material-feeling for the first time is expressed in new form, in new vesture. The poet does not portray a single or isolated picture, rather a world of pictures. The reader or the connoisseur is presented not a iota of feeling, nor a detached idea of poetic feeling or experience, rather sum-total of the poetic sensibilities, and what he thought and experienced.

So, when we read poetry, various forms or ingredients of poetry become revealed to us. We feel with him his feeling, his thought, his experience. These are predominant in the poetry. But what distinguishes poetry from other literary form is its own way of expression, its diction, its metre. Every form of literature has got its own way of expression, revelation and manifestation.

Every one is luminant. But, poetry is different and distinguished from other form of literature in diction, metre, in its peculiar and succinct form of expression, that is not meticulous in description. As for example,

> "Beauty is truth, truth beauty
> That is all, ye know on earth
> And all ye need to know."[5]

Poetry expresses the nature of beauty and that of truth making them identical with each other. The form expressed is metaphoric and succinct. The peculiar picture, the outburst of ecstasy, the calm, deep experience is contained in the form manifested in simile and cadent expression.

We observe that whichever the thing the poet presents to the readers and connoisseur, he simply paints a portrait with the words, his sensibility, his emotion being the dominating factors in painting the portrait, of which expression is a vital element. "Poetical image is created with the help of expression, or in other words a poetical image is a picture made out of words."[6]

The expression of the poetic sensibility or poetic experience is to a greater extent influenced by the general regulation of the science of language. Supposing, a poet speaks of the touch "so exquisitely poured through the whole body, with a languid will perform its functions"; here it is clearly the sense of temperature that is uppermost in Wordsworth's mind when he speaks of touch. Words, Wordsworth speaks of the similitude of touch, not a real touch. But readers experience the same sensibility, the same emotion as the poet himself feels. The genre through which the poet presents himself is through expression and that also is testified to by the common experience of the human being. So, "it is also an undeniable fact that whatever passes current in our thought is determined by an articulate verbal form. It is apparent that the creation of image is constituted not only of the poetic sensibility, his experience, his way of using the metre, diction, but of the pragmatic significance of the expression also."[7]

"The permanent position enjoyed by the expression – element in the system of grammar is traceable in the science of literary, criticism as well, which analyses the importance of expression competent to transfer the unrivalled experience of the poet into the mind of the appreciator."[8]

To make it more clearly, we may say that in the creation of image the expression-element plays a vital role. Poetic sensibility and emotion possess a good deal of importance and significance, because of the fact that that poetry is poetry in its peculiar form and embellishment, without which, and if it is bereft of the existence of the said ingredients, it will cease as poetry, and will be enmeshed in the quagmire of nothingness. So, the definition runs as this.

"Poetry is a peculiar type of expression possessed of the literary excellence and the poetic figure, and capable of bringing the emotive content into comprehension."[9]

This particular type of expression contains the expression-element of the system of grammar. Dandin, the author of 'Kavya-Darsha'—describes the word-element as the highest luminosity, which through its absence makes the universe blinded by darkness and through presence makes the world worth-living; and describes the texture of poetry as one constituted of the expression competent to bring the charming content into light.

So, poetry is identified with expression itself.

Jaganath also in definition of poetry enunciates the diction in which language-element receives permanent importance, but still the importance of contact-element is recognized. Literary critic also cannot deny the position of expression as the vehicle of communication in poetry and it is through the medium of expression also that the idea of the poet sharing the feelings of the original personage is communicated to the reader.[10]

The poet, then is a man endowed with a more than usual capacity to percieve and to feel and to revive his perception and feelings in the absence of their object : to be a great poet, let us add, he must have thought long and deeply. In all this he differs from his fellow-men only in degree, all men are able to perceive, feel and think in same measure and many are able even to imagine.

> "Oh! many are the poets that are sown
> By Nature, men endowed with highest gift
> The vision and the faculty divine
> Yet wanting the accomplishment of verse.

It is this last figure, the accomplishment of verse that distinguishes the articulate poet from other makes even from other poetic nature. The poet can communicate his experience and communicate them in such a way as to give pleasure. " What the said critic means to say is this that the poet presents his perception, experiences and poetic feelings which do not differ very widely from that of the laymen, but the difference between them lies in the artistic creativity of the poet and the laymen. Laymen lack in the faculty of "the accomplishment of verse."

The readers appreciate the accomplishment of verse presented to them along with the similitude of things, the image of objects, seen by the poet. The accomplishment of verse is of no value, if it does not accompany the poetic emotion, sensibility in the contents of the poetic image itself. The said critic further says that "poetry is not a mere entertainment, a diversion for a Patron's idle hours. It is the breath and finer spirit of all knowledge, the impassioned expression that is in the countenance of all sciences."

All these qualified evaluation pinpoints our question as to what sorts of presentation or what quantum of objects are placed before the readers by the poet or what the readers do seek in course of their study of poetry?

A systematic search in the works of Rabindranath is our present 'treatise'. We come to our point.

Mr. De la Mare also speaks in the same vein.

"Burdened with complexity of the lives we had fretting over appearances, netted in with anxieties and apprehensions, half smothered in drift tiped thoughts and tiped feelings, we may refuse what poetry has to give; but under its influence serenity returns to the troubled mind, the world's crumbled loneliness shines like flowers after rain, and the further reality is once more charged with mystery."[11]

What he means to say is this that some sort of calmness, tranquillity are infused by the poet in the mind of the readers burdened with complexity, smothered with anxieties and apprehensions. In his dictum he clearly states the poet's role. But he fails to point out what the objective-relative is presented to the readers. The readers get the very image of what the poet experiences. This feeling, this appreciation is wanting in the mind of Mr. De La Mare. He also fails to point out that the aspects of all pervasive ideas are "related to the root idea that the substance of poetry is the image and resonances".[12]

Now, we come to the point of considering the major structure of poetry. In poetry we observe different ingredients, divergent aspect and formal contents. In classical poetic theory (by classical I mean here one that prevailed generally from the Greeks till some time in the Nineteenth Century) this order of poetry is an order of events or thoughts. Events are capable of casual connection, thoughts of logical connection; the one is the structure of narrative or dramatic poetry, the other of philosophic or reflective poetry. To get it vividly and widely, we have to take all the credit and debit side of the structure of poetry. First comes the syntax, of events, and syntax of thoughts. The linguistic, phonetic aspects are of no little value. These are the primal basic and fundamental starts, on which the entire world of poetry depends. The order of events and the order of thoughts come simultaneously. The metre, the rhythm, the lilt have their distinguished role to play. These are the ingredients of poetry.

One cannot claim poetry as poetry if it is divested of its relative structure or its peculiar order of events and thoughts. It is poetry because of its expression, its mode of thinking, its genre of concentrating on one intense impression. Its pattern is made by simple juxtaposition, but this simplicity differs from that of other form of literature.

The ingredients are peculiar no doubt. But we cannot but feel the importance.

First, we look at the organization of the "waste land". The opening twenty lines of the poem can be seen as an elliptical narrative, with fragments of reflection and direct speech a poem about frustration, aridity, fear and the perversions of love. The ingredients create the base of poetry, but what really makes the poem a totality, that is image, which is allied with structure, the order, the experience of the poet, and his emotion and aesthetic feelings, which play a dominant role in the creation. We can cite an example from on Indian alankarika, Vamana, the chief protagonist of the Riti school. He begins his *Kavyalankara Sutra* "with the most significant aphorism—"Kavyam Grahyam-lankarat", where he lays tremendous stress on the term Alankara. According to him, poetry under consideration applies to the sabda and the artha sound, and sense beautified by Guna and Alankara. Bhamaha also has the same money towards the conception of the definitions of poetry. He stresses on the combination of sabda and artha. But Vamana on the element of Guna and Manhara. Vamana agrees with Bhamaha and Dandin in accepting the Alankara on the fundamental principle of embellishment. The Alankara that plays a vital role in a poetic creation is to be taken—not in its ordinary sense of a poetic figure, but in a special sense of poetic beauty in general."[13]

It is obvious from the role of alankara that it adds extra quality to the poetic truth. It has got the qualification to beautify the vestures of poetry. It is identical with ornaments of woman. It simply embellishes her or it adds some degree of beauty to her original beauty. The ornaments are of no use or value to her ugliness.

Anandabardhana, the greatest exponent of Dhani Theory lays emphasis on Dhani or suggestion. Neither Alankara nor Riti or Vyakrakti is the soul of poetry. Rather all-important suggested content, according to him, is the soul of poetry, 'Dhvani-Vastudhvani', Alankaradhvani and Rasa Dhvani. Anandabardhana lays much importance on Rasadhvani, which, he says constitutes the essence of poetry. To him essence of poetry is neither the expression nor the expressed contents. What imparts charm to the Sahrdayas or Sympathetic Readers and connoisseurs is the suggested content, otherwise called Dhvani, which is of supreme importance in poetry and the expressed content is the basic stratum, on which all-important suggested content is based. Although there are three types of suggestion—Rasa Dhvani is dominant over other two Vyanjona. It is the Rasa, that subdues the contradictions between other two and constitutes the soul of poetry. The Rasa Dhvani, according to him, is the Dhvani par excellence, since Vastu Dhvani and the Alankara Dhvani may occasionally be conveyed through the function of Abhida as well. To him Alankara like Upama, Rupaka are simply the creator of embellishment. They serve to augment the beauty of emotional mood in poetry and attain the status of Alankara. But he prefers Dhvani to Alankara. Still so, the structure, form and good physique of Alankara help to enhance the suggestive content of poetry. Alankara, rather is identical with expressive element of poetry.

But we are of opinion that Anandabardhana through his theory of suggestion helps us to a greater extent to imbibe the quintessence of poetry. Rasa Dhvani is the very element of poetry, nothing else. It is based on the expression or expressed content and that is the outcome of his emotion sentiments, consciousness and manifestation of his experience. It is the totality which is related to consciousness and manifestation of his experience. It is the totality which he assures, constitutes the very soul of image.

It is not simply the combination of words and meaning,

rather it is the total output of poet's emotive experience, his sentiments, his poetic idea of life and the world that may be philosophical, material and egoistical.

Another school of criticism opines that neither Dhvani, Upama, Alankara Guna, Riti constitutes the fundamental aspects of poetry. Vakrakti indeed, whose chief protagonist exponent is Kuntaka, is the vital force of poetry. Bhamaha gives his distinguished coin to the same by his dictum that Vyakrakti is the "highest means of embellishment and consequently as the universal element in all the poetic experiences." Kuntaka conceives of vyakrakti as the decorative principle of the expression and its content. It is the poet's originality and ingenuity which helps to augment and sharpen the strikingness of expression. It is the extra quality that has been added to the school of Vyakrakti by Kuntaka. Vyakrakti, strikingness is a peculiar mode of expression or it is the Visesa (special) aspect of expression. Poetic expression will be devoid of life inspite of its being endowed with Alankara and Guna, if their excellences are not peculiarly designed by striking expression i.e. vyakrakti, so, it is firmly stated that "thus since this Vyakrakti is an act of the poet's imagination, the visesa according to kuntaka, is the peculiar way or the work of poetic genius and not the attribute of the external expression or of the inward content."[14]

We admit of the importance of the strikingness of expression. It is the peculiar trend of expressing the elements of poetry. The combination of words and meaning sometimes lose their edge and keenness. The Abidha and Lakshana being repeatedly used become devoid of its original sharpness, Vyakrakti replenishes new blood to the dull expression. So, we admit of its importance and utility. But it is not the soul of poetry. It is one of the ingredients of poetry. If the subject matter, emotive experience and sensibility cannot cross the periphery of dullness and insipidness, Vyakrakti or the strikingness will carry only the dead body of poetry. Hence strikingness is of no avail. We are of opinion that strikingness may be considered as one of the original factors in constituting the soul of poetry. We may consider it in the sphere of image also. The striking and novel expression creates the groundwork of image and the striking image constitutes the soul of poetry.

Ksemendra, the reputed author of *Auchityavicaracarcha* propounds the theory of Visesa in his own way. According to him "Aucityam Rasasidhasya Sthiram Kavyasya Jivitam". Rasa or the supreme aesthetic enjoyment is the final point, and that also is determined by the element of poetry, that is auchitya or propriety. The propriety is the very basis, which imparts charmingness to an idea and finally becomes the very life of Rasa. Alankara, to him, plays simply a decorative role and Guna is merely a quality which can augment the limit of its periphery only. But what infuses life to the expression is auchitya, not Alankara or Guna. It is, we deem, related to the fundamental basis of poetry i.e. consistency, the practicability and its reasonableness. In his attempt to define the term auchitya he says that what is suited to a certain thing is called proper or appropriate, and therefore its abstract idea is called 'Propriety or Appropriateness'. We are of opinion that Auchitya or Propriety, one of the distinguished element of Poetry, "Auchityan Rasa Sidhasya Sthiram Kavyasya Jivitam" is a simple hyperbole, because of the importance imposed on it. It is an item of the component aspects which constitutes the soul of poetry. And it adds a distinguished colour to the VIBGOYR of Poetry.

Another school of thought propounded by him in his 'Kabikantha Bharana' is the school Camatkara the Relish, or Delight, which is conceived of as the very life of the Poet as well as of poetry. poetry will become dull, insipid and devoid of grace and delight, even though it is endowed with high thought and fundamental aspect of life, it its expression, lacks charming quality or its modus operandi is given no exciting and charming exposition. So, it runs. "Kavysyatma Chamatkrtih" i.e. the soul of poetry is the camatkrti or the strikingness of nature, It may be mentioned in this connection that Jaganath also is the propounder of Camatkara that differentiates a poetic expression from the ordinary one. He extends recognition to camatkriti as constituting the Visesa of poetry.

We are agreed to the dictum that Chamatkara is related to the external elements of poetry only like Alankara and

Guna. Camatkriti is an element, which differentiates poetic expression from ordinary expression and upgrades the poetic expression from the ordinary scale of expressiveness. But whatever be the role played by the striking element of poetry, it is the poetic experience and sensibility, which is identical with the poetic image, that constitutes the soul of poetry. We admit of the importance of its being one with cardinal ingredients of poetry, but thus far and no furthcr. Because mere strikingness is no factor in the totality of poetic expression and wide impression. We should be careful of the significance and importance of the role. No such emphasis would be laid on it, so that it can mar the poetic truth and direct the readers to the quagmire of hyperbolic expression.

Now, we come to the vital portion after proper explanation as to what is poetic integrity and its relation to poetic image?

We have dealt widely and meticulously with the problems of poetic integrity in Indian poetics. No systematic mode has been adopted by them to define poetic image. But they have seen the form and vesture and pin-pointed on the outward Alkankriti, modus operandi and genre of exposition and revelation. They failed to feel how the poetic experience, Poetic sensibility become manifested through the striking images; sometimes they become identical with poetic image. That is to say, all the ingredients of poetry such as totality of emotion, sensibility, conception, metre, rhythm and the peculiar mode of expression would be isolated, detached, insipid, if a striking and consummate image would not take them on her cornet. So, decision may be drawn that image is the basis and focusing instrument of poetic truth and reality. Readers, connoisseurs feel exulted by the feeling and emotion which is nearly the same experience of the poet himself.

Now, we come to the main problem. In the very dawn of his poetic career Rabindranath creates the images, but those images are not striking, embroidery of which is not so varie-coloured and texture is not so beautiful. An example will make the point clear. (In) Deep dark night crematorium becomes awful. As if fear has laid its dark seat. Here fear is attributed to with human feeling. Transferred epithet, Samasakti intensifies—the poetic passion and transplants the image in the mind of the reader.

In the next stanza we see texture becomes close-fastened and poetic feeling has been expanded. Hence darkness is stimulated to action.

> "In the crematorium deep darkness lays herself
> Heaps of bone creep themselves amidst ashes here and there
> Streamlet glides caressing the garlands of the lovers
> Cleansing the pile of ashes, putting out the flames."

The texture of image plays a vital role being "Characterised by a gracious and picturesque style and it is this fragrant quality that has kept his work sweet and appealing and commended it to later days." So, we see image helps the readers and connoisseurs to catch hold of the general truth of poetry and feel the sensibility of the poet himself. As the image awakens the emotion lying latent in the mind of the readers, it becomes possible for them to perceive the general truth and have the same experience with the poet. And through the image it will be revealed that the feeling-element, therefore, is the supreme, controlling factor in poetry. Employment of the device of Samasakti supplies the fibre of the embroidery only, it is not dominant all over the image. It is simply a device, it can add brilliance to the poetic image. It actually remains subservient to the poetic image and poetic feeling. Here Rabindranath aptly has applied it. Even in his early works we feel and see his image-making power. Taking an example, everyone is tormented by the sunrays and all is fearless, as rain promises help. It is clearly an image, because of the fact that the elements which are treated as animate objects are attributed to with human feelings. And same annoying and battering experience of common nature have been depicted brightly catering to the practical passion of the afflicted persons. The experience is grossly portrayed. No artistic and striking expression has yet been achieved by Rabindranath in this phase.

These images are no new contribution to his image making power. In this stage freshness, intensity, suggestiveness, propriety and evocative power are absent. Some gross and common place pictures are found, as he creates a picture of Himalaya where there is utter silence, and plants and trees are reticent. In this atmosphere the sage Vyas begins to sing, and as a matter of consequence big banyan tree becomes silent having its leaves unmoved. Birds are speechless and stop moving, wind, that is as cold as dew-drops, tremulously blows, the brook flows quietly. A common picture has been depicted. But what is impressing and striking is its easiness and meticulous descriptive sketch. The practical objects and experience of the day-to-day existence are moulded into artistic things and subject matter of his poetry. We shall mention here a occurrence that is tinged with political aspects. Rabindranath wrote a poem in animadversion to the severity of the Zamindars and kings of India, who assembled to give ovation to Viceroy, Lord Lytton when India was devastated by famine. In this poem also Rabindranath creates an image which is marked with poetic feeling and his patriotism. He writes that even in this affliction they (Zamindars) are overenthusiastic to wear the golden garland. It is no audacious and striking image, but in this sort of image we get poet's unmixed feeling and unadulterated poetic experience and which (image) we are sure, is more than decorative and embroidered embellishment. In the poem Banaful (wild Flower) Rabindranath is emotive, his passions and feeling are wild; sorrow and pensiveness have become beautiful. We may refer to Keats

> "How beautiful if sorrow had not made
> Sorrow more beautiful than Beauty's self."

Rabindranath in this state has crossed that periphery of poetic device, where some sort of hyperbolic expression haunts the readers. But what we get here is 'sorrow more beautiful'. Kamala's imprecation on Bijoy, who murdered Nirod is a superb expression of sadness as well as mental wild ejaculation. Here oblivion is attributed to with human quality and elements. "Oh oblivion! Do not keep Bijoy under the quite shade of yourself." Another citation will prove of its being identical with image itself. The image of rivalry and hatred is dominated by love, which is of ideal and abstract one lying between men and women.

> "Ah! Kamala loves you much
> That makes you relationless and cruel."
> And she promises that she will replace love
> By oblivion.

Here an image has been constituted out of the common and practical feature of the earth. Still so, some sort of strikingness and animation of abstract quality is predominant in the image and there lies the difference.

In 'Bhanu Singher Padabali' Rabindranath has followed the foot-print of Viishnava Poets. The picture and portrait which he has drawn are similar to that of the Vaishnava ideals and concepts. In this sphere some sort of originality can be claimed by him. But the Juxtaposition of image is a new thing in the Bengali literature. Attraction for the Vaishnava poets is not so much as for the new and rhythmical words used in the padabali, other collection of poems. His mind is arrested by the lilt of music of Vaishnava padabali. "It is an evocation of beauty, which is both earthy and enchanting, full-blown roses, soft air, crystal streams, freshening shades and songs of fairies build up a romantic retreat." He also admits in a letter dated 20th Ashara 1317. "When I am thirteenth or fourteenth years old, since then I with much delight and desire have been reading Vishnava Padabali, its metre, language, its rhythm, emotion have beguiled me. Although I am teenaged, I have entered with inarticulate, and vague way, into their dogma of Vaishnava religion." What is of much importance is his attraction towards rhythm, language, and moving quality; but its religious side is touched by him through the media of rhythm, Rasa and metre.

In "Kabikahini" Rabindranath catches hold of the hand of Wordsworth. Like wordsworth he causes the Nature to come with her openness, vastness, quietness. Even the hero of the poem forgets the warmth of the lap of his mother, and takes recluse in to the nature. Here we see natural phenomena is the dominating feature of the image. The Golden cloud, wind's singing of wild song and dawn's smiling, (which is compared with a deity) creates a novel atmosphere. The elements used are of common nature. But attribution of human quality to nature and its peculiar manifestation give rise to the consummate and striking image. Kalidasa, Valmiki, and Banbhatta created this sort of images. But what we find in the works of Rabindranath is the texture and weaving of words lacked in Bengali literature, even in the works of the said poets. The pictorial art is found in texture of words in his poems, and in their different and divergent uses and implications that create the image, which is used by him as the canvass of painting literary truth and poetic, emotive experiences.

Another aspect is quite clear to us. That is, the readers having read the poem Kabikahini feel with the poet his emotion, his sensibility and experience. But what the poet experiences has a original form and material shape. But the readers will be given information only. It is divested of its original form and shape, rather it may be said that they will get similitude of things only. But the poetic sensibility and perceptibility is so keen and acute that similitude of things seems to them as original as anything. We are of opinion that such happens due to the striking and consummate poetic image. Sometimes readers become struck dumb at the sight that image is identical with poetic emotion and sensibility.

In "Rudrachanda" he follows the same modus operandi. The story of Chandkabi and Amiya and the story of Prithiraj are the dominating elements in Rudrachanda. Here presentation is not so beautiful as in Manashi, Chitra and later works of Rabindranath. But what is striking in these poems is the grossness, the audaciousness and poet's subjectivity. The poet Beharilal Chakraborty is the pioneer. Rabindranath in description of Mahakala Bhairab writes:

Mahakala, Embodiment of Bhairab
Oh God! Hear the prayer of devout
By wink of your eyes Annihilation occurs
The world trembles by the pressure of your feet.

Here image of boisterousness looms large in the vast sky and there Trilochan emits fire from his three eyes; in these images grossness is dominant. The poet finds an accomplishment in his fructification when lyrical elements along with pensiveness are depicted. He creates an image of a flower named Malati. She opens her eyes in the dawn of the spring and looks around. She is not mere flower, rather she is attributed to with some girl's feminine qualities. She resembles a beautiful sweet girl. We see that a flower having puberty of a young girl and poetic sensible experience has presented her on the poetic carnet. There is another portrait that Malati has been cloven from the plant and lies prostrate under the tree. Her eyes are being closed slowly and she looks around her for the last time. Both the images are striking because of the fact that Rabindranath feels with the poet, Chandkabi the sad music of his heart and feels also the exultation of the blossomed flower, and at the same time songs of separation and weeping of the flower. This is one side of the poetic truth. There is another, i.e. the readers and connoisseurs feel the whole things and appreciate the poet and his creation, the poet with all his creation sensibility and experience comes to the readers and connoisseurs through the image, it is clear to us that it is image, the striking and consummate image that reveals the whole thing, the total presentation made by the poet.

In the poem Bhangahrdaya (The Broken Heart) cluster of images are created, which are not all striking and paving new path and development. But they are all sprouted blossoms. They do not attain sweetness and fragrance. But they are paving the path and arranging preparation for the blossoms of Manashi, Chitra etc. in this phase passion, sensuality is predominant, and the image emanates accordingly.

As if a sea of heart lies in this soul
The ocean of great delight is confined in the small shell
This obstructed stream of mind rending the sky,
Wants to inundate the whole world.

Here we find an image of outburst of passion and swelling of emotion. The sound of the of 'Nirgharer Swapnabhanga' or the awakening of the fountain from the dream is heard in this poem. In this phase poet's experience is tinged with sentimentality, the outburst of passion and subjective elements. In his reminiscence (Jiban Sariti) of his life, he writes about the emotive passion of that period.

> "When I an eighteen years old I begin to write Bhagnahrdya, and the time is neither youth nor childhood. The age is at detour from which there is no scope to get the light of truth."

So, it is obvious that image in this phase is not of much importance and distinction. Rather it is similar to that of non-enthusiastic and redundant continuity ot the preceding Poets. Still so, there is fervent emotions of the poet communicated with compelling force to the reader result in the transport described by Longinus.

In 'Sandhya Sangit' images are smeared with subjective sadness, and the genre of exposition is still inarticulate and ambiguous. But metre and mode of expression is having new outlook. The confinement and periphery of mode and boundary of environment in which the poet Rabindranath was so long engaged, has fallen off. He finds his own modus operandi and his poetry has tested the new light and novel outlook. That is to state that his poetry takes a new detour and from this phase it becomes free and open from the fretters of dependence and imitation.

And he admits that in his "Jibon Smriti". He also admits the reason of his being confined in the subjective, sensible ejaculation. Still so, some of the poem written in this phase is of fundamental nature and of original sensibility touching universal aspect. Image of these Poems are dominated by pensiveness, sorrow. The poems 'Star's Suicide Disappointment of Aspiration', Deserted, Lamentation, Of Happiness, Calling on Sorrow, Unbreakable Love, Nectar and Song of Defeat, are all heavy with poetic sorrow and subjective elements.

In the image of Sandhya the poet expresses his deepest sorrow and wants consolation from her. He calls evening to come close to him who is desolate and alone, and to be enwrapped with her care of heart.

Here we feel the keen perception of the poet and his feeling with the heart bruised with the deep pain. Although its expression is confined in subjective elements, it is based on objective qualities and it is drawn to the propinquity of universal expression. In the poem "Calling on Sorrow" Rabindranath gives a profound expression to sorrow. He wants to nurture it with motherly affection, which is in the habit of sucking blood from the veins of heart. Image of this phase are heavy with pain, sorrow, deep feeling and tears. To sorrow is attributed human feelings-and passion. It plays a dominant role in poetic feeling and ecstasy. At the end of this phase, we see that the poet is struggling to have new vesture of life and novel implication. In the song of struggle, he desires to struggle with his heart. Now, he is determined to struggle with life also. It is no newer phase of life, no fundamental change, nothing of that sort. It is simply an iota of desire to go beyond the boundary of confinement. Almost all the images of Sandhya Sangit (Song of Sandhya) are the offspring of the poet's sense, sensibility and perceptibility of natural phenomena. The poet feels how Nature reacts on his mind and he observes:

> 'Oh Evening! Under the eternal sky
> Sitting alone with braidless hair
> Speaks to yourself very softly so
> Staring in the face of the world.'

The poet hears the song of the evening every day, but does not understand the meaning. The poet finds in the pictures of day-to-day existence some sort of romantic idea of far-off centuries. He feels the existence of Udashi, Prabashi i.e., of alien and exotic nature. Here we are confronted with cluster of images, which are direct and vivid emanation from the poet's subjective perception. The readers and the connoisseurs are brought to the new world, the alien and romantic world, which is peculiarly unknown to them. Some sort of eeriness is added to this Rasa of the poem. The words that originates from poet's emotive experience and which is caused to inspire the readers to feel the emotive content of the Poem constitutes the song of the image. The words are the corner stone and foundation-stone of the palace of the image. Inspite of the vital role of the words, they are different from images. Images are created by the words no doubt. But mere words are no factor to the creation of image. The figure of speech, Alankara, rhythm and all these radical factors are vital in the process of creation. But what is of foremost value is the Poetic feelings, imaginative passion and the Poetic idea of life. The image of Sandhya is luminous because it conveys the sensibility of a young beautiful woman who speaks softly, gently and sings sweetly. The Alankara personification being introduced deepens the poetic sensibility and thereby helps the poet to create striking and consummate image. The phase of Sandhya Sangit is earmarked as that of subjective confinement. The phase of Prabhat Sangit (The morning songs) is the breaking point from the preceding vision of life. So the images of this period are also manifestation of the realization and bright elevation from the previous age. The "Awakening from the Dream of the Fountain" is the very tenet of his poetic experience. It may be described as awakening of poetic genius. The happenings of the previous phase that occurred in the life of the poet as described by himself in the previous phase that occurred in the life of the poet as described by himself in the previous works are identical with the dreams. The images of this period are marked with restraintless elements. The poet (in the form of subjective 'I'.) could not restrain the effusion of sensible emission. The poems of this phase are called an emergence. The mind of the Poet was so long in the dark cave. The images of Sandhya Sangit are dominated by the poet's subjective sensibility which resembles the darkness of the cave. The images in Probhat Sangit is identical with an emergence from the dark cave of sensual confinement.

The poem, "Awakening from the Dream of the fountain" is an image itself inspite of its having cluster of images. The poet christens the awakening or emergence with the epithet" Prabhat Rabin Gan – the song of the morning sun. The images of the swelling water, the pangs of heart and its passion are all the factors of the consummate image. It may be said that the images portrayed by him are the focusing forum of his poetic experience and his feelings. So, we must not lose our point, if we are of opinion that sometimes images and feelings of the poet stand juxtaposed with each other. When the poet expresses his outburst of joy thus:

> I'll pour the shower of compassion
> The stoney jail I will break down
> Throughout the world
> I will walk
> Singing as fervent as craze-striken.

We cannot detach the poetic feeling and passion from the image. We see the poetic outburst of joy, passion and sensibility are crystalised in the poetic image. So, it is clear to us that poetic image is nothing but the attributed feelings, personified passion and sensibility, emotive intellect, intellectual emotion and imaginative passion.

In the poem 'Prabhat Ceremony' of the 'Probhat Sangit' volume the image is of free and open nature, i.e. sensual element are not so predominant. The poet finds himself in the vast world. The subjective confinement which is symbolized in dark cave doe not haunt him again. He wonders how this same morning appears to him with luminous entity. He wants to look at the sky. He enjoys the bird's chattering on the appearance of the bright light. Some sort of metre pervades everywhere. The sky is a close relative to himself. The poet desires to add extra mirth and joy to the heart of breeze. All these images are distinctive and distinguished from those of preceding phase. Personal elements are given universal nature. Subjective awareness is brightened and expanded. The Natural phenomena with all her bounteous blessing are one of the foremost factors. He requests the sun to take him in his crossing of the ocean of sky. So, we see that images of the boat compared with the morning sun leads us to perceive the sensibility of poetic rasa and poetic emotive experience.

In the poem 'Love of Rahoo' subjective effusion is dominantly portrayed. But deep sadness, dark face, tears, broken heart are all the dominant factors to constitute the image of emergence or going out from the subjective confinement.

Now, we sum up the ingredients of the poetic image found in the early poems of Rabindranath. The ingredients are as follows:-

1. The Natural Phenomena and the atmosphere of "Sandhya."
2. The words and its association with embellishment and coinage.
3. The poet's sense, emotion and keen perception.
4. Poet's desire to create a romantic picture and to present to the reader and the connoisseur.

Above all, a perfect and consummate assimilation is of absolute necessity. As perfect and meaningful coinage is necessary, so also is needful the keen perceptibility, imaginative passion, emotive contents and an unblemished love for the life and the country.

2

Image and Universalization in the Poetry of Rabindranath

In the preceding chapter the ingredients of poetry have been dealt with meticulously in contradistinction to image. We have touched on the point that neither the decorative alankaran nor the high-flown dictum of idea constitutes the soul of poetry. Rather image, to speak the truth the novel and striking image is the soul of poetry.

Now our attention is being directed to the generalization and universalisation of image. The actual fact is this the poet's sensible ejaculation is found by its limitedness. It is affluent within its periphery. The first strata of poetry is this. Here is no difference and distinction from the words and images of day-to-day usage. But on this radical foundation the generalized and universalized realization and recognition is based. Taking an example that :

The pomp and grandeur of marriage ceremony, of a girl, its delight and sun-burnt mirth is of no value and importance to the people who are not relative to her, but the marriage ceremony of Aja and Indumoti is of universal nature. It pleases both the readers Western and Eastern. Here is the distinction between them.

Indian aesthetics regards Rasa as the corner-stone of poetry and mentions the Vibhava, the Anubhava and

Vyabhicaribhava as the factor leading to attainment of poetic experience. So, it is stated that through these steps the poetic experiences of Rasa is realized. Vibhava is an alies of the expression of Karana but it is distinguished from the ordinary expression.

To say more clearly, when love of an ordinary girl is elevated and upgraded from the ordinary strata, her love, her stimulation takes the vesture of yielding the universal delight to other sympathetic readers and connoisseurs, the cause becomes Vibhava bhava. Anubhava is an idea. Vyabhicharibhava is the helping hand and component aspect of the totality of Rasa Nispattih (accomplishment).

The role of the aforesaid theory is based on impersonal aspect of poetic experience. Sakuntala to the Indian aesthetician is an impersonal entity, not an objective co-relative. The aesthetic realization signifies the impersonal and baseless idyllic nature. But what impression as a sympathetic reader we have about Sakuntala is not impersonal or impracticable, but a young girl with flesh and blood having stimulation of passion and great love for her lover is revealed to us. And this revelation is identical with the poetic image.

It may be said in another from:

> "The poetic image which extends to the readers an opportunity of seeing the entire universe before him is brought into being by the word and the meaning, the expressed and the suggested poetic figure, the main role in this matter being played by the supernormal function of suggestion. Since the poetic experience is a total and indivisible whole, the structure of poetry communicating such experience, in its turn is a totality." *Alankara and Aesthetic Realisation—A Critical View*, Ramaranjan Mukherjee

Here lies the aspect of universality. We are citing an example which shows that personal emotion and feelings are conveyed into poetic exultation and generalized. Sight of red twilight and moon-lit evening of day-to-day existence, gets the colour and hue of universalized nature. Rama expressed his profound sense of sorrow and rancour in the mind of the readers and connoisseurs. This capacity of revealing character is thus implanted in the following poetical image.

The branches laden with flowers bright
In shining luminaries while rays
In gait of tusker of superior might
Approaches autumn granting grace.
Touched by rays of shining moon
And closing in joy the starry eyes;
Crimson-red doth Evening soon
Silently leave the zone of skies
River in Autumn after rains
Doth slow and slow its banks display
Like a bright enjoying dalliance gay
Showing her things in amorous play
In face of lotus the nights
As eyes of stars do sharply twinkle:
Decked in embroidery of lunar light
Like ladies clothed in garments white.

Here Simile and Metaphor play a great role to enunciate and to make the personal experience to be universalized and extends a wide field in the image.

Upto this we rare rounding[2] about the circle of image and other ingredients of poetry and the feeble portion of poetic image of Rabindra Kavya is touched upon. The language of Kari-O-Kamal is varied, broad-based and its metre is sweet. But what is striking in poetry and for which poetry becomes endowed with universality and modernity is wanting in this phase? The poet is deeply and greatly influenced by his subjective qualities. He is within his aperture.

But whence the detour commences or new phase originates is *Manashi*? In *Manashi* he has attained perfection, that is to say, the qualities or poetic peculiarity for which we call him *Kabiguru* or poet laureate is found in abundance in *Manashi*. The characteristics of perfection in poetic Art looms large in idea, imagination, adornation and creation of portrait or image, language and manifested wavy metre. *Manashi* is the original and perfect conglomeration of all these qualities and poetic genius. In the poem "Awaking from Dream of the fountain" we have seen new detour; it is emergence or ushering from mere subjectivity, but the overflown condition and outburst of joy which emanates from the same sources i.e. subjectivity still dominates the poem. In *Manashi* we see all the qualities which are in crude form or rude qualities in preceding poems in exulted manner. But what is original and object of universality is its novel and striking image. The pre-*Manashi* creations of Rabindranath lack in perfect and striking image, for want of which we think and think it perfectly that poet's experience and sensibility could not find its medium of expression, all those ideas and poetic aspiration were bogged in the quagmire of sentiments and unproductive feelings. The poems of this Phase are luminant for the portrait of natural objects. The poet has identified himself with the flora and fauna of nature and all the objects of day-to-day existence. In his poem 'Kuhudhani' or the song of the cuckow Rabindranath has given us a varied pictures of natural objects which may be termed as galaxy of portraits by a master artists. The detached items of portraits are mingled as if they have been depicted on a single canvass in different manner. The grinding of wheat by twin sisters in the corner of the floor and their pauseless singing, raising of water by two teen-aged girls, whose faces have become dull due to hard heat, from the brick built well, river is far off in between two sides, the farmer being seated on the platform watching the field of corn are the objects of the artist. The pictures are all depicted in a single canvass, which we call image or the similitude of things, Rabindranath's creation of image is not so striking in this phase. He has followed the foot print of previous poets like Beharilal, Madhusudan Dutta etc. But the creation of galaxy of portraits or weaving the texture of various fibres or stringing of the garlands with various flowers are but new and enchanting things. The role of the song of 'Kuckoo' is vital, it pervades all over the poetry and pictures.

In the dream of death Rabindranath has shown new coinage. The transferred epithet plays vital part. The movement of Ganges in summer season specially in 'Vaisaka' is slow and feeble, because in this season the flow of water is scanty and is unable to thrust to it. It is of common place-mater of fact. But Rabindranath instills a new outlook into the old happening. The thin bodied Ganges paves her way slowly and moves with idle merry-making. Ganges is conceived of a young lady having slow-movement and who plays with her idleness. The natural phenomena is of no curious object, rather when it is thought of in a novel way and queer manner with the main purport being kept intact, it touches our imagination and gives novel spice to our dull experience.

In the poem "Exultation due to Separation" the poet was happy in the state of separation. He was there like hopeless stranger with indifference and callousness and he felt the swelling of the forests' outbursts of joy coming in contact with the gale. He prefers sadness to the mirthful condition. The exulted condition in the state of separation was like this that the lying of the poet under the shade of a tree, the mind full of separation, the memory would come with the sleep daily the pigeons coos sweetly sitting on the branches, days elapsed yielding itself in the sky, the cuckoo called his sweet heart, and heavy coldness pervaded in the dead forest. The image is constituted out of the poet's experience with the various status of mental conditions. The coinage are becoming closebound, the detached mode of expression are being closely knit. The texture of weaving is fine and bright. The subjectivity is still a predominant factor in the creation of image.

But the objective element are being given emphasis. Readers feel with the poet the sting of separation. The presentation has become lucid and it touches on the worldly phenomena. Here is the emergence from the subjective confinement. The texture of the poem, the wave of the sea is peculiarly woven. The idea lying in the context originates from the sad experience of the poet. He had seen the Pilgrims of Puri drowned in the sea with their boat. He felt that some boisterous ceremony was held. The gale bullied with an authority as if it flapped with violent stroke. The common natural occurrence are given a tremendous momentum by vesting it or endowing it with force and might. To it are attributed some animate and living qualities. The force behind the gale and waves who are annihilation-incarnate are compared with eyeless, earless, homeless and cruel, frenzied Demons. They are breaking the bondage and rushing towards death.

The image of this poem emanates from the poet's concept of the natural force and calamity. He also feels with the pilgrims who had experienced the sad and pitiful condition. On the other hand another picture that has been depicted is the portrait of Nature's power of creating calamity and disorder.

In 'Fruitless Desire' (NISPHOL KAMANA) the image of the transcendental love and beauty has been portrayed; and the atmosphere along with it the natural phenomena is enwrapped with deep sadness. The poet with wistful desire is craving for some one.

I am seeking where you are
Where are you?

The atmosphere of the poet is that the sun sets, darkness in the forest, light in the sky, evening with her eyes directed downwards in pursuing the day slowly, the breeze of the dusk is wearied with sadness-due-to departure. The poet is seeking his consort because the poet seeks:

Where is the entity?
In which nectar is kept hidden
As the luminant endless mystery of the Heaven trembles
In the sky of dark evening
Amidst the solitary galaxy
(So) The mysterious flame of the soul trembles
On the deep dark surface of that eyes.

The image of Manashi is closely related to the perceptibility of the poet.

The figure of speech Upama introduced above maintains the very tone of poems; the sensibility of the poet; the emotion is deepened by the said figure of speech. So we see this poem is a conglomeration of poetic emotion and feeling. The weaving of the image is connate with the origin of the emotion. Anandabardhana therefore, is perfectly justified in maintaining that a real literary embellishment is improvised though the same effort as is necessary for depiction of the feeling, at the same time this is incorporated after due deliberation keeping an eye on the emotive content, that constitutes the centre gravity of the specimen of Poetic Art. (*Imagery in Poetry,* Dr. R.K. Mukherjee)

A kind of sum-total consciousness emanating from sorrow, happiness, day and night, misery and good day, death and life, and from the rounding of the season is conceived by the poet as a lotus having multipetals. This consciousness has no direct connection with bodily experience. It is apparent in the beauty of the body. Rabindranath requests the lovers to love, to make love only dominant in life, but not to hanker after the lady-love in person. The soul is not the wealth of desire.

Here we see an image of the perfection of love. It has an overpowering quality. It pervades all the human existence. Evening is quiet and uproar is stopped. We can presume that profligacy in love can stretch its hand in the domain of natural phenomena. With the quietness of desired evening also is conceived of tranquillity, peacefulness.

In the 'Expressed Love' the lover wants to keep the veil and the veil is of modesty and shamefulness and it is over spread on the natural objects and living beings. The lady-love is engrossed in herself. The image of the hidden love is sacred to her. But the blooming of the blossoms, the grandeur of the rainy season, the varied movements of the clouds are all the qualities related to the "Expressed love".

But her expressed love makes her prostrate in the wide street like the cloven flowers. She leaves the glossy leaf and tender-shaded enwrapping and leads herself to the dusty ground. She becomes outstripped of the modesty and shamefulness. This fall is a unkindest out of all. It denotes her treading along the vast world alone in nude condition.

In the 'Hidden love' the contradiction of the expressed love is depicted. The dramatic monologue in the Hidden love. provides greater scope for the use of audacious metaphor and novel imagery than a lyric or a contemplative one. The poet moves through many images—images of dark cloud, the early rays of the sun, the combination of these images turn the face-value into deeper meaning. That is, coming in contact with the early rays of the sun, with the dark cloud, beauty emerges in the morning. The wild love sitting in the darkness blooms itself in the blossoms. The image of the Star's desire is to light up her heart with her own light. All these emotive experiences of the poet make us assume that the juxtaposition of the images is dominant in the exposition of the poet's feelings, sense and sensibilities.

In the poem 'Wait' Rabindranath takes a very common feature of day-to-existence of the world. The epithet 'wait' constitutes the particular-universal relationship. This experience has been conceived of from all the natural phenomena, which are attributed with human qualities. They are waiting ever not to bid farewell to their companion.

> The morning is over, and afternoon is waiting
> At the end of the day time is all weariness
> Still so, the sun is not willing to go
> Looking through the earth
> Asking no leave of departure.

The lover is anxious of his union with his lady love. The married women come to the bathing ghat; there is no shade. The wave is broken by the strike of the Kalas or earthen pot, the sunrays become fractured and the wearied breeze sometimes kisses surface of the water of the border. The image of the "waiting" is tinged with poetic emotive experience. The sun is supposed to have imbibed the beauty of the parting day. The day-to-day happenings are conceived of as beauteous and the sun is supposed not to part with the day. The day gradually comes to an end, the light starts vanishing out, the outline of the deep dark forest is discovered at the end or at the meeting of the sky. It is as dark as the eyebrow on the eyes asleep due to fatigue.

The image of the parting day and the portrait of the wearisome sleep is new thing to the readers of Rabindra-Kavya. The compound words, device of the use of adjectives and Emotive Embellishment and perception like presentation shine in its undimmed splendour as one of the most living images. When finally the time of union comes they come from different sides with much eagerness and anxiety only to be immersed in the deep ocean of midnight. As a matter of consequence the restless current is stopped, din is over, and the reticent union is drowned in the darkness and a complete unification becomes possible in the surface of annihilation.

The images depicted in the poem are of immense moving and living. Although the subject of the poem denotes the old and common experience of human beings, it expresses something living. Broadly said that 'whatever its subject may be' a poem must express something living—"Something living in the mind from which it comes and the minds to which it goes."[15] The famous critic Charu Chandra Banerjee has given his opinion on the poem that "the lover is waiting for the moments of the union with his lady love and musing over her present engagements". It is very common feature of relationship between lover and the beloved. The poet of the preceding age has dealt with this common happenings. But the poignancy of the poem comes from the living aspects in image emotive experience, peculiar treatment of the theme which emanates from his personal meanings. "This marriage of personal meaning with set subject creates a theme, and by virtue of this theme the poem is a living image it reveals to us something that is alive in our own minds.[16]

The prayer of Suradasha is important in the history of love and gradual achievement of feeling of beauty of the poet, Rabindranath. It is the relevant opinion of one of the greatest critic of Rabindra Kavya, Dr. Upendranath Bhattacharyya that the poet, SuraDasha or the blind poet desires for the formless existence of beauty which is crept hidden in the love of the corporeal beauty of the women. The unity of this incorporeal beauty is an endless, supreme and luminous, and which remains beyond the reach of the sensual desires. The poet Suradasha in his early poetic career had set this incorporeal existence of beauty on the level of sensual aspiration. The image of this sort of experience comes through this vitality. He depicts a picture:

> Were that cravings of mine, enchantingly fickle
> (which are) as black as bumble-bees
> Humming with tears on your sight?

The perfect presentation of sensible desires with theirs being compared with black bumble bees and the portrait of modesty and shyness and the treatment of sensible and incorporeal beauty testify to the fact that Rabindranath is of high vitality and originality and we are opinion that he "alone, there-still forming, still inchoate, his work also holds good for posterity may indeed hold more meaning for later times than for his own."

The poet Suradasa wants to tear off his eyes, by which he enjoyed the carnal and sensible pleasure of beauty of the body of women. He requests her to extinguish the desire of his eyes with annihilating the existence of eyes. It seems that world would be as dark as anything. But he feels that in the deep darkness a sacred faced sweet embodiment and tenderly downwards-bent eyes become luminant before his blind eyes. He craves in the sky of his heart her incorporeal effulgence. This poem is a assimilation of the cluster of images. Besides, some harmonious thread lies prominent in the poem, which constitutes the single image of incorporeal Beauty. In the poem "In the days of Rainy Season" an image of seasonal ecstasy having its border the saddest experience is constituted by Rabindranath. In this day sweetheart is near at hand. But there lies on ocean of separation smeared with salt of tears in between them. And, they feel sadness at the core of their heart. It is raining incessantly and there is none in the world. Except themselves none is to be looked upon and the society becomes insipid and throbbings of life is of no value. Only to enjoy the feast of eyes with these eyes and to feel the heart with the heart is of much value. Remaining objects are in the womb of the darkness. In this poem Rabindranath creates an image of exultation being bordered with pensiveness. These picture reveal a highly sensitive imagination.

In this poem Rabindranath is peeping through his window of subjectivity. He looks round him the world of material world. Here he creates a picture of universal nature. What he realizes and experiences is presented in his poem, we also can look at with him and by virtue of his own genius. We can see them almost as vividly as he did.[17]

The individual experiences has got the form of universality and generality being divested of its crude and raw elements. The individual temperament takes a new detour by the intense, sympathy of the poet. And the propriety which is the most essential trait of a living image, and which serves as the symbol of the artists' unrivalled experience is emphasized in this poem. At the same time poignancy of poet's acute feelings and sensation causes the poem itself to take a shape of the complete and consummate image.

In the 'Infinite Love' the image of infinite, internal and unlimited love which pervades different births is depicted out of the poet's emotion, outburst and ecstasy of personal love. Alfred Noyes in his 'The Progress of Love' harps on the same lilt as Rabindranath.

> "In other words I loved you, long ago,
> Love that hath no beginning, hath no end;"

Shelley also has got the same coin for us:

> "For love, and beauty, and delight
> There is no death, nor change"[18]

In the poem 'Megh Dut' (the cloud as a messenger) Rabindranath identifies himself with Kalidasa. This poem emanates from the deep regard of the poet for a poet or it is an image of tribute. The poet looks into the slokas and evaluates that in the immortal portrait of words of Meghduta which bears the deep sound and rhythm of the cloud all the people devoid of their lady love keep their pangs and sorrow in the dark care of their heart amidst the deep songs of exaltation.

The poet concludes with the poetic and imaginative truth that some sort of separation pervades all over the world. The lady love who is laid in the bed of pangs of separation situated on the bank of imaginative lake and which is in the land of dusk devoid of the sunrays and luminent by the pearls lying beyond the mountains, and rivers of the world.

The lilt of Meghduta is dominant throughout this poem. The image is marked by the congruity and evocative power of the poet. Because this poem is written pursuant to Kalidas's Meghdut, but Rabindranath by his deep perception and imagination presents a new and striking finished goods out of the old and used raw materials. The experience causes an overflow of poetic exultation and emotion in the mind of the readers and connoisseurs. The whole poem "To Ahalya" is an image itself. The story of the Purana is endowed with new form, new meaning and novel atmosphere. Ahalya has been petrified by her husband for her sexual relation with his pupil. This insipid and worthless happenings are lost. The poet looks into her in a different way. He gives new poetic truth.

"You lay down in the dumb immense
Where faded days drop, like dead
Flowers with seeds, to sprout again
Into new dews".

Again

"You felt the thrill of the sun's kiss
The roots of grass and trees that are
Like infants fingers clasping at
Mother's breast."

Here is an image, of all power full and all pervasive entity who has got the large and placid motherliness of the earth.

"In the night, when the tired children of the
Dust came back to the dust, their
Rhythmic breath touched you with
the large and placid motherliness of the earth."
Wild weeds twined round you
their bonds
of flowering intimacy."

The image reveals the feeling step by step and as it acquires prominence it controls more and more the employment of image.

"When she haves the new birth
She forgets the surroundings and beloved environment and
Atmosphere of previous one. Still so,
The dew of that unfathomed night
Trembles on your eyelids
The mosses of ever green years cling to your hair."

"You have the wonder of new birth and the wonder of old time in your awakening. You are young as the new-bloomed flowers and old as the hill."

An image of wonder lying with concept of familiarity, with the apprehension of acquaintance is depicted in this poem with a view to create a total impression on the perspective of the poet. So it is concluded that "as the poet communicates the result of this perception—the total experience, he is to take naturally the help of an indivisible medium—the whole having an integral pattern of its own.

In the 'Golden Boat' Rabindranath has matured himself

in art and artifice, the image being in this phase consummate and full-bloomed. In the first poem a common and practical happenings of the village life have been expressed with symbolic revelation. The juxtaposition of the activities of the farmer with the natural phenomena and the novel outlook of the poet in the sphere of his looking into the natural objects are all painted on a single canvass. The poem Sonartari (or the Golden Boat), although it consists of many images, is an image itself-image of poetic sensibility and emotive experience.

The poet is alone in the solitary field laid on the bank of the river and by his side lies accumulated paddy cut by him and the river having strong current. The corn-cutting continues upto the rainy season. It would be insipid to the readers had there been none to haunt him and to knock to his silence.

"Oh! There comes someone singing
She seems to be familiar with me
She goes off sailing looking neither
The waves become helpless
Break sides either."

Here is an image of new outlook and novel outburst of his imaginative passion. The poet requests the sailor to stop her journey to turn her boat and take sojourn in his shore and to take the golden paddy away with slight smile alighting on this shore. The Golden boat is filled in with the poet's golden paddy with which the poet so long was engrossed being indifferent to this world and at last requests the sailor to take him to her boat.

There is no place, no room in such a narrow boat. It is filled in with his golden harvests.

The poet is again alone. The deep cloud floats on the sky of July-(Shravan). He is left on the solitary shore of the river, all of his own being carried away by the Golden Boat.

In this poem we see many images, but there is a golden thread over all the images and one single emotion and poetic experience throughout the poem, i.e. the poets' novel idea of life, and imaginative passion. The common occurrence bring in new outlook, novel imagination and that is also due to poetic emotion and experience. Here we see the activities of the rule of generalization or universalisation. Rabindranath while giving explanation of this poem pinpoints on the atmosphere and this reaction of the climate that supplies the raw materials to the poet in composing this poem.

But actually what vesture he endows with is not the picture we got from his explanation. The common things have become uncommon due to his power of generalization. The farmer of Sahajdpur or Silaidoha experiences this fact but unlike Rabindranath they express purely in crude from, but what he expresses or gives expression is beyond common modus of experience. Here we feel the power of image. The portrait he paints is different from that of real objects and things.

In the poem "The lady laid asleep" images have attained perfect from and revelation, especially when the poet in the form of a lover along imagines himself to have entered into the apartment of the lady. The bed is as pure as the lotus in which her soft body is sunk. Her cluster of hairs is like the cloud, falls abundantly covering the pillow. Her one hand lies on the chest, and another lies on other side. The outskirts of her clothes becomes loose on the side and the bracer is about to tear and it seems as if the two fruits of worship are covered by the leaves."

Here the texture of the image is woven by the poet having in his mind the romantic idea and sensibility. The image is constituted out of the poetic perception and emotive feeling and romantic idea of the lady love.

In the poem "Jete Nahi deba" or 'I'll not allow you to go' an image of common incident along with it an uncommon and universal element is given expression. A common feature is that while a person goes abroad he has to cross the river of the pangs of separation and his wife and children to bind him at home. This fact has been universalized and the pensiveness is felt throughout the Natural Phenomena. Rabindranath gives description of atmosphere and melancholic condition of outgoing person actuated by the teen-aged daughter of four years. The car is ready, time is noon, the rays of the sun at Autumn gradually are becoming hot, the dust is flying out in the desolate rustic path. The old begging women is lied asleep on her torn clothes under the tender shade of pupil tree. It seems that the sun-burnt night is husing all round, there is pindrop of silence. There is no slumber of rest at his home. The atmosphere is tinged with pensiveness and melancholy; it pervades all over the natural phenomena. The portrait of this departure is no new thing, but what is presented to us is a new item, we have no experience with this, though the incident is identical with that of ours. The sensibility and the emotive expression which has been focused with the portrait of the image becomes generalized and universalized.

In the poem 'Manas Sundari' or 'the Ladylove of his imagination' the poet struggles towards a condition of novel consciousness and new-inspiration, in which vitality and permanence combine. The idea and consciousness prevalent in Manashi parva (era) or stage do not involve a dissolution of the contour of poetic passion and emotion. That is to say, these poems lack to some extent poetic restraint, and are based on high-flown fancy and outburst of sensible joy and pensiveness. But in this phase Rabindranath establishes his poetic consciousness on granite strata and that also is based not on the sparkling rainbow of fanciful world, rather on humble, simple and honest atmosphere of the day-to-day happenings and in which he meets the poetic purport.

The image of Meghduta and that of Manasundari differs, because of the difference of poet's perception, contemplation and the perspective of the poet.

It would not be out-off-the track if we mention that the poems of "Sonartari" or the stage above-named still does not get over the subjective stratum. But it would not be tenable if we thrust with the decision that the mere subjectivity and sheer sensible feelings loom large on these poems. The image of "Manas-sundari" and texture of the poem along with the poet's emotive experience denote the said dictum. Side by side we should remember that it will be of paramount value to note that it is image from which we can perceive the poet's new outlook, contour of poetic inspiration and more beautiful texture of words then that of weaving by words of early stage of Rabindra Kavya. The poet appeals to his ladylove, who is also the creation of poetic mind, and who is also the wealth of his accomplishment since his poetic birth, addressing her as a poetry, a Paradisical creeper to come to him by his side. There is no work, only gossiping, lilting with his ladylove, only enjoying and drinking the red wine of evening rays until the veins and its subsidiaries become filled in with the stream of beauty, until in the great pleasure and ecstasy the bondage of consciousness is torn. "I forget completely which desires are not satisfied what sort of nectar in this shape of delight there is? Which, coming in the outskirts of lip and not satisfying the desire of the mind has withered. Let this peace, this sweetness impart on the sorrow, poverty and dissatisfaction of the reticent, dull, tender life, the soft (due to pity), deep beautiful lustre. Libidinal experience when the lover appeals to her to come to him leaving aside the lyre and bind him with amorous clasping round his neck. As a consequence his chest becomes restless and start quivering, eyes are about to shed tears, charmed body becomes beguiled, mind is illumined in the farthest corner of the body by the fact that the restraint of sensible organs are about to tear out. "

The libidinal experience of the poet is not new things, but what is striking in this phase is its vitality and universal perceptibility. The relation between a young man and woman resembles this. The presentation and embellishment of the poet is unique and unprecedented. An image is woven, when we see that the poet requests his Manassunduri to raise her peerless face, that is similar to newly bloomed flower, binding her neck; and another image of the happiness is constituted of the brightness, redness, abundance of honey. The happiness, what sort of happiness? Happiness, to the poet is red, bright and full of honey. The poet weaves various types of network. His textures of weaving is variegated, multi-coloured and multi flavoured. It has got the capability of giving satisfaction, satiety to the mind, pleasure to the ears, enjoyment to the eyes, the galaxy of pictures to the persons interested in artistic creativity. The image of the coming of the evening star is beautifully depicted as if a lady with a view to meet her lover goes out in the midnight very cautiously. The evening star marks her foot-prints on the bank of the river situated in bed of the forest slowly and cautiously. The transferred epithet is used to beautify the canvass of the painting and intensify the emotive contents of the poem. The image of the night that arranges for a bed in the dark endless earth denotes the tranquillity and peace prevailing in the atmosphere. The total picture is embodied in the existence of unification of fear, desire and soft love full of tears existing between the two souls. This lady is his first love, the moon of beauty in the sky of his fortune. He remembers that they used to meet together in the garden of blossomed Juthis in the time of early childhood. She resembles the blossomed flower. She comes to him to take him in the garden to collect Shephally and in the lonely mysterious nook of the house and in the solitary roof of the house under the sky.

The image of the Manassundari is constituted out of the common factors of existence, and day-to-day passion and sentiments; Rabindranath utilizes them and paints a universally interesting and charming picture. Manassundari first comes as his wife on path of blossomed flowers, being efflorescent with modesty wearing red clothes. His core of heart is always shivering, which is too tender to bear any touch. The inward urge is awake with his happiness, sorrow, while his beautifulness, desire to bear any touch fear are too quivering, tender.

Rabindranath creates an image that is as much marked by congruity as by audacity and freshness. This portraits of image is unprecedented and unique. Here we can claim that by creating an image Rabindranath has fulfilled and been able to evoke the emotion and feeling of permanent value and reliability. The role of the image and its retaining capacity of its value beyond the boundaries of time-limit has been explained by a great critic. "If an image is to retain its value and relishability to members far removed from the artist by boundaries of time, it is to present new relations between ideas and things in such a way that permanent emotions lying latent in the reader of all time to come are evoked, making it possible for him to find is own self in the miniature universe caught in the painting."[19]

The idea of the poem 'To the Sea' emerges from novel outlook, imagination, the sympathetic treatment and strong consciousness of humanity of the poet. He compares sea with an affectionate, perturbed mother who is always anxious about her only daughter, earth. The poet gives us a scientific truth addressing sea as a primitive Mother and Earth as her only daughter on her lap. Like the affectionate mother who caresses her only daughter and haunts every abode of gods for health and good fortune, the sea by raising her prayer makes resonant all over the sky. She clasps her daughter, by the tides of waves falling in her numerous kisses enwrapping her body with her blue skirt with much care and caution in soft genre. The poet is amazed at her tricks that lies in her going back stealthily as if she wants to leave her but again she jumps on the chest of her daughter with boisterous outburst of joy in abundance of unmixed smiles and makes her drenched with smiles, tears and pride of happiness. The poet asks us who can realize her unfathomable peace, her limitless anxiety, her deep reticence, her warbling, her smile, and heaps of tears. The idea of this poem originates from single experience, but when that experience is given expression it covers much wider field, it is engrossed with total life-experience of the poet. C. Day Lewis expresses the same dictum in the following passage. "And we must bear in mind that, though the theme of any given poem may well have arisen from a single experience, its images will usually have been drawn from a much wider field—from the total life-experience of the poet so that, in helping to create a whole poem, they also hint at the existence of a coherent order underlying all things which gives its general authority to each several theme."[20]

The image of young girl who becomes for the first time mother is attributed to the sea. The outburst of affection is so great that it cannot be restrained. The sea also clasps her daughter, earth, with merciless emotion, coming to her with affectionate swelled breast. The earth cannot bear her torture and oppression. The mother then repents for her action. The consort evening touches with her tender hand and gives her consolation. The night as a friend hears her suppressed grief in chocked repentation.

The image of motherly affection with its variegated

elements is depicted by the poet giving rise to its bearing on a wider field of experience and we feel, although the poem is based on a single emotive experience, the image of this poem is multi-coloured and multi-formed. The poet creates cluster-images. But its guiding principle and the thread of emotion is one and single i.e. creation of an image of a mother full of passion, feelings, tender, anxiety, and all those qualities of a first mother attributing these qualities and qualification to the primitive mother of human beings. The poet remembers very slightly the condition when he is absorbed in her vast womb with the unborn foetus of the earth. The incessant warbling that has been going on for crores of years is writ large in the mind of the poet. So, when he sits on the desolate bank of the sea with down-cast eyes he bears that old warbiling. Here is an image of the mother of pervasive nature. In that primitive state she was alone, undividied, endless and absorbed in herself being ignorant of the vastness of the great mystery of first pregnancy. Some unrevealed anxiety over love for day and night, an affectionate or amorous attraction of the pregnant, an unprecedented sympathy on the childless desolate heart of the mother. The image of the affection marked by frivolousness-desolateness and devoidness or destituteness of the sea, that very wakeful desire full imminent waiting, that very unknown pages in the deep core of the heart for this invisible great future arisen in mind like the memory of the epoch-making revolution. The image of an invisible pain and unknown aspiration is constituted by the poet. Here we cannot but admit of the role and importance of the power of words that are identified with the universalised form of expression. The role and importance of abidha and lakshna is emphatic. The treatment and the peculiar use of words that give expression to the experience and emotive identification with material facts and happenings are rudiments of the poetic image. In Rabindra-Kavya, we observe the same guide-line, the principle and the modus operandi. In Sonartari or the "Golden Boat" we see the perfect assimilation of these factors. The aspect of sensuousness which is the pivotal mark of his early works is symbolized in this phase.

In this early works it has played the role of vortex, but

here it is an aspect; it is one of the ingredients devoid of its previous acuteness and keen-edged bearing on sensuality. The poem 'To the sea' denotes the poet's desire for coming into the world of human being, whose lives are distinguished with passion, feeling and throbbing of sun-burnt mirth. It is simply emerging out from the dark cave of sensual feeling to that of the world of Chitra, "Ebar Ferao More", "Turn me now".

The Earth (Basundhara) or the Holder of Wealth is personified as the mother-earth in the poem. The image of mother-hood along with her affection and the pervasiveness, poet's identification with the mother-earth has been portrayed in this poem. The image of the consciousness and eagerness of the poet to identify himself with the water, earth and the sky and to pervade himself in the every nook and corner of the Nature is dominant. The unsevered relation with the nature of the world, an ever-old identification and oneness attracts the poet earnestly and time without number. The profound savour of the evergreen beautiful earth personified as vivacious and beautiful mother beguiles the mind of the poet. He is pervaded by this mother-earth in form of idea and in vitality. The pression of one scientific truth in the following image.

> Oh! Mother-Earth :
> I' am pervasive amidst the soil all
> Expanding myself throu' quarters
> Like exhilaration of the Spring.

He wants to tear out the darkness of the inner cave of his heart, to break the story bindings of the narrow barrier of the blind cell of his joyless existence, to swing to scatter, to thrill, to startle in illumination and delight, and to glide throughout the world from one frontier to another, from north to south, from west to east. He wants to be juicy admidst the moss, fern, corn, branch, bask, leaves, in the vital savour of the life and touches with the tip of the finger the surface of the cornfield downcast with golden apex. The flora and Fauna has been portrayed by the poet and the image is constituted with the keen, symbolic and meticulous insight of the poet.

The image of pervasiveness of the poet is symbolized in the desire of his spreading himself on the peak of the mountain which is compared with white scarf, on the taciturn silence of the unmixed snow, on the soulless solitariness.

His peculiar use of words and their coordination, the adjustment of their meaning and implication are all the vital and dominant factors in creating image. We should always remember image is not based on words and phrases only, it has its own way of expression, words have a great role to play. The impression of the image can be realized by its own expression and modus operandi. It is a pattern a new and novel pattern of giving expression to the poetic ideas and experience. When he states the idea that lies in his desire to have expanded himself in the blueness, only to dance in endless warbling of the silent earth, we have behind the moments of intensity, passion throbbing[21] although the expression is nearing the propinquity of hyperbolic expression.

The poet stretches imagination to the remotest corner of the earth which is impassable to go through it and is devoid of way, trees, there is only vast land, and arena of great Thirst. The burning sands in the sunshine pierce the eyes like the needle.

The poet depicts a picture of scorching heat looking out of his window. The sick mother-earth is weltering on the ground with hot breath, dry voice, being consortless, speechless and cruel. The image of the day-do-day existence with its familiar objects is painted to intensify the emotive contents of the poem. The net is spread in the sunshine, the boat is floating on the water, this sail is flying in the air, the fishermen are catching fishes, the narrow streamlet is somehow managing to flow out in zigzag way in the hilly-pass. This descriptive features are painted on a single canvas by the poet with a view to create a consummate image. His desire to enwrap with the hands the hamlet of the people which is resounding with the happy warbling of the people, situated on the lap of the secluded mountain is identical with the image. Here, poet's pervasive outlook, his emotive passion and sensibility, his intention to identify himself with the flora and fauna create the living image of which we have different yawning gap between them. The epithets, 'Secluded' in the lap of the mountain laid image the use of the poetic generalization helps largely to portray the image out of the limited periphery of words and their limited implication. He wants to be the child of the desert and to drink the milk of the camel and to walk on the Buddhist Monastery situated in the detached hilly abode of the mountain. The image of oneness with the every objects inanimate, animate, human beings, rivers, mountains is painted on a sketch comprising in itself the cluster of images. He wants to be born in the house of Persians who drink grapes are inhabitant of garden of rose, of the fearless equestrian Tartar, of the lively, modest Japanese, of the old, wise Chinas engaged in action day and night. The perception and feelings of the poet denotes the distinction between the particular and the general vis-a-vis the universal through which 'the reader is conducted to the new world of reality which effects transition from individual experience to universal experience giving rise to the living image endowed with the power of liberating the man from the conditionings of life.'

Rabindranath states that when he sits being unmindful on the shore of Padma stretching his charmed eyes, he feels with his body and mind how the sprout of the corn is shivering in the earth-mother, what sort of savour of life moving always in her heart, with which great delight the buds blossom on the stock and become anxious. The creepers, shrubs become delighted in the bright sunrays tinged with secret outburst of joy, become glad with the savour of mirth and joyfulness, like the child who is wearied of drinks of mother's milk and is over-satisfied; he creates a cluster of images painted on a single canvas. The Alankaras Upama and Samasakti and Swbhavyakti being used are engaged in embellishing the structure of the image. They have no dominant role to play in the main melody of the poem, they simply brings a splendid beautifying device and nothing else, where 'a living image points out to the main melody of the poem and consequently is a feeling-vector'.[77] The compounded words bring into the readers the particular and individual experience of the poet, but when the feeling elements of the poet touches on the feelings and emotion of the readers, they experience the material feeling along with the poetic sensibility, presented in the form of poetic image. The poem, Basundhara although it comprises so many living images, is symbolized in one percent living image and that image is of the poet's desire to pervade all throughout the Mother-Earth and to experience the variegated feelings and emotion of this earth. So, we conclude that the Basundhara", that one of the best poems of Rabindrakavya has become the laurel and masterpiece because not only of its bearing on emotive and sensitive contents, on beautiful and grand style and adornation or embellishment, but of the living, consummate and perfect image. All throughout the poem we find hundred of images and these seem to be apparently of broken nature, but these images are painted on single canvas; and there is a deep co-ordination between those having powerful chord of feeling to form them into a tuneful whole.

The last poem in his phase, is symbolized in the awakening and emergence from the sensible whirl pool and individual consciousness and subjectivity. In the first poem we see that poet is left alone in the shore of the river, and the golden paddy with which he was engrossed so long had been carried away by the golden boat. Here he has got his room in the boat but does not know to which end the alien beautiful girl will harbour her golden boat. To this question she does not respond, but laughs only good laugh. He does not know what sort of things she is having in her mind. She simply points lifting her finger silently to the impatient sea, and the sun sets in the corner of the sky in the far-off west. He does not know what for they are going and what sort of things there are?

Here, an image of uncertainly, anxiety and purpose-less journey over the sea of the poet with the alien sailor is constituted. The poet wants to know the destination, the abode of the sailor, when he says to her.

> Tell me I ask you oh strange :
> That place, where burns in the evening the day's pyre
> Water dazzles like liquid fire
> Where melts the surface of the sky
> As if Dikbadhu* becomes tearful;
> As your abode situated there

Beyond the sea resonant with waves
On the bottom of the setting mountain* kissed By the clouds
You laugh only staring at my face speaking nothing.

We become confronted with the image of deep consciousness and keen-edged perception. Although there lies the shadow of mystery over the atmosphere, there is incertitude of sensible love and human feelings between the poet and his Jibandeva symbolized in her lady love, and she is nothing but the poetic inspiration and experience of the poet; so the desire, to live amidst the day-to-day existence with an overall adjustment with the universal world is emerging out, ushering out from these limited periphery of subjectivity and personal activities. The image of the emotive experience with the alien sailor in the boat floating over the impatient sea, and his eagerness is depicted, what appears to us 'slightly unfocused impression which goes with nostalgia. He urges on the lady and asks.'

How again I ask
Does tender death there lie?
Is there peace, slumber in the darkness?
You are laughing lifting your eyes
Remaining speechless.

The image of last stanza is depicted with masterly touch. The expression of the emotive contents, the sensible experience with the lady is pictured in a powerfully evocative force. The images of the dark night, the evening sky, the flavour emanating from her body, the warbling of water of the sea are all symbolised in a single consummate image. The poet comes near very near the lady. Being exhausted and benumbed appeals to her,

Oh! Where you are, coming near touch me
You will not speak, I'll not see
Your silent smile.

We quote below the distinguished portion, of the poem of Francis Brett Young Invocation and Tennyson's, "The voyage" for denoting the analogy and marking the distinction between image of F. B. Young, Tennyson and Rabindranath:

Whither, O my sweet mistress
Must I follow thee?
For when I hear thy distant
Footfall nearing
And wait on thy appearing
Lo! My lips are silent; no words come to me
Whither, o divine mistress, must I then
Follow thee?
Is it only in love, say is it only in death
That the spirit blossometh
And words that my match my vision
Shall come to me

- Francis Brett Young
"Invocation"[23]

For one fair vision ever fled
Down the waste waters day and night
And still we followed where she led
In hope to gain upon the flight
Her face was evermore unseen
And fist upon the far sea-line
But each man murmured, O my Queen
I follow till I make thee mine
For my purpose holds
To sail beyond the sunset, and the baths
Of all the western starts, until I die.

- Ulysses, Tennyson.[24]

There is an affinity in mood and ideal between two English Poets and Rabindranath, but what is striking in Rabindranath lacks in the said poems. Because the images that are constituted in the purposeless journey of Rabindranath are not found in young's Invocation and Tennyson's 'The Voyage' When Tennyson says "Her face was evermore unseen' Rabindranath creats a consummate image. The poet does not say in prosaic method. He says that the savour of their body comes to him with the air, the warbling of the water haunts him only and the locks of hairs come flying on his body. The cluster of images denotes her existence.

Here we simply give the outline of *Chitra* or Variety to intensify the feeling element, sensuous content of the poem

"Niruddesh Yatra" (or the Endless Journey). The poetic image in Chitra or 'variety' incarnate symbolised in a young women is compact and consummate in form, colour, rhythm, song and sense. The poet conceives of Chitra setting her in blue sky, who is sparkling in endless light, who is merriful in the bower in great delight, who sports in fickle movement in the earth and in the space. The poet comprehends her form and exclaims how variegated she is, she is variocoloured also. The image of the poem is revealed by the figure of speech Prativastupama in which 'the particular is linked to another particular or the general is linked to another general either by a similar attribute or by the same attribute, expressed in different language only to avoid tautology'. Her rhythm of dance is resounded by ringing of the anklet in the remotest sky, flavour of the hairs are flying in the gentle breeze, the universal mind is bloomed by the sweet dance; how much the pleasant Regini there are :. The Chitra is conceived in various forms and figures in multiformed songs colours and books. She is variegated amidst the objects of the world and she is multiformed. This image is created by the various settings and by colours and odours. There are cluster of images although there is a connecting link and co-ordination between them. Another image is created by the idea and feeling that the Chitra is symbolised in single unity. She is crystalised in a dream in the charmed tearful eyes, in a lotus in the bed of the heart-stem, in the moon in the endless sky of mind.

2

In the poem "Farewell and curse" the image of farewell along with pensiveness and the sensuous experience of Kach and Debyani is portrayed. Kach after his attainment of learning comes to Debyani, to bid farewell to her with a view to return to Heaven whence he comes to her father to learn the use of weapons. He solicits her blessing so that the learning, he has attained becomes for ever in the heart like a bright pearl resembling the sun that shines in the pinnacle of mountain in undecaying brightness. The simile and the comparative genre is no new pattern of technique. But the coherence and just a position placed by the poet and the imaginative statement which hears testimony distinguished from the original story of Mahabharata, lays the granite strata of the living image and helps us to assume that 'image pattern must be in fact patterns and not random assemblages of word pictures' although the importance of word-power cannot be denied.[25]

Debyani reminds him of his attainments of the learning comprising of rigorous studies and austere and arduous practice, and asks him whether he desires anything more than that. She appeals to him to look into the unfathomable deep heart and to find if there lies any desire in the outskirts of the mind that desire is like the shoot of the kusa grass which is so small that it is invisible, yet of keenest nature. We are acquainted with this sort of perception in our daily life. We feel this sensuous object, but what is presented in efflorescence is novel to us; we know the every epithet used in the said poem, but its dramatic consistence, coherence of impression and assemblages of word-picture are peculiarly and consummately manifested. The arduous practice that had been run by Kach is no factor, but only an item of the total image-patterns. The sensuous poetic mind is resonant with the feelings that have been related to rhythm, touch, smell and sight, and he deals much with the sensuous experience of Debyani with Kach and her pensive and melancholic mood in the time of bidding farewell to her by kach. She stress on his austere practice and on the grand picture when he returns to heaven; and on what sort of grand ovation they will give him! The Heaven will be filled in great delight and auspicious conch will resound, the goddess will shed in his head the shower of flowers that is cut-forth-with from the spike of Mandarin true of the Heaven. On the Heaven-path there will be auspicious commotion in the sweet toned goddess.

Side by side the poet paints contrasting picture of the life of Kach which he passed in great trouble, in austere studies and in solitary alien land. There was none to remind him of his happy and warm home to avert the pangs arising out of alliances. But whence will she get the happiness of Heaven? There is no cheerful face of sweet girls of heaven. But it is not the real happenings of Debyani and purport-striking images.

It is simply a pensive and melancholic consolation she tries to give herself. And on this pensive and sensible manifestation his poetic image does not lay its foundation. The image of the heart-felt desire that lies in the core of the heart resembles the worm lying hidden in the flower and the desire which seeks the desired like the insulted bumble bee who files time without number to the unblossomed lotus is the bearer of real feelings of the poet. The petal of sensible mind of Debyani with slow and pensive opening is depicted with much care and felicity. The beautiful forest, the warbling of the birds, the murmuring of the leaves have no bearing on the mind of the kach when he is bidding farewell to all these animate things with which he had passed his long arduous years. This is the pertinent question of Debyani and the poet also. The trees have become pale, the shadow of the forest has become deep dark due to sorrow, air begins weeping, the dry leaf starts falling, but kach only will go with smile like the dream of the departing image of this poem is of love and pensiveness, which also is due to pangs of separation. The cluster of images are dominated by the reciprocal love. Kach, while tending the cows would fall asleep off and on under the shade of a baniyan tree, affection to the guest which is very kind enough to spread its long shadow over him, the cluster of sounded leaves fanning in mild sound brings in the pleasant sleep to him, Kach. Then he may go, but there will be no harm inflicted to anyone, if he would sit under the tree and for the last time get the accosting of this affectionate shadow. He admits of their creative influence upon him, of the purpose of spreading their new affectionate net to bind their feeling-friend and this is their last request symbolized in unprecedented abundance of beauty. He then salutes to the largest and deep shadowed tree. He visualises then countless travellers would sit under his deep shadow, the silent solitary seat of grass like him and would study in low humming sound like the insects. Then Debyani reminds Kach of the religious cow (whose milk is used in religious sacrifice) and requests him not to forget her in pride and boastfulness. The portrait of the tender, soft-bodied cow whose movement is slow and beautiful due to idleness and her ruminating and lying under the corn-field the whole day, who occasionally opening her large eyes full of gratitude and peace licks his body by her sight of deep affection, is allied factor to the consummate image. He promises he will remember that tranquil, tender and opaque, robust white oily and slippery body. He will not forget the warbling stream of Benumati (its shore is covered by the bamboos, hence this name). She passes through many flowered bowers with the voice full of delighted warbling like the rustic wife who is always swift-moving.

She is his alien consort being engaged in observing auspicious vows. Now Debyani opens the petals of her mind so long closed. The question "Is there any companion beside you engaged in taking care day and night to avert the pangs caused by the residence abroad is the dominant factor in constituting reminiscence of Debyani of first meeting with Kach. He appears to her as the luminous rising sun his body being white and saturated with tender effulgence, the forehead being smeared with ointment, with garland round the neck wearing vesture, in the lips and eyes there is delight and innocent smile, he comes then to the garden, the image of kach with the pleasant atmosphere, the very incarnate of love, appears to us, being allied with poetic feeling, and emotive experience." The image created by the poet invokes in the mind of the reader and the connoisseur the very feeling and emotion, sensual relation between them and the total emotive experience on the peculiar natural influence. The stream, the blossoms, the dark forest the religious cow are no mute objects, rather they are caused understood. Their dominant role in the creating total 'Kavyavastu' or the purport of the poem, this is identical with consummate and perfect image. And Debyani appears to him like one who has taken one's bath just now, she is dawn-incarnate bathed in lustre having long lock of hair wet, wearing new white clothes, taking a wicker tray flowers in hand she is plucking host of newly-bloomed flowers for worship. He earnestly requests her that labour does not befit her and to give him leave to pluck flowers. Then we see the image of love that has grown out in secrecy. But that too is beyond their reciprocal exchange of love and affection. Debyani requests him to remember the happy occurrences, if the song of delight and pleasure rings inside and outside of his mind, if at the same dusk in the shore of Benumati the unprecedented abundance of mirth arises in the mind at the leisure of the study, while staying in garden if the outburst of delight of the mind like the fragrance of flowers pervades the evening sky, the bloomed groove. Here the poet creates his poetic image on the canvas of natural phenomena. The Alongkara Upama, Smile, Samaskti have been used to make a bridge over the streams of the feelings, passion, emotion of the poet and natural phenomena. He attributes the poetic feelings to the mute, dumb objects of Nature. The still view unbloomed love and affection is symbolized in the cluster of image comes out in flying colours when Rabindranath describes the grandeur of heavy shower of Asara which haunts the minds of Debyani and Kach with mirthful fancy. The image of blue matted hair of Asara in the horizon of the new cumulus of the tender dark coloured rain, of the body begin ailing due to deep fancy in the workless day in incessant showers of rain; the image of appearance the youthful ardour being impatient of the swing of hilarity independent and boundless of the unwarranted spring, the image of this stream of emotion resonant with songs and its pervasion of the deluge of delight in creepers in leaves, flowers in this and another forest through the train of waves, are all the living images giving rise to the invocation of emotive experiences and feeling experienced by the poet in the mind of the readers and connoisseurs. Besides, we feel through these images peculiar characteristics of both the characters and their inarticulate exchange of love and affection. Debyani requests him to recapitulate the past happy days; requests him to feel that he could not detach the countless dawn, moonshine, deariness, the verdurous gloom have identified themselves with his life in this forest. Amidst those were there not found such morning evening, charming night, such hearby rejoicing, such happiness such face which would delineate in the mind as sketch of universal picture and which will be remembered for all times to come? Is benefaction not more than that? There is no beauty, no love and affection, nothing more than that (benefaction). The Image of that unexposed stream, which flows in the heart being full of blood and that cannot be manifested outside, is the novel and striking one. The cluster of images has been painted having this image been placed in dominating and all prevailing position. She appeals to him not to go to the Heaven. There is no happiness in the glory of the pride. She requests him to create a new heaven here in this shore of Benumati mixing this solitary tenderness of the forest with the secluded, tranquil charmed two hearts unaware of the world. Although Kach did not unlock his mind, Debyani had observed that hearing her sweet voice his body had trembled like the diamond that if it moves, the light comes out flashing. Is it unobserved by her? He is caught red-handed. He is captive to her. He is unable to untie this binding. Indra is no more Indra to him. Then we see image which brings in the picture that manifests Kach's secret love towards Debyani. The image of the atmosphere of the evening that comes silently as tender eyelids of loving eyes in which Kach sings the songs of the heaven – is the image of Love and poetic emotion. Rabindranath characterizes Debyani not as a stern-hearted haughty girl, but as a loving, passionate, kind-hearted sweet coy who longs for love. Here we see the images are marked with the amorous glance, the longing for love, not with idyllic foundationless platonic love. She requests him to forget heaven of ideality and to create a heaven resonant with human feeling and throbbings of human life. Kach admits it but he cannot break the vow. Then we see the image that is marked with her tears, softened with love. What does she do with that undone and disappointed life? She will remain alone secluded and aimless. She will not bear the pricks of memory of him which he will leave every nook and corner of the forest. This image is characterized with common human feelings and passions. The story and character of Mahabharata have attained a revolutionary change in the hand of Rabindranath, and that change of tremendous character is given suitable expression through the striking and novel image. Here we quote a portion of the poem Don Juan who states the common feeling and passion of a young girl who is longing for love and is disappointed in love.

"Man's love is of man's life a thing apart
'Tis woman's whole existence; man may range
The court, camp, church the vessel and the mart

Sword, gown, gain, glory, offer in exchange
Pride, fame, ambition to fill up his heat
We but one,
To love again and be again undone."[26]

At last Debyani utters fie on Kach who is similar to cruel traveller sitting under the tender shadow of her life; in pretext of beguiling a few hours he has woven the garlands of happiness; tearing the happiness like the flowers in one thread in the time of departure he did not take the garland round his neck and making that acute thread torn it down. The glory of her life has been smeared with dust.

We are confronted with the image that are predominantly marked by the common and ordinary human feelings. The characterization and the emotive contents of Mahabharata are of no permanent importance or of original nature. Rabindranath depicts the common feelings of amorous character on the granite strata of day-to-day existence. Here the features of material life is not absent. But what is peculiar in this poem is its striking and novel images. The utilization of natural phenomena and the attribution to them with human feelings and passion along with its consistency and coherence are of permanent value, which is of universal nature and of typical character to charm the contemporary artistic sense as well as the same of the feature.

3

Image and Symbolization in the Poetry of Rabindranath

We have observed importance of expression-elements and have given much emphasis on the expression-element and the ingredients in the previous chapters. The expression-element or the Abidha-Sakti is symbolized in the foundation stone of the sky-kissing palace of poetic image. It will not be off the track if we take an example in elucidating this.

"In poetry the expression-element is of permanent importance, since it is through the medium of language-experience into the mind of the refined reader and the connoisseur, who is supposed to identify himself easily with the passions and actions, events and character introduced in Poetry".[27] But what appears to us is not the direct stuff of poetic experience, it comes through the modus of purgation and modification. The total experience is transferred from the mind of the artists to the receptionist, the readers and the connoisseurs. The lunch which is served on the table of the kitchen by the housewife is not the raw materials direct from the field, rather it comes through the rigorous action and through various bye-laws of modification. Still so, it is no other than the raw harvest. It also follows the same rule, the rule of suggestiveness. The scientific use of language is the very basis of emotive and peculiar use of language of the poet. But what we get from poetry is not what we have in the dictionary of science of language, we get poetic and emotive language of the poetry. It is divested of the grammar-predominant language. But in "arriving at the concept of the process of suggestion the science of literary criticism derives considerable help from the system of grammar, and it is not difficult for the discerning mind to find out the extent of help received by literary theoretician from the formulators of the Philosophy of grammar on this account. As a matter of fact, the entire doctrine of suggestion as enunciated by the learned Dhanikara is backed by the authority of the theory of Sphota, that is regarded as one of the most notable contributions of the science of language, to the field of Philosophical speculation."

So, it the quite tenable in the portrait of the image of happiness. The image of happiness is symbolized in the sketch of natural phenomena, and that is as follows : To day is cloudless day; the bright sky smiles like the friend, the gentle breeze touches face, eyes and the chest so softly as if the invisible scarf of the sleeping Dikbadhu (Diety of the quarter of the globe) flutters over the body. The image of the happiness is manifested through the smile of the bright, clear sky, through the sweet touch of the gentle breeze. The Romantic Dikabadhu being brought in and caused to come in contact with, intensifies the solidity of the atmosphere. The figure of speech Upama bears the testimony to suggestiveness, Vyanjona. The expression content is the very basis of symbolization. Symbolic expression is a peculiar mode of expression, it is a modus operandi. Rabindranath has used this every now and then to have clear expression of poetic feelings and idea and to give much stress on the same to bring in the mind of the reader and connoisseur the totality of poetic experience and feelings. The image of this poem is as follows : - the boat floats on the quiet Padma in fickle delight of warbling. The half sunk bog is seen to have been left alone afar, as if a long aquatic is basking in the sun. The high-bank remains broken, and deep-shadowed. With trees hamlets are covered, the curved thin path appears to have come from the far-off villages and to have gone into water like the thirsty tongue crossing the cornfield. The wives of the villages spreading out the outskirts of their Sari on the water are engaged in jocular conversation. The loud sweet smile mixed with warbling of the water is entering into the ear of the poet. The old fisherman sitting on the bound boat with down-cast head weaves a net in the sun. All these portraits are arranged a galaxy and painted on a single canvass. Although the portraits are distinguished from others, there lies a common and fundamental coordination between the pictures painted in the poem. The common and ordinary description of the occurrences happening at the villages of Bengal are painted in details. In form and figure they are no new things to strike the readers and charm the connoisseurs. But at what they are aiming at, which ideality they are denoting, and to which they are subscribing is the new and novel thing? Their expression is symbolic. The question may be asked whether the function of symbolization plays its role in the evocation of the feeling and emotions. We may quote the remark on this points of discussion. "The word-essence is the impression of the universal word, those evocation follows comprehension of the momentary sound, technically known as dhavani in the terminology of the Indian aesthetics; the symbolic of the system of poetics also is an impression, which is called into play in the mind of the refined reader on comprehension of the expression and the expressed, that remain inseparate in the realm of his intellect."

The image of the happiness is symbolized in simple and honest delight which resembles the smile of the children, the state of the full-bloomed flowers of the garden, which is, pervasive and manifested, and which is craned in eagerness for the nectar of kiss with the lip and looks at all being speechless ever day night in infantile belief. It is crystalised in the song resounded from the universal lyre, which makes the sky motionless and calm. The state that the blue sky is calm and quiet, water is motionless and tranquil causes the poet to assume that happiness is simple and honest. The image of the happiness is constituted out of the natural flora and fauna and the poetic outlook and mode of looking into the core of the heart of the Nature. The pictures and the word essence by means of which the image is created are no striking objects, but its co-ordination, juxtaposition and its suggestive impression make the image come in flying colours, along with it, nearly identically, the poetic feeling, sensibility and poetic outlook. Here also we feel the paramount role of the science of language.

"In its endeavour to explain the process of revelation of this significance word-essence the science of language extends recognition to the function of suggestion that is conceived of as an impression called into play by the intention of the speaker and the person spoken to."[29] The image of happiness, which Rabindranath draws from the commonest objects of the earth is similar to that of wordsworth. One of his critics states that the source of joy from which Wordsworth draws is the true and most un-failing source of joy accessible to man. It is also accessible universally. Wordsworth brings in therefore

'of joy in widest commonalty spread.'

The device which has been adopted by Rabindranath to make the images striking and novel and to present the objects as real as anything and to personify the sentiments and emotions reminds us of the adoption of the same:

And joy
With his hand over at his lips
Bidding adieu.

The texture of weaving is tinged with sensuousness. The image conveys the same emotive contents to the readers and connoisseurs.

In the "Initiation of Love" (Premer Abhisekh) Rabindranath creates an image which is identical with the feelings and emotion of the poet that are luminant beyond the indigence and humiliation of day-to-existence. Love honours the poet giving him the throne of Monarch crowing him with a coronet of glory and adorning him with a garland. Her holy mark of coronation is always glowing the form of flame of glory on the forehead. Due to her favour imparted to him the poet hears daily the languages of countries far and near, that come from far-off lands, words of the age old and new, song of day and night, Saga of union and separation the impatient melody of satiety-less, fatigue less eagerness. The poet is brought in the galaxy of beauty, in the abode of nectar by the deity of love, where, in the dusk the chaste Damayanti walks with Nala being exhaled in sad murmurings of the forest, where is seated Sakuntala on the row of flowers, who is engrossed placing on her lotus-hand with her face pale and who is meditative, where Puraraba loiters day and night in the forest-spreading unbearable separation in melodious tone in the world, where the devout Mahasweta sitting alone in the temple of Mahesha with lyre in hand is playing ragas made of pangs of the heart tinged with consolation, where on the bed of the mountain, on the seat of the rock Phalguni in the pretext of speaking the message of love kisses the flowers-soft check flushed with shame, where the lap of the beggar-shiba guards his beloved always with great eagerness. The Mandakini of tears that flows with waters of weal and owe, makes the flowered forest pale-pictured in pity with her tone of solicitation, the pensive tone of the flute finds its beloved in the shadow of the trees in every bower."

The image of love is intimately related to the grandeur and pomp of glory of the past, the poetic revelation of the poets of ancient age. The readers and the connoisseurs experience the beauty and glory of the past. Rabindranath gives expression in his own genre which he has experienced studying the works of Kalidasa. The image is created with its bearing on feeling-element of the poet. Here we again feel the role of image in the action of transfer of the actual and entire experience into the mind of the absorbed readers. We are quoting an infallible dictum of a great critic Dr. R. R. Mukherjee from his book *Imagery in Poetry–An Indian Approach*.

"Poetry communicates experience in this sense that the blissful experience generated in the mind of the creative artist is recreated in the mind of the connoisseur, who comprehends not only the stuff of the experience but the experience itself along with the moment in which it is derived. It is not enough for the poet to give the reader what has been experienced nor is it enough to show how the experience has been obtained; he is to translate the actual experience along with its bliss and passion into the mind of the absorbed reader. And transfer of this actual and the entire experience is capable of being made with the help of the complete image. This explains the urge felt by the creative perception of the poet to link the component parts and present a unified and complete picture of the theme."[30]

Love brings him in the world where there is no small responsibility, no favour. In this limited atmosphere he has to bear all these dishonour, neglect he is given treatment carelessly. The epithet of abstract perception has been pictured. The poet sets this experiences, this passion of love in the form of libidinal experiences with his lady love. Her touch, her love making, her amusing words, her kisses, her sweet winking are all symbolized in the image of love, He compares this mode of keeping nectar with that of the Moon, who has kept for eternity the secret nectar of the gods making himself an ambroisial cup, like the sun who had kept the sacred fire of the god burning with much care, love has made him the Monarch of all. Here we see that the poetic passion, sensibility have been given effulgence and predominance; and the poetic image comes out as spontaneous as anything. In this poem the sensuous nature, emotive experience of the poet and the passionate sincerity shine in the splendour of the brilliant image and as a matter of consequence the sensuous and subjective experience becomes universalized "making possible the brilliant confrontation between the generalized experience and the universalized image, symbolizing the elevated experience of the poet."

In this phase Rabindranath writes a masterpiece i.e. "Turn me Now" (Ebar Ferao More). The poet has alighted from the tower of fancy and sensual subjective confinement. He has so long seen the earth through the fanciful glass. Now, he feels the pulse of the oppressed and humiliated common mass. He fails to attune his lyric with the lilt prevalent in "Manashi" and "Sonar Tari". He addresses himself as one who plays the flute all day long in the air that, conveys the sorrow of far off-forest, is tardy, wearied and hot, under the solitary, pensive shadow of the tree in the noon at the field like the restraintless, truant boy, when all in the society are always engaged in various works. This image emanates from the attitude towards activity, from the change of outlook arising out the combativeness of the poet. The poet is no longer engrossed in the collection of flowers for the garland to be offered to the beloved of the poet. He asks himself to get up and arise to respond to the action which is symbolized in the burning fire. There bellows a conch-shell to keep awakened the people of the earth. Where from do the weepings come to resound the vacuum of the earth? In which blind cell the worn-out helpless women does ask help? The swelling humiliation sucks through its innumerable sucking feeders the blood from the heart of the weak. The injustice arrogant in self-interest mocks the pain and infliction. The contracted, afraid servant lurks in disguise.

All these images, and the predominant passion and poetic feelings luminant in the said images are the turning point; here the flow of Rabindra works turns its movements and creates new atmosphere, novel phenomena and new outlook. The poet has confronted himself with the material world. He breaks the barrier of aristocracy and makes himself ready to mix with the common place-people, who is pale-faced, mute, dumb, who carried in their shoulder the load of the earth, the responsibility of the society, the poverty and humiliation. The poet comes to their hamlet to peep through their barless window and observes their miserable condition and reads on their foreheads, wherein is writ large the pitiable saga of century-old sorrows and miseries. These people neither chide their fortunes nor censure the gods, nor find fault with this human beings. They are ignorant of their sensitiveness. They are in certain way keep their worn-out lives, living picking out minutest portion of rice only. If some deprives them of that food, inflicts them with boastful cruel oppression, they are not even aware of the court where from they will expect justice.

As a matter of consequence they will pass silently calling once again the god of the humiliated in great sigh and disappointment. The image of despair and disappointment and side by side the image of boastfulness pride and oppressive misery are all painted to create "Turn me now" a single and consummate image—the image of human feelings, poet's combatism and his unimixed humanity. He wants to look into the nook of their hamlets and presents before himself the programme of activity to give and expression to their stupid, pale, dumb mouth i.e. to make them conscious of their situation and vocal to inspire in their worn-out wearied, broken hearts with aspiration, to call them loudly to arise with elevated head for a moment and they will see that the man whom they fear much is more coward than them, when they will forsake their down trodden state, he will flee so soon, when they will confront him he will loose all his pride and boastfulness in fear and contraction. Gods are averse to him, he has no consort, he conceits himself, but is aware of his meanness at heart.

The poet is pained at heart and asks himself to rise from the state of sensible and fanciful imagination and face the pain-stricken society, where there is great sorrow and pain, there is poverty, vacuum, great smallness, closeness or contraction and darkness. As image is constituted out of the dark sides of life, every items or factors are brought in indistinguished manner as to make an emphatic expression in the mind of the readers and connoisseurs. So, by this side an image of food, life, light, open air, strength, and vivacious chest is presented to the readers. He wants amidst these diffidence, meanness, misery an image of faithfulness, belief, which he asks his poetic self to bring from the Heaven.

Now, he requests the deity of imagination to turn him now towards the society. Not to swing him in the restless breeze and tremulous waves, not to bewitch him anymore, not to keep him seated in the solitary, pensive shadow of the groove of the heart. The image of his desire to emerge from the fanciful world, from the bewitched snare of imagination is embedded in this poem. His feelings, emotive experiences play the pivotal role in constituting the images. The factors and cardinals of the image are drawn from the day-to-day existence. The texture of the image is woven by the fibres of great poverty, vacuum, meanness, darkness along with its contrasting aspect of nature, strength, light, open air, savour of life, vivacious chest and the picture of faith and belief drawn from the heaven. We are confronted with the contradiction of the poet's experience, which was so long engrossed with sunburnt mirth, merry making and restless playfulness. Here we see in image of the emergence from that out look, idea and feelings of the poet. The feelings, emotive experiences are largely marked by his combination and creative outlook towards life. The poet then emerges from his egoistic confinement and alights on the grey-expanded road under open sky, amidst the people. It is a new fact to them, who asks the poet, where do you go, where? The poet feels his difficulty and admits that he passed his days alone day and night without consort in the unusual creation. So, his vesture is bizarre, and his customs are more novel. Because of this he is affected with somnambulism and his heart burns from the fire-hunger. He states in his Reminiscence that with his birth he is given a flute, by means of which he invokes speech in the mouth of sorrow, from deep sleep emerges great desire for the nectar of the heaven, he thinks his song will be endowed with praise, and so man's displeasure will become tranquil in the great song.

Here the poet creates an image with which his passion and feelings are entwined.

The poet comes then to the most fundamental and most focal point, which is a predominant portion in image-pattern of this poem. The poet confronts the material world, where beauty can't keep its lustrous eyes, where din, bustle, sorrow, pain are the happenings of day-to-day life. The poet constitutes an image of selflessness. He preaches a dictum i.e. he who is averse to the great world, and who is engrossed in himself, he does not learn how to live a life. Keeping abreast with the waves of the great universal life, one should pave one's way apace fearlessly taking truth as one's firm guide. Then we see an image of transcendentalism, he causes us to feel some entity who goads him through the great world. He has been surrendering himself for this and another life. He is not recognised by him. He resembles the unknown invisible alien crew of the golden boat. He knows the only fact that for him the travelling human beings have been passing through the ages in the darknight through storm, hurricane, and lightning, kindling the candle heart of the with much caution. This also is known to him that he who bears His call, runs headlong to the whirlwind of the danger fearlessly forsakes the world and bears the innumerable oppression. The alankara being used intensifies the purport of the poem; and he abstract idea has been given expression through the living images. The poet does not pin-point the Being he refers to, he simply depicts different and typical pictures on a single canvass the passion and feelings being the same and identical with the living image.

The image of that Transcendental Being for which the Prince wore the torn cotton clothes, became averse to the attachment and became beggar, is identified with poetic passion and feelings. For this identification has he, the poet turned his imagination to the mundane earth? To that Being the honoured has surrendered his life, the rich has abandoned his riches, the valiant has given up his life, the poet has composed innumerable poems.

The image of the Being that is pervasive in the great deep, auspicious songs, found in the vastness of the gentleness of the breeze, is identical with the outskirt of the loin that is spread round the blue sky, with the image of love that is of consummate and universal nature, which is bloomed at keen moment at the feet of the beloved. The images of the beloved in universal form and the poet's directive to pave alone through the hurdles of life, and to do work without idleness making all happy and at last his coming to the world, devoid of sorrow, for the unfatigued peace in wearied footstep after long journey at the end of life are all living images, having bearing on the different and variegated walks of life and typical feelings and passions of human beings. When we come to the concluding phase we see the consummate image of the satiety of thirst of love crystalised in one love.

The poetic image in Chitra or variety-incarnate symbolised in a young blonde is compact and consummate in form, colour, rhythm, song, and sense. The poet conceives of Chitra setting her in blue sky, who is sparkling in endless light, who is merriful in impatient delight florescent also! The image of the poem is revealed brightly through the figure of speech Prativastumama in which "the particular is linked to another particular or the general is linked to another general either by a similar attribute or by the same attitude, expressed in the different languages only to avoid tautology". Her rhythm of dance is resounded by the rising of the anklets, the flavour of the hairs are spreading in the gentle breeze, the universal mind is bloomed by the sweet dance; the poet exclaims what a pleasant Ragini there is! Chita is conceived of in various forms and figures, in multiformed songs, colours and looks. She is variegated amidst the objects of the world. With a view to impress the idea of Chitra on the mind of the readers and connoisseurs, the poet creates another picture which is apparently contrasting to the said form and shape i.e. image is created by the idea and feeling that the Chitra is symbolised in a single entity. She is crystalised in a dream, in the charmed tearful eyes, in a lotus, in the bed of the heart-stem, in the Moon set in the endless sky of the mind.

The poet describes her as demure lighting. She is identical with firm, deep magnificent, reticent glory, with the blueness of the eyes of opaque, endless and tender nature, with firm smile like the light of the dawn symbolized in the unlimited form. He addresses her as one who smiles with restraint. The poet muses over the fact. She is alone in the love of his heart, she lives in his mind.

The cluster of images are all sensuous and lyrical. The collection of words and their coherence, the setting of atmosphere, the psychological analysis and the descriptive sketches are all interlarded with one another as to create a bright and effulgent image. The image of variety of single entity and the image of diversity in one and single experience are depicted in this poem. But this feeling and emotive experience are marked with susceptibility. It also appears to us as an experience based on the sensual perception that is distinguished with throbbings of lively human relationship.

The image of an 'Appeal' is one with the desire of peculiar and romantic character. It is peculiar, because of the servant's indigenous desire, that is based neither on material outlook, nor on any pecuniary gain. It simply caters to his romantic idea and imagination. It is romantic because of the fact that it simply fills the mind of the servant with romance, imaginative habits.

The image of the Appeal is identical with the desire of the servant to sit at the feet of the Queen who is alone in the solitary meeting. He wants to enjoy the smile of the Queen, to become the weaver in her grove (Ami taba Malancher haba malakar). For the material desires, needs, demands he does not appeal to her. Rather he wants to sit alone with her to enjoy the sweet smile of her and to be her garlander in her garden. The poet presents contrasting picture also through the poetic dialogue. The servant wants retirement from all activities of life. He leaves the armour, archer on the ground taking the crown lying prostrate under her feet. He requests her not to send him as a ambassador to another country, and not to send him to conquer the new countries. He spreads his sign on the vastness of the activities, with which her men, her soldiers, watchmen are engaged. He then directs his vision towards the sequestrated high island, where lies her place as white as ice amidst the coloured clouds, which is faultless, pure and is adorned with Chandrakanta mani i.e. gems bearing the moon light. By her leave he will pass his days in secluded sweet note of the parrots under the window of the south, under the canopy of the bloomed creeper, that resembles the moon. The flow of the fountain bursts out in the cry of warbling coming from the water-pump in the crystalised floor, making the noon overwhelmed with poems, impatient with pity and in the corridor spreading out the tails the home-peacocks will dance out of swelling pride. The herd of swans will swim over the moss making noise with their white-bent-neck. All these images are denoting the romantic aspect of poetic nature. He wants relief from din, bustle of this world, he wants no honour, respect, glory, award, rather he wishes to pass his days idly and romantically by the side of the queen and to string the garland for her. The image of the feeling, to be idle in the sphere of activities useful for the day-to-day existence is painted vividly and beautifully. He wants to engage himself to make the avenue of the garden lively, through which she strolls at the dawn at the time of rising sun forsaking the hot idleness of sleep from the relaxed body in the tender wave of the breeze. His eulogium of her feet writ in the script of flowers will be revealed in every dawn on the surface of the host of grass delighted in longing of her touch, The beautiful garland with which she entwines her forehead enclosing the braid in the evening, will be woven by the servant himself setting it on the golden plate stringing that variegated garland putting the evening jasmine in and he will hold that before he silently with his face downcast, when she will plait the braid of her wave-crouched with her white lotus hand look of hairs that is dishevelled and impassioned like the fountain in the darkness, and that is lying loosened and spread out on her back, with golden mirror on her lap. Here the image of romantic idea and emotive experience which are identical with the libidinal experience of common place nature is not painted simply but of some elevated strata is crept therein. The common power of the words which speak of common sexual experience are used here denote the highest form of ideality and greatest form of revelation and manifestation. What is of importance and strikingness in this phase is his creative, evocative, sensuous and passionate image? The images that are created by Rabindranath in this phase seem to be living and impress much on the mind of the readers and the connoisseurs instilling the confusion that they are seeing real things and experience not through the eyes of the poet but through theirs. They visualize that the servant sits beside the queen and sees that servant solicits to be the weaver of the garlands of her groove.

The readers see that when she will sit on the cradle of Malati on the root of the Saptaparna Taru, i.e.. Tree with seven leaves, on the bank of the tank of lotus where lotus blooms predominately. In the interval caused due to detachment in between leaves thousands of kisses of the curious Moon will caress and touch on the forehead, eyes, chest and clothes. The savour of the forest overwhelmed with desires will entwine the delightful body like the respiration, the servant under that atmosphere and the circumstances will rock in gentle rhythm like breeze that moves gently and pleasantly. He will lighten that candle bringing in it the scented oil, which burns steadfastly on the upper portion of her bed and spreading its sleepless, steady, moveless sight on the sleeping good physique of her, which is beyond the imagination of angles and human beings. He will colour the garment with pink dying and with the stalk of the sephali (while fragrant autumnal flower) he will adorn daily the foot stool with new idea, new form and with auspicious paintings with flowers and sandal with imaginative writings. Being the consort of the groove he will become the weaver of her groove. He will demand no prize for his activities. In every morning creating armlet of flowers he will bring that on the leaf of lotus, he will put that on her hands clasping her small hand that resembles the bud of lotus; he deems it as a prise. Every evening painting her feet with the red brightness of Ashoke he will kiss and wipe out the smallest particle of dust; this he considers as his prize.

All the images of this poem carry suggestiveness. They are not mere pictures, sheer portraits. Rather they bear the dominating stamp of symbolization. The appeal of the servant does not aim at the fact that is identical with material desires, rather on the appeal all the romantic atmosphere and suggestiveness are kept brightly. It does not end in itself, rather it bears the testimony of peculiar things, peculiar habit of nature. It has a bearing on the minds of the readers and connoisseurs, so that they will feel with the poet the passion and emotive feelings of the appeal. The peculiarity in the creation of image in "bedai Abhishap" (Imprecation on the eve of departure), Happiness, Appeal is remarkable. The difference in imagery in the said poems is arresting and very indicative of the difference in mood and temper in which they were written. The image in 'Urvashi' is almost different from that painted in other poems in Chitra-Phase. The image in 'Urbashi' is so distinguished that it places this poem in the pinnacle of glory, endows it with melodious joy and radiant touches giving impression of different mood, feeling and emotive experiences than that given in Bejoyini, Jibandevata etc. The image of Urbashi is symbolized neither in the form of mother nor of daughter, and wife but in beautiful woman. She is a woman living at Nandan i.e. which is gladness incarnate. She is not connected with the material world. To state this atmosphere Rabindranath creates an image denoting the common experience of the existence.

> When evening comes with weariness, dropping in the
> pasture
> Drawing the golden loin
> You light no evening candle up in a hamlet
> Or any hut of some one.

The image of an abstract beauty—the beauty which has no bearing on a material life and existence is woven here. She is not like the loyal wife who goes to the bridal chamber with sweet smile in silent mid-night with much modest hesitation with trembling heart, and having looks bent downwards. Urbashi resembles the rising of the dawn. The atmosphere with which we are confronted in this poem is unique and distinguished to create such a consummate image. The transferred epithet and attribution of human feelings and emotion to the inanimate objects, the coherence and juxtaposition of word-element, imagination of evening as a fatigued young girl are all peculiarly portrayed. We visualize that some young girl, exquisitely beautiful is before us. We try to pinpoint her on the granite foundation of common experience forms, shapes and natures of mother, daughter wife. She belongs to neither of them. Yet she is beautiful having good physique and form. Again we see another set of contrasting pictures that she has no origin, she is bloomed in herself. She is like the stemless flowers that blooms in itself. Now the poet gives us a picture or portrait of a young girl who was the outcome of churning with a container of nectar at right hand, and with that venom at left hand, and the great boisterous ocean like the charmed snake was lying prostrate at the bottom of her feet having thousands of impatient fangs bent downwards. She is as white as Kunda flower, she who bears brightness of the nude is worshipped by the Monarch of the God. She is beyond censure, she is iewge weibliche—the eternal woman of Goethe. The poet wants to depict a portrait of eternal beauty making her identified and endowing her with the common human feelings. He attributes to her with such qualities that are based on concrete materials. A cornet of constrasting portraits, aesthetic interrogations, some negative features, and above all consummate, full-bloomed portraits is presented to the readers and connoisseurs. The poet visualizes her childhood and her childish activities. He is rather confounded whether she was in her adolescence. If it is so, with whom did she pass her those days, in whose house in the dark ocean. She played with gems and pearls and on whose lap on the bed of prabal stone illumined by gems with unblemished smile in the warblings of the ocean did she sleep? Rabindranath wants to enjoy the beauty, to imbibe the fragrance of beauty which is manifested in women's beauty—the beauty which is abstract, which is intellectual, which is stemlees and beyond material reach. Still so, there is no yawning chasm between the concrete and abstract beauty. Every revelation, portrait, figures, testify to the fact. The poet eulogises of her beauty. She is the loving consort of the Universe. She is an unprecedented beauty. The hermits after breaking their meditation surrenders their outcome of penance to her feet. By the infliction of her side-glances the world become restless. The blind breeze carries with it the sweet savour of her body all throughout the places. The charmed poet like the bee avid of honey is after her in convetous mind singing indomitable songs. She being dishevelled in loin and as restless as lightning makes her anklet resounded. All the portraits signify and aim at pointing to the eternal and abstract beauty of woman. It is to a greater extent identical with the highest form of expression, Vyanjona or the suggestiveness. It is one of the poetic forms of expression. The function of suggestion, also is a function, which is required in addition to the normal functions of Denotation, Indication, and Purport recognized in the speculations of early theoreticians in order to cause manifestation of the symbolic of supreme importance. The form of eternal beauty is also largely dependent on the material objects, the feeling and emotion-contents, the poet wants to present the beauty as devoid of material lassitude, lust and desire. We see that it is like the charming beauty of the puberty of woman, which depends on the symmetry of her body, her colour, her dark eyes and hairs, on all round symmetrical form of her body. So, we observe the image comes out with flying colours. The readers through the images see that when Urbashi dances in great delight on the meeting place of gods, the waves in the sea start dancing in rhythm, the loin of the earth-mother trembles shivering in the apex of the corn, the stars fall detached from her pendant of her breast on the sky, all on a sudden man becomes impatient and his blood becomes restless; her ornamental girdle shatters in the horizon. He addresses her as dawn-incarnate, as fascinating the whole world. The image of her beauty is manifested in the thinness of her body that is bathed by the shower of tears of the world, the flush of her feet is marked by the blood of the three world's heart. She is of dishevelled hair, she is nude. She places her lotus-feet on the centre—the bloomed lotus of the universal desires very softly. She, being the consort of dream, plays limitless frolic in the boundless heaven of the imagination. Rabindranath creates an image of Urbashi who is incarnate of abstract of beauty no doubt, but her attractiveness is not baseless, foundationless. He feels that her beauty has a tremendous attraction and charming bearing. Even today men feel attracted with her world fascinating body. The poet involves her beauteous appearance with drenched hair from the surfaceless, shoreless ocean. But she with her boastful glory has set in the horizontal setting mountain, her influence is felt even today. The world becomes pensive and melancholy. The outburst of mirth comes with hot sigh of eternal separation. In the full Moon, in the world fascination mirth and pleasure the remembrance of the past happenings play the impatient flute and shed shower of tears. So, we see the poem Urbashi is an image itself, although we see cluster of images poetic feelings, passions, his idea of abstract and concrete beauty in it. The poem is a masterpiece; we may ask on which ideality its being masterpiece is based? "It is because the poetic sensitiveness is there that the object undergoes a miraculous transformation, and enables the reader savour blissfully his own feelings. This transformation leading to evocation of feeling is incapable of being caused through denotation of work a day world, that follows the path of logic and rationality, and consequently postulation of Vyanjana is an essentiality." And due to the keenness and evocativeness images come out with abundance and affluence.

The poet again comes down to the mother-earth, he is again tormented by the misery, sorrow, pangs of separation of this earth. He is not annoyed with these revelation, rather he prefers it to ideal and fanciful world. He wants to turn himself from the tower of imagination to the lowest hamlet of this earth. In the Poem "Farewell to the Heaven" he expresses his love for human being who is always afflicted with sorrow, separation and melancholy. He loves this world and he creates an image of his affection, love, and feeling which shines in a unique and luminous suggestiveness and symbolisation. The story of this poem runs thus "One young man happens to come to the heaven and after the expiry of the term he bids farewell to heaven. On the eve of his departure he expects pensiveness, sorrow, tearfulness of the inhabitants of the heaven. But to his utter disappointment he looks round him an atmosphere of grieflessness, heartlessness. The happy Heaven looks indifferent and unperturbed at the departure of him. For thousand and million years they have no winking of their eyes. As much pain the most worn-out leaf feels when detached from the branch of the banyan tree but the Heaven fails to do so, when we in thousands like the fugitive lustreless start fall of at a moment from the abode of gods in the endless stream of death and birth of this earth. If that would pain, the spectre of separation would appear, the ever luminosity becomes dull like earth in soft vapour of dews, cold, sigh due to sorrow and separation. His (Poet's) love for the mundane world and deep affection for the human beings are crystalised in unmixed emotion and passion, and that involves the image of this poem. The human feelings of the poet is manifested in the image of worn-out leaf's emotion and its feeling of pain when it is detached from the branch. This is his distinctiveness and peculiarity of expression. He finds no tears in the eyes of Heaven. Heaven is indifferent and unperturbed. The transformed epithet plays double role in intensification of emotion and feeling dominating throughout the poem. First, by means of attribution of animate emotion to inanimate and passionless objects the poet deepens the emotive atmosphere. Secondly, the entire circumstances become attuned with one lilt of song. The negative quality is given no importance. The Heaven's indifference and callousness are no dominant factor. What is striking is the image of pangs and melancholy. If the Heaven would feel pain Mandakini, heaven's river in her every shore sings the pitiable story with her warbling tone, the garden of Heaven exhales in murmuring, the indifferent evening at the end of the day would go towards the horizon beyond the solitary meadow, the secluded, silent midnight would sing before the galaxy the song of stoicism in the tune of cricket. The poet in the eyes of the said man looks into the indifferent and unperturbed life of the Heaven and feels that in the city of the heaven the dancing Menaka fails to maintain the measure in the golden anklet off and on. From time to time the golden lyre binding on breast of Urbashi all on a sudden jingles in hard torture the deep pitiable tune. The gods feel perturbed and their eyes are filled in tears without reason. All these images are marked with the poet's deep affection of human beings and the mother earth. Even in the unperturbed Heaven he would find the mark of sorrow and pensiveness. But the scene is different. He bids farewell to Heaven. Let them drink the nectar in full-throated ease. The Heaven is their happy place, human beings are alien and exotic there.

The poet creates an image of earth, the affectionate mother-earth not dull, withered and harsh, rather she like a terror-stricken mother wants to put all the children on her small lap spreading her anxious embrace over all the small, thin, the wretched with a view to bind all in her soft breast—She gets relief and delight with the touch of the body smeared with dust. The man, referred to, who is no other than the poet himself leaves the heaven with the impression that Heaven is heaven, it is not mother land; here only flows the eternal flow of nectar nothing else; but on the contrary, the earth is full of the stream of love, mixed with happiness, sorrow and that makes this cloven parts of the earth evergreen with tears. Here we feel the poet's keenness, love of humanity and affection over the earth and all the animate and inanimate objects of this world. He loves the mother-earth, who seems to him living being and who is marked with mother's anxiousness, pensiveness, sorrow and happiness.

He speaks in the mouth of the man referred to in the poem sarcastically and asks her (lady love of the man) not to let the lustre of her eyes become pale due to pangs of love. He is bidding farewell to her. She never longs for one and she never feels sorrow for anyone. The image of Apsari the goddess of the Heaven, who becomes immortal due to drinking of nectar, and who is ignorant of sorrow, pensiveness, invokes in the minds of the reader feeling of sorrow and melancholy and fluidity of human passion and love. The poet then brings forward his experience of this world. If his lady-love is born even in the house of most indigent nature, in the hidden hamlet under the shade of banyan tree, in the border of some village on the bank of a river, that girl will preserve the treasury of nectar for him in her breast with much care. In her childhood creating an image of Shiva on the shore of the river in the morning she will pray to him as her husband. In the dusk causing the burning candle to float on the water with anxious and trembling mind and looking steadfastly she will count her fortune standing alone on the bank. She will come once in auspicious moment to the house of the poet with her eyes downcast, with her forehead marked with sandal paint, wearing red silk cloth amidst the song and rhythm of the ceremony. Then in the days weal and woe with the auspicious bangles in her hand, with the mark of the beneficial vermillion on the parting-line hair, she being fortune-incarnate passes her days in sorrow and happiness resembling the moon light in the sea of the earth. The poet will remember his experience with the Heaven and inhabitants of the Heaven as a dream of far-off event and this will be remembered when awakening from sleep in midnight he will see in the light of moonshine on his clean bed, his sleeping lady-love, her relaxed hands falling on the ground, the knot of the modesty has been undone. She being startled with the soft kiss of caress will awake and lie prostrate on his chest in deep embrace. The south breeze will bring the savour of flowers, the awaked cuckoo on the far-off branch will sing. All those cluster of images are typical and all emanate from the poet's deep perceptibility and sensuous nature. He wants to imbibe the pleasures of this earth making these identified with the experience with his lady-love, and thus also comes from his deep love for this earth and for her inhabitant, her indigent, poverty-stricken children.

The poet through the eyes of the man visualizes the scene of the earth, her eyes marked with tears. The man again feels deep pain for her, the earth after a lapse of time. When his dried eyes become full of tears, at the very moment the heaven like the idle fancy, the shadow of the heaven vanishes. The blue sky, the human habitation, her light, her long beach, white crystal of ice on the apex of the blue mountain, the silent rising of the sun, the evening with downcast eyes on the secluded bank of the river-all the images are visualized and appears in the mind of the man so as if the reflected image comes on the surface of the mirror.

The image of the earth which resembles the sorrow-stricken portrait of human beings is created by poet. The image of heaven and the reservoir of nectar are no lucrative aspects to the poet. It is similar to idle fancy. All these images are symbolized to pinpoint on the deep love and affection towards these images are symbolized to pinpoint on the deep love and affection towards this earth, her happiness, sorrow, her weal and woe.

He remembers the departing day from his mother-earth, and the flow of sorrowful tears, shedded from her eyes, which drenched her breast has now withered.

The image of her portrait, her anxiousness, eagerness full of sorrow, happiness, fear under the shade of life, is created to make a consummate and perfect portrait of love and affection. She always apprehends to lose him, whom she has taken to her breast.

The poem "Farewell to the Heaven" is an image itself. The image of humanity, deep love and affection, deep keen feeling and passion of the poet, his emotive experience is depicted. This is not all, the juxtaposition, the coherence, the sensuous nature become obvious through perceptibility and peculiar consummate ingredients of his poetic image. The transferred epithet is a dominant aspect of his image. The earth is painted on a canvass of a sorrow stricken mother; and this image invokes the portrait of the shore of the sea, crowded human habitation, the long sea-shore, the white crystal of snow in the apex of the blue mountains, the evening with her eyes downcast. The outburst of the long sigh that comes in the wave of the breeze is also woven in the texture of image.

All these poetic images are peculiarly and perfectly created by the poet. The Abidha-Sakti of the words-form is the foundation-stone of the image, that is identical with the Vyanjana Sakti or Suggestiveness. "The image of the earth mother drawn by Rabindranath transforms the ordinary earth in which we move and have our being into an extraordinary one in which it shares the feelings of the sorrowing humanity at large, in this way, the object is raised to an elevated status, it no longer remains the ordinary object of the emperical plane."[31]

Still so, the words-contents are the very basis of the poetic image. The word-contents along with alankara converts the objects of experience into a universal one; the form may be of symbolized nature or it bears the testimony of subjectiveness. All there feelings and passions are crystalised in the novel, audacious and striking images. Rabindranath creates an atmosphere, an outlook and philosophy, which represent the contemporary social life and its way of thinking, love, desire, freedom and humanity. Capitalism creates a condition which revolutionises the preceding mode of social relationship, fundal relation ceases to be and bourgeue is relationship dominates. Romantic outlook emanates from this circumstances. The poet has to create new means of expression to give form to this new attitude.

In the poem Santwana (Consolation) Rabindranath weaves different, typical texture of images. The lady-love of a lover consoles him and dresses the wounds inflicted on his heart. She wants to restore the tranquillity in his restless mind. In one part of the city beyond the limit of the prairie lighting the candle up in the darkness of the dusks she is seated on the seat of flowers being the queen of the Basara. She addresses her lover as a bird who returns to her nest being inflicted on his chest. The bird is tortured, wearied and wants consolation. The image of the sensual pleasure and the libidinal experience is created by the poet having in mind the contrasting picture of infliction and disappointment in life. The image of infliction is drawn in the short canvas, rather in the canvas of sketch only and that also in symbolic genre.

The beloved has created an atmosphere of perfect love and the world where there will be pursuant two human beings only, She and her lover. Pursuant to this atmosphere of love there will remain the dark-night and the doors will remain shut in. There will be perfect sensual pleasure between them.

The house will be worthy of such union. They will create a new world of love and happiness. Only a candle will light in that vast darkness.

The idea of this poem is no new and novel aspect of nature. But the images through which the atmosphere, their sensual union, their emotion, passion and the touching consolation are revealed, are new and novel things. The situation, the atmosphere and circumstances are marked with traditional outlook of life, but the choice of place, the time, the perception, the contradiction are all different and distinguished, and these are all the ingredients of perfect and striking image. The exchange of garlands between the bed's consort and imagination to lay the loin drawing in from the breast are all new and audacious images. The libidinal experience is of striking nature to have kiss and take it into division by both of them and to bring a rose in near the breast are all objects of high-flung imagination and from that emanates the striking image.

The image of the atmosphere of love-making that has been created by the beloved and by the activities of the passionate girl allows the readers to experience the anguish and anxiety of the lover, who happens to have been turned out by his another lady-love. The beloved wishes to enthrone him in her kingdom, and to entwine the immortal honoured garland round his forehead, to adorn him with the auspicious candle and make him seated on the throne of flowers. For that she has strung the garland and attuned the golden lyre with new string. The galaxy in the sky waits with great reticence in tranquil curiosity. She asks whether this garland will be moistured with tears. She means to say that such arrangement, elegant preparation will be of no use of their union. She has felt anguish and pangs of his heart and requests him, who is gagged in voice and in song, not to speak anything. She also will not ask anything. She will feel his silent pain as her own. She will put out the candle and lift his head in her breast and will touch on his wet check with tender hands. The dishevelled lock of hairs will touch the hot forehead with the movement of the breast in slow and gentle measure. By the fanning of her respiration his lock of hairs will tremble, he will close his eyes. In the mid-night in peaceful breeze she will give a kiss on his sleeping forehead. The image of consolation created by the poet does not resemble the ordinary form or genre of solace. It is a poetic alleviation of misery. Here, the role of misery, disappointment covers no dominant portion of the poem; rather it is a factor which claims prominence, because of its spring-fountain from which the consolation-stream originates. The image of consolation is identical with the relationship between a lover and a beloved. The beloved creates an atmosphere a loving and verdurous gloom where they are the only inhabitants; that is the only world they will know and the rest will be in the womb of ignorance and beyond their knowledge. The poet creates an circumscribed world where lovers only reign. This passion and sensibility is the root cause of the creation of the living image.

The poem, "Vanquisher" (Bejoyini) is a consummate and beautiful image itself. Rabindranath, like a painter who makes his portrait lively applying variegated colours and forms, creates an canvass of multiformed and coloured images with the paint-brush of words.

The image of this poem is identical with the handiwork of a craftsman or the beautiful painting of an artist, it is so much a painting as much a poem. The day the woman gets down into the water of lake having crystallized form, the new spring was strolling throughout the world like a first love with shivering and horripillating expression at every moment. The breeze was talking delirium under the deep shake of leafbed, the lustre of the noon became pale in the wood, the parrot-couple sitting on the peaceful, unperturbed branch of the flower, champaka was making solitary warbling at the leisure of deep kisses with their beak. It is a sensuous portrait having a sensual and thrilling feeling of the Poet.

It is similar to the following image of the poetic passion and emotive experience.

"Beauty sat bathing by a spring
Where fairest shades did hide her;
The winds blow calm the birds did song—
The cool streams fan beside her

My wanton thoughts enticed mine eye
To see what was forbidden
But better memory said fie
So vain desire was hidden."[32]

The woman in this poem is a beauty-incarnate. The modus of creation of images of both the poets Munday and Rabindranath is different; they have similarity in their description. The images of Rabindranath is far-flung, more descriptive and more sensuous. Munday's is not so, rather he expressed his wanton desire to see the forbidden and being debarred by the better memory. It is an image of a moralist, not of a poet.

The descriptive features of this poem (Bejoyini) such as getting down of the lady into the water, the desultory talking of the breeze, the stralling of the new spring, the sweet warbling of the parrot couple, the swooning of lustre of the noon in the wood are painted in a single canvas aiming at a perceptive and sensuous image. The figure of speech, Samasakti, plays a vital and dominant role in realisation of aesthetic sense and feeling. Splendour of Samaskti reveals itself at its full height in the brilliant painting of the spring.

The description of the poem runs thus:

On the bank of the lake on the corner of white slab-stone the blue clothes stripped of the glory of the sweet touch of the lady have been left, the hot fragrance of the beautiful body was still with it. It is like the last animation of life in the swooned body at the and of the longevity. The waist girdle was sprawling leaving the waist of the lady in reticent dishonour, the anklet was lying prostrate, the corset of her breast was weltering on the hard stone leaving the grace of breast symbolised in heaven. The golden mirror remembering someone looks at the vacuum. The paste of sandal and saffron were arranged in the golden pot, two red lotuses were wallowing and full of bashfulness, the garland of white karabi is brightfully beautiful, the white washed garment is like the bright luminous sky of the full Moon. The waters of the lake was full-brimmed, blue, peaceful and frictionless; and in every bank there was an expansion of abundance of charming, deep embrace. In the corner of the lake, under the deep shade of the Bakul sitting on the white slab of stone sinking herself upto breast, stretching the tremulous shadow on the opaque water was carousing the white swan that was brought up with much love, clasping her on her breast. Enclosing the two soft wings with nude hands, keeping the tall neck on her shoulder was talking again and again the incoherent utterance of affection, the soft check was touching the back of the swan bewildered with touch with soft hand. Here we see the image of the abstract beauty, and that is symbolized in the naked beauty of a lady. The sketches surrounding this overwhelming beauty of a lady is consistent with the consummate form of the image. The feeling element and emotive experience are given much importance. The briskness, the tenderness of the spring and the passionate lady keep in the total emotion and lilt of the melody of the poem. The result is the emergence of a complete image, so it is essential to the attainment of poetic experience. We have seen her caressing the white swan in the breast-dip water in the lake. Amidst the beautiful sketches she, the passionate lady is identical with a jewel at the centre.

There was resonance of the sweet melody in Ragini everywhere i.e. in the water, the earth and in the sky. Some one was creating a beautiful story with the shadow and the sun rays, with the silence of the forest and the murmuring of the leaves, with the tremor and the throbbing, respiration and outburst with language, hint, hummings, with flash and spray.

As if the strings of sunrays of the nebulous lyre was weeping bitterly due to the stroke of champaka finger of the girl of the heaven tormenting and causing the reticence swooned with pain. The benumbed Bakul flowers were falling loosened silently and sparcaly under the tree, cuckoos were singing incessantly, the fruitless warbling were weeping bitterly from one forest to another having indifferent resonance. In the shadow a bit far-off in the corner of the lake the small fountain was getting down into the roaring wave having rung in the warbling dance the jingling anklet made of gems.

The tuneful image achieves another major success in the painting of spring. The feeling-element and the psychological trait is prominent in creating images, but what we have seen there is a poet going all out for intensity of expression; sacrificing certain points for it, and in the result achieving also consistency of impression. The sympathy with the natural work, rather aesthetic utilization of the natural world has supplied the poet with an image of his thoughts and ideas.

The images of the atmosphere is allied with that of the sensibility of the poet. In the bank covered with grass in this mid-day breeze in the warbling, the stork was asleep having his nape of the tall neck bent in beautiful gesture turning it across his back into the grey wings; the herd of swan in a flight in the sky, who is always restless, leaving the merry-making on the sand of some far-off-river were soaring like the melted snow towards the mountain Kailash.

All these nude beauty of the passionate lady before Madana, the consort of the spring, who was lying in wait in secrecy under the trees of Bakul sitting on the heap of flowers, setting his body on the person of the tree, stretching his feet on the bed of the new green corn. The border of the yellow scarf was wallowing on the ground, the woven garland of Malati flowers was round the curling hairs and round on the white nape of the neck. With smitting winking of eyes he was observing out of curiosity the charming lady and her dalliance in bath. The restless, wanton fingers being eager with the arrow of flowers of aiming at naïve and soft chest was waiting for the opportunity. Thousands of bees were humming round the flowers; the stag with charmed eyes was caressing frequently the sleeping antelope under the tree, the shadow of the forest as a consummate one in idleness and desire coming in touch with the spring.

The beautiful lady ascending the borderline of the water marked with the perturbed and saddened tremor, marking her watery foot-print on every step got up on shore, lock of hairs became dishevelled on her back. The swelling up wave of the puberty expressed in every limb had become firm and motionless captive by the charm of the physical beauty. The apex of these became luminous by the meridian sun; that fell on the forehead, on the lip. On the thy, on the waist, the summit of the breasts, the twin arms, on every streak of her wet body in gushes. Surrounding her the endless breeze and vast sky sitting on the same hamlet with deep eagerness had kissed all her body, like the servant who wipes the wet body with hot loin with much care; this shadow like the for-shaken garment remained prostrate under her red-feet, the forest remained stupefied being widened with amazement.

Leaving the root of Bakul the God Ananga (having no body) got up with gentle smile.

Coming in front of her he stopped with a startle. He stared at her winkless, motionless eyes for a moment, just after that, sitting on his knee with reticent amazement, with his head downcast, surrendered at her feet the flower-bow, the flower-arrows as the religious offer emptying his quiver. The lady looks with peaceful, pleasant smile at the armless Madan.

The purport of the poem is simple and innocent. The lassitude, the lustfulness, the libidinal activities are vanquished by the nude and perfect beauty of woman. The portraits are depicted catering to the requirements of the atmosphere that are created by the poet to intensify the feelings and passion of the poem. The images are tinged and earmarked with romantic idea and imagination. The images of the flight of the swan who left the sportings on the sand of the far-off river, the image of small fountain which was getting down into the warbling of waters are the corset through which the poetic feelings, sensibility, and emotion are revealed. The cluster of images are marked with sensuousness, the perceptibility of natural savour, sight, fragrance. The murmuring of the leaves of the woods, the reticence of the forest, the throbbings of the spring, this swelling-up of the outburst of mirth gush are the factors that create the living and striking images.

In the Poem 'Jibandebatá' a peculiar sensitive experience has been expounded. When he asks "Oh! Lord of my being, has your wish been fulfilled in me?" the readers are presented with the corset of sensuousness, perceptiveness, and poetic sensibility. An image of some entity of elevated and majestic character is revealed to the readers and connoisseurs. The image of the Lord who, is an alien sailor in 'Sonar Tari' i.e. Golden boat, who directs the egoistic existence of the poet in every sphere of his life. The poet on the other hand prepares himself to reach the elevated strata of Jibandevata and to make an arrangement as to quench the desires, lust, wish by opening an avenue to his heart for her. His preparation is this: With the cascade of weal and woe he has fulfilled the pot and given her the same wringing out from his heart, by cruel torment like the kneaded grapes. With so many colours, so many fragrance, melodies and so many matters he arranges her bed. Having melted the raw gold of lust and desire, he creates every day new and novel incarnation for her momentary sport. The said poetic feelings and passion invokes the poetic image. The poet, as it were, tries to satisfy the desires and wishes of this elevated self. The elevated self has been given expression through the sensuous images. An abstract entity along with the poetic passion and emotive experience has been depicted. The articles of common experience of the life, and common items of gratification are the religious offering to be given to the Jibandevata of the poet. Whether has she received him or not is not known to him? He asks whether she is satisfied with his night, morning, his sport, his activities in her solitary residence. Has she heard the songs sitting alone on her throne that are resonant in the rainy, autumn, in the spring, winter? Does she weaves the garland stringing the fanciful flower on her loin-cloth and put on the same round the lion. Has she walked on the bower of this youth? This images emanates from the emotive feelings and libidinal experience of the poet. It is an aspect of romantic thought of the poet. The basis of the elevated and majestic experience is founded on common passion of life and that common passion is expressed through the pictures made of words, which also is of common nature. But the sum total portrait along with it the aesthetic experience of the poet makes the poem a consummate one. And that is the pattern of poetry-the pattern which gives us pleasure because it satisfies the human yearning for order and for completeness. Beneath the pleasure we receive from the verbal music, the sensuous association of a simile or a metaphor; there lies the deeper pleasure of recognizing an affinity. It has been called the perception of similar in the dissimilar; that will do very well, but the perception would not cause pleasure, unless the human mind desired to find order in the external world, and unless the world had an order to satisfy that desire, and unless poetry could penetrate to this order and could image it for us piece by piece. The poetic image is the human mind claiming kinship with everything that lives and has lived, and making good its claim."[33]

So, it is clear that the image is a galaxy of anything and everything that is depicted to give an impression of completeness and wholeness.

The following image is identical with peculiar romantic experience, common psychological experience presented in a universal suggestiveness.

> Days have passed without
> Service and nights without love.
> Flowers have dropped on to the dust
> And have not been gathered for your acceptance.
> The harp strings strung with your own
> Hands have slackened and lost their notes.
> I slept in the shadow of your garden and forgot
> To water your plants.
> Is the time over now, my lover? Have we come to the
> End of this play?
> Then let in bell ring of departure, let the morning come
> For the freshing love
> Let the knot if a new life be tied for us in a new bridal
> bond.[34]

The romantic service which the poet has rendered, the exquisite song that he, his egoistic self (Symbolised in subjective (Ami)) has tried to sing and his tearful failure to fulfil all her desires are expressed as closely related to some permanent human impulse. All the subjective, objective emotions, agencies and convulsions, and his feelings of these agencies and desire to go beyond this tangles and convolutions are all expressed being transmuted into something rich and universal suggestiveness. When his egoist entity 'Ami' states,

> Embrace of our arms being loosened
> Divested of madira are our kisses
> Does the night of love tryst dawn
> In the bower of life?

We are confronted with a peculiar, romantic expression of love and relation to lady-love. Still so, it is not an ordinary exchange of love, or it is Ami's self dedication to Jivandevata, his higher entity. The fact is this that the poet prepares himself, tries to elevate his small contracted strata to a universal one. In 'Manashi', 'Sonar Tari' we have seen his arrangement, his preparation to know the elevated self, to recognize her and tries to understand her words and her activities. In this poem he goes a long way and prepares himself to ask whether her desires are fulfilled in his arbour of life.

All these sensuous, perceptive expression are tinged with psychological and libidinal relation of lover and the beloved. The image of Jibandevata and the relation of 'Ami' with her is the canvas on which Rabindranath has created anything and everything that has bearing on some permanent human impulse and emotions, although these are based on his personal likings, personal agonies and desires that are moulded by the socio-economic condition present in his age. On this poet T. S. Elliot has harped beautifully and exquisitely.

"The essential is that each (poem) expression in perfect language some permanent human impulse. What every poet starts from his own emotions. He is occupied with the struggle which alone constitutes life for poets to is transmute his personal and private agonies into something rich, and strange, something universal and impersonal. The great poet in writing himself writes his time".[35]

Our point is that some permanent human impulse cannot express itself, it must take some modus operandi, i.e. which we emphatically can say that it is image which expresses that permanent human impulse. To take an example:

"The brightness of her cheek
Would shame those stars
As day-light doth a lamp."[36]

Here the poet Shakespeare pinpoints on Juliet's brightness of her check and through this image comes the rush of feeling, the overpowering realization and immortal expression of the transforming glory of love.

So we are of opinion that one poet will be distinguished from another in their creation of images, expression of permanent human impulse and that also is expressed through living and striking images.

4

Images and Its Relation to the Aesthetic Experience of the Poet

Before dealing with vital aspect of discussion—image and its relation to the aesthetic experience of the poet, we shall quote a famous dictum of Whitehead which will radiate light on the image-pattern of Rabindranath and its relation to the aesthetic experience of the poet.

"There is nothing in the real world which is merely an inert fact. Every reality is there for feeling : it promotes feeling, and it is felt."

"..... an actual fact is a fact of aesthetic experience."

In the preceding chapters we have given preference and predominance on the Abidha-Sakti, Lakshna-Sakti and Vyajana-Sakti of words, on whose coherence and juxtaposition, the foundation of literature is based. The luminosity of one factor, which directs, dominates all said factors and ingredients is that of feeling, sensibility, and emotive experience of the poet.

Aesthetic experience is no other than man's aesthetic relationship to reality as creation that conforms to the laws of beauty. To be precise, the creative power of man unfolds in the creation of humanised objects and of his own nature. Man is already a creator since he produces objects they satisfy human needs; a new product images from his work, one that is human or humanised and that exists our human in life and for him. The aesthetic, akin of a particitor relationship between man and reality, his been forged historically and socially in the process of transforming nature and creating a hold of human objects. And the aesthetic sensibility strains from the human process of affirmation. The aesthetic sen seasars when human sppensibility has been enriched to such a point that objects are, primarily and essentially, human reality, reality of the essential human powers. The qualities of objects are perceived as aesthetic qualities when they are grasped without a direct utilitarian significance, when they are thus experienced and essence of man himself. Although creation in particular, and the aesthetic relationship to thing in general, are thus the fruit of the entire history of humanity, and are at the same time two of the most highly developed means by which man conforms himself to the objective world. The practical activity of man has created the condition necessary to advance the humanization of things and of senses to the level required by the aesthetic sensibility. By creating new objects by discovering new qualities and properties in them and human relationships among them, man has own desire that extended his forms, and has enriched and raised sensual consciousness. The aesthetic sensibility is both a scientific form of human sensibility and superior form of this human sensibility in as much as it confirms to the essential human powers objectified in the products of human labour.—*Art and Antiquity*, A.S. Vasquez, pp. 77-78

And these feelings and emotions are given expression through the novel and striking images. So, it is a system of logic-actual fact, happening, the occurrence which did not and will not occur at all, but which is identical with the common happenings in occurance in light of the aesthetic sense. To sum up, reality is meant by the reality felt by the human beings and the literary truth, which is one with its universal, being, must essentially be human.

Here we quote a poem from 'Punascha' of Rabindranath which portraits the particular passion and poetic sensibility touched on the material fact experienced by the poet as one of the material life.

Here I send you my poem
Densely packed in this writing book

Like a cage crowded with birds
The blue space, the infinity around
Constellations
Through which flocked my verses
Is left outside.
Stars, torn from the heart of night,
And lightly knit into a chain
May fetch a high price
From some jeweller in the suburb of
Paradise,
But the gods would miss from it
The ethereal value
Of the divinely undefined.
Imagine a song suddenly flashing
Up like
A flying fish
From the silent depth of time!
Would you care to catch it in your net
And exhibit it in your glass vessel among a swarm of
captives?

The poetic passion and feelings are not like that which becomes manifested in 'Sonartari', 'Manashi', 'Chitra', 'Chaitali', 'Kalpana', 'Balaka' etc.

Some critics may propound—that it in every sense bears the aesthetic experience. It's outlook is related to human feeling and sense. The poet's objective quality is revealed much in this sort of poems. It is an image of actual fact which emanates from aesthetic experience. But the poetic experience and sensibility which we get in Chaitali is also human feelings and passion. But the presentation and manifestation of the human feelings in this phase is peculiar, because of their mode of expression and cluster of images.

In the poem "Dedication" the poet has attained the power to create a perfect and tuneful image-the expression being romantic; and the identification of the poet with natural objects which appeal to his sense is the initial step in image-making.

To-day in my bower of grapes
Bear the fruits in cluster
They seem to burst out at a moment

Due to heavy weight of pain
In the gale of the spring
Perhaps bend down the ground
In the unbearable outburst of passion
Bear the fruits in tier
One upon.

Here we are confronted with the experience and romantic feeling of the poet. The romantic consciousness which finds expression through the corset of the grapes bower is new thing in this phase. In Jibandevata his sensibility is of different aspect. He bends himself, prepares himself for her linking. The image of modesty, humblencess and his desire to fulfil her wishes are manifested. Here in this phase he prepares himself. He requests her to come to his bower as one, who gratifies his desire, to plunder all the viaticum of his life, that resembles all yielding of the spring extremely down-cast silence. He requests her to take the those melancholic representation of the forest. He requests her to tear out the knots of the plants with nails that sucks blood and sitting on the root of the creepers in trance of happiness (she) culls the flowers out of sport with idle fingers for all day long.

"Let the ripe fruits be torn by her bite of teeth".

The poet sees that in the bower of grapes hum the restless bees. All day long the ruffled gale is exhaling the murmuring respiration and the leaf trembles due to the throbbing of the chest of the forest. In his bower of grapes bear the cluster of fruits. The romantic experience has been impressed on the mind of the readers and connoisseurs and special care has been taken for creation of successful images competent to present the symbol of the poet's experience to the refined-reader, who is required to work out this experience in his own mind. The perception of the passion-feeling and the intellect that has been grasped at by the poet is symbolized in the fact,

"Today in my bower of grapes
Bear the fruits in cluster".

In his image we see the uninterrupted manifestation of sensuousness and perceptibility. The intellectual emotion, the emotional thought, intellect, emotion are all guiding aspects or principle to direct and mould the images. The poet creates a symbol of his blissful experience with the help of image, that focuses at a given point of consciousness the brilliant experience along with the unique moment in which the experience is obtained.

In the portrait of the 'Noon' the poet is engrossed in the sights and sounds of nature. Here image comes out due to emotions produced by the visual organs. These images are included in the class of personification or Sama-sakti. The natural objects being attributed with human consciousness give rise to the living images of this poem. We are giving examples of the image of this class.

It is noon. The small thin river is motionless due to lack of current, because of its being stricken with moss. On the half-sunk-boat is seated king fisher, on the bank two cows are grazing on the cornless field. The buffalo remains sunk in the water of the shore, raising his mouth in peaceful eyes, on the shore is bound the desolate boat. On the desolate ghat the hot black crow is taking his bath flapping his wings. On the green bank covered with tender grass the wag-tail dances rocking her tail. The chequered insects on the strength of their transparent wings are floating in the wind, taking momentary rest on the moss. The swan on the younder ghat of the village making sweet cackling noise washes her white wings with the drenched beaks. The hot winds rushes carrying the savour of dry corn, and goes out far. The dogs of the villages bark by fits and starts being engrossed in quarelling. Sometimes the peaceful lowing, the chirping of the Shalika*, Sometimes murmuring sound of the worn-out banyan tree, sometimes the harsh sound of the gull on the remote vacuum, sometimes an outcry of pain of the bound boat due to momentum of the wind, the pathetic inarticulate harmony of the noon, the tender shadow of the forest, the reticent tranquillity of the village are the objects of nature, human feeling-attributed objects, on the centre of which the poet is lying as an alien inhabitant. The poet identifies himself with all the natural objects and realizes that he has come to the origin of all after a long of time. That also not alone, rather with all creatures of nature, to that previous birth when in the first outburst of feeling of life he clasped at the sky, breeze, the water, and the earth like the child at mother's udder, sucking the aboriginal savour of delight.

The sensuousness and keen feeling along with romantic outlook of the earth and nature create the images that like mirrors set at different angles which do not merely reflect the matter, they give it life and forms it is in their power to make a spirit, visible. The theme of the poem "the Noon" is a sum-total picture or sketch of the village of Bengal, and that is marked by the poet's keen observation and passionate outburst and that also is manifested through the prism of images. We deem it correctly that images through which poetic passion and outburst of delight and melancholy are revealed are identical with those. Sometimes they loose their identification and distinguished marks of identity.

We see that the factual occurrences are the basis of the aesthetic realization of the poet. The theme, the passionate experience of the poet, the metre, the rhythm and the alankaras of the poem are the factors we receive in the living images, and the factor that creates these images are drawn from the very walks of life and thus emanates the aesthetic experience of the poet, with which we are confronted while observing the living images of the poem.

In the poem "Rtusanhar' (Revocation of the seasons) the images of the sensuous aspects of the seasons and their impact on the poet kalidasa are created by Rabindranath, when he states:

"At youth's coronation, Kalidasa,
You took your seat, your beloved by your side
In Love's primal Paradise
Earth spread its emerald-green carpet
Beneath your feet
The sky held over your heads
Its canopy gold-embroidered;
The seasons danced round you
Carrying their wine cups of varied allurements,
The whole universe yield itself to your loneliness of
delight
Leaving no trace of human sorrows and sufferings
In the immense solitude of your bridal Chamber."

Here we are confronted with the peculiar and unprecedented typical imagination of Rabindranath, although it is manifested through the poetic sympathy common to all men.

We are quoting here a dictum of a famous critic relating to the poetic imagination and sympathy of wide nature.

"When we speak of poetic imagination, then, we speak on the one hand of sympathy common to all men, though in the poet specifilished, cultivated and intensified, and on the other hand a perpetual reaching out of this sympathy towards objects otherwise unattainable – towards the past, the future, the absent, all that lies outside the compass of present experience without which the meaning of this experience must be so much the less distinct and complete. The nature of poetic sympathy is revealed in images and I do not know any better way of defining it than by a selection of images in which poets have embodied this sympathy, or attested to it."[37]

We see the poetic sympathy through the poetic images. He makes us see the love's primal paradise, earth's spreading out of emerald green carpet. He pays majestic tribute to Kalidasa and expresses poetic sympathy towards objects which are unattainable, specially the natural phenomena which adorns the poet Kalidasa. And that is manifested through living images of the loneliness of delight, the immense solitude of his bridal chamber, emerald-green carpet; the world is imagined as one Harem, one bed-chamber. The next poem Meghduta (Cloud messenger) reveals the opposite and contrasting portrait of nature.

> "Suddenly god's curse descended
> From on high
> Hurling its thunder bolt of separation
> Upon the boundless detachment of youth's egotism.
> The season's ministry in a moment was ended
> When the veil was wrenched
> From love's
> Isolation
> And on the tear-misted sky appeared
> The pageantry
> Of the rainy world of June

Across which journeyed the sad notes
Of your bereaved heart
Towards a distant dream."

The alankara 'Samasakti and 'Vachyotpreksha intensified the poetic sympathy towards objects referred to. Through the image of separation that is hurled on the boundless detachment of youth's egotism, the poetic sympathy is revealed. The sad notes of thc Meghduta's bereaved heart towards a distant dream is given expression of the poetic sympathy and that also through poetic images. Such as the beautiful world of the tearful June or Asara, through the sad notes of separation of the universal lyre sung at the heart of the world.

In the poem 'Unsuitable time' the poet requests his consort to stop all vain attempts of activities. The all-round reticence will be predominant. The heart of the poet is compared with the hermitage, which is afraid of the fear of the interruption in austere ascetic mediation. It is not the time for his beloved to come to him with the garland of the flowers with the loin full of youthful reminiscence. The time is most unsuitable for the song of the secluded bower. Only her two anklets will resound in the path of the murmurless forest.

The image of the peaceful hermitage and the unsuitable time of the arrival of his consort, the secluded bower bereft of the outburst of song are all passionate experience of the poet. The passionate experience, anxiety that is manifested through the blooming of the blossoms that are attributed human feeling do add new blood vigour of the living image.

Kalpana (Imagination)

Endless

The images of Kalpana are magnificently created by the poet. The aesthetic experience, feelings, passion of the poet are distinguished and different from that of Chitra, Manashi and Sonartari. The romantic outlook has been endowed with the element of the detour whence new stream of consciousness flows on. The ego of the poet after a long journey in his life has taken repose in night. He hears again the call of his guide, Jibandevata. He exclaims? The activities that are entrusted to him have been aptly done. Again she calls him. The atmosphere of the nature is full of the poetic passion and feelings. The natural phenomena suits to his repository situation. The bright dawn went away a long while ago causing the garden of Madhabi flowers bloomed, the noon has gone withering the dews lying with the flowers and making the atmosphere very thirsty. In the west outskirts of land the afternoon ends with pale smile. In this wearied situation the Ami is about to get up the boat bound for the another side of the river and hears the call of Jibandevata. The repository situation of Ami and the atmosphere of rest is revealed through the image the drowsily idle evening in her hand alights. On the warbling of the day draws the humming of sects, the deep dark curtain. The image of the evening which is animate with human feelings are created to intensify the atmosphere of the evening and situation of silence and seclusion. The alankara, Samasakti or transferred epithet is used here to make the image more distinguished and perfect. The call of Jivandevata would have been less poignant but harsh, should the atmosphere be depicted with less intensity and less comforting. The portrait of the black bank of other side is deepened by the blackness of the night. Into that deep black and unfathomable night his eyes do sink. The dream clasps the eyelids and song is stopped. Fatigue grasps his body like the request of his beloved and at that crucial moment she calls him again. All the inanimate objects and natural phenomena are attributed with human feelings and passion. The experience of the poet resembles the ordinary one, but how does this ordinary and subjective expression change its form, colour and strata? It is due to juxtaposition of the poetic feeling, the peculiar use of alankara and above all the aesthetic experience, which is revealed through living and perfect images. If the portrait of the drowsily idle evening is not presented to us, if evening is not compared with a sweet girl with a candle at her hand and not pictured before us, we do not understand the atmosphere on which the poet changes his outlook, philosophy of life. He wants to break out the periphery of egoism or egoistic outlook and respond to the urgent call of his guide.

Then he addresses her as cruel and blood-monger, hard-hearted fiend, because of the fact that she wants to make him engaged at night also, the day being already scarified to her work. Rabindranath through these images wants to manifest his feeling that emanates from the materialistic outlook and philosophy of life. It is the duty of the poet to engage himself with the activities congenial and beneficial to the impoverished, poverty-stricken, illiterate people of the world. He has got no tranquil moment on his life. His life is filled with works which demand careful wakefulness and vigilance day and night. This idea, feeling element invokes the images of negative, contrasting nature and character.

He appeals to her and enquires whether there is peaceful repose in her palace or not.

Oh' awake Queen!
On the door of your palace on the shore
Of the south sea
Does not the maxim of stoicism ring
In melodious tone and wearied metre?
Do not the birds sleep on
The black branch of the mute forest?
Do not the stars rise slowly in
The apex by their soundless wing solitary
Do not the lock of flowers create their solitary bed
Under the canopy of the creepers?
Oh unwearied, calmless! The day is coming to an end.
Even at this moment there is call!

The character and form of the image lies in the form and stratum of poetic reason and dictum. The night is meant for peaceful and tranquil rest. Even in the palace of his Jibandevata there is tranquillity, peaceful quietude pervading all the natural phenomena. The all-round motion of activities are involved in this maxim of poetic perception. What we have seen there is a poet going all out for intensity of expression of the poetic experience and passion. "If we follow the cluster of alankaras along with the poetic process and stages by which the poet penetrating ever more deeply into the meaning of his perception, outlook, and aesthetic experience has at once been guided by it and directed it, as a sculptor may be guided by the grain and contour of the rudimentary block from which he is extracting a finished form. The sympathy with the natural world will supply the poet with an image for his thought gift so gratuitously and-unobtrusively into his hand that he is unaware of what he has been given".[38] The ego of the poet responds to call of Deity Jibandevata forsaking all his own, the flame of the lamp of his evening, the couple of eyes that look on his way, her weaving of the garland with care. "Let the ferry boat sail with the home-going persons to the village of the opposite bank of the river, and let the thin-shaped moon third lunar day set slowly on the north of the hut. "

His night, peace, the obsession of the dream, the tender tranquillity are left untarnished. He starts again responding to her call with his head downcast being wearied.

· All these images emanate from the common experience of the poet, from the common walk of life. But the poetic feeling, passion and poetic urge toward action are all depicted on the same canvas on which traquil, peaceful quietitude, along with the tender, calm atmosphere are pictured. The image is thus created out of the aesthetic experience of the poet. Conversely the aesthetic experience is revealed through the living and perfect images. Aesthetic realization is helped by the poetic figure in another also. The poetic figure effects the integration of images and consequently plays a vital role in attainment of the aesthetic delight. But all these experiences and realisation depend largely on the word-contents, wherein lies the foundation stone of aesthetic experience and perfect, living images.

The psychological state of the 'Ami' of the poet is similar to the first state of mind, with which he for the first time responded to her call. Remembering that he puts pertinent question whether he is again able to adorn her, to beautify her. He asks her pardon and appeals to her good sense and sympathy. If drowsiness forbids him to do his work as previously, the slackened hand forgets preceding skill, if the losses strength of mind, if his eyes become full of tears, he requests her not to chide him, not to dishonour him. This sort of behaviour he does not deserve as he responded to her call untimely. We are confronted with passionate behaviour, the slackened hand, chiding element, drowsiness, writhed with blood, adorning with flowers, that have taken shape of symbolic images, which augment unconsciously in us the same sensation the poet experiences.

At last we see the ego 'Ami' of the poet awakes from his slumber and drowsiness, and promises her to fulfil her call and he will not falter in his word, will not tremble, he will wait for the new bright day with lustre of lamp in his hand and hand over the load of work in novel morning to the new servant and in his last declaration he will announce her call.

All these sensible and sensuous activities are not mere statement of fact or reportage, but these have an impression no doubt and these become crystalised into an image. There is a process, stage and continuity. 'The creative process up to the emergence of formed images from the unconscious, is described by Dryden in his introduction to the Rival ladies where he speaks of the time when the play was only a confused mass of thoughts tumbling over one another in the dark; when fancy was yet in its first work, moving the sleeping images of things towards the light there to be distinguished and then either chosen or rejected by the judgement."[39]

We see in Rabindranath that sort of experience, process and a confused mass of thoughts that are the foundation stones. These are all a confused mass of thoughts and sensible and tears- marked occurrences and facts. It is aptly said that these are all the sleeping images of things towards the light. It may be stated otherwise. "Trains of thoughts are continually passing to and from the light into the dark, and back from the dark into the light. When the current of thought flows from within our ken to beyond our ken, it is gone, we forget it ..... After a time it comes back to us changed and grown as if it were a new thought."[40]

The poem 'The end of the year' is a masterpiece due to its elevation, idealized concepts and striking and living images. This language, its rhythm, metre by no means resemble that of "old servants" – the poem of this phase. So, it is clear that as language has got its vital role to play, it is also of the same importance that the portrait, painting with words, the image are of permanent value to the realization of concepts and aesthetic experience of the poet.

The 'end of the year' bears the evidence of the natural description. The accumulated rubbish, the old thoughts, and aspiration are brushed aside by the advent of the south-western. The poet takes the south-western as symbolic, as the wester which wipes out all the smashed, withered objects. The poet while biding adieu to the old, to the past year wants to sing the last song of the wearied, old year. At the advent of the south-western the natural phenomena becomes disruffled and everything is at topsy turvy. The pasture becomes dust-grey, cows run having their face upturned, the farmers are hasty towards their home. The boatmen quickly strike their sails of the alarmed boats lying on the river. The flow of yellowish brown colour of the dust, the scattered clouds of the west looks with angry eyes. The anxious birds fly in flocks through lightning-rent vaccum.

The images of dust grey pasture, of the running of the cows having their face upturned, the striking of the sails that are alarmed and the flow of the yellowish brown colour of the dust lying with the scattered clouds in the west are created by the poet's concepts of life that emanates from the aggrieved mental state of the poet in the contemporary political background. The advent of the south-western is symbolic. He portrays his agitation that chides all round meanness, cowardice, timidness of the contemporary people of India, and eulogizes the victorious songs of the greatness, magnanimity of the Elan vital.

The aggrieved mental state of the poet takes shape not in the disappointment leading the people astray; rather the symbolized image creates an atmosphere that is marked with throbbings of accomplished concepts of life. The advent of the south western brushes not only the amassed, withered rubbishes of the nature, the worn-out concepts of the poet also. The Poet directs his 'Ami' the ego-self to strike the lyre with the sharp jingling and clattering sound, and to raise the lilt and let the heart fall in boisterous affluence by the cruel stroke. He directs his Ami to sing the song like the hurricane, full of life, which soars high in the endless sky. Let the colourless, emaciated and wornout leaves fly out and go out of sight in great respiration. Let the frantic south-western dance binding the anklet of hurricane in it feet, let the fruit-less accumulation of the old year be destroyed like the dust and the grass by the whirling stroke of her loin cloth, in rhythm and in every step. The natural whirlwind is wiping out all the emaciated, worn out accumulated objects of the earth. It is no new and striking fact. But what is striking is a novel, boisterous change and revolution in the mind of the poet. The attribution of human feeling especially of dancing girl who will dance binding the anklet of hurricane is new and unprecedented fact. The poet at this stage is worried of the political fact of his contemporary age. The desire to leave the old world, old customs and behaviour is a crying need of the age. The image of his feeling, passion and aesthetic experience of the poet is created by the symbolized aspect of his concept and doctrine. The 'end of his year' bears the evidence of the afflicted state of the mind of the poet, which is identical with the net work of communication between its images.

"I have unlocked my heart to the rains and storms of the sky."

Let a whiff be puffed into the face of my heart like conch; let the auspicious loud noise pierce the cloud in the roaring sound of victory awakening in the illumined mind the stern satisfaction that resembles the nude purity of the hermit."

The images of stern satisfaction that is compared with the nude purity of the hermit, the image of pervasion of the auspicious sound, the whiffing into the heart like the conch emanates from the poetic sense and sensibility. This image pinpoints the afflicted state of mind and his desire to achieve a vivacious and vital life. . So, it is clear that he is more sensitively alert than his contemporaries and we see for his reason that he is connected with contemporary age by an invisible tie. The freshness and audacity of image will also be realized by the same measure. From image pattern it is obvious that a poet can create an image from any given object, provided his imagination responding to is strong enough. Rabindranath was emotionally stirred by the contemporary happenings and occurrences. The subject matter of the poem

'End of the year' (Barsa Sesha) is symbolically presented. The poetic emotion, poetic experience, through the alankara, rhythm, metre, metaphor, simile denotes the said fact. Rabindranath paints his image on the canvas of traditional antiquity of India.

Let that consummate high and deep tone like the incantation of Samaveda and the saga of veda, which is candid and deep, emerge at a moment in the icon of entirety from the whole heart. At the emergence there is no weal and woe no old anger and lament, there is no trembling, shame and fear. That is only sounded with the victory of the life that is just bathed, straight, white pure and open. The image of the poetic dictum is beautiful and impressive because of his concept of life that marks vividly the image. The emergence of the consummate deep tone also illumines the image. The poet prefers to present the simplest truth, illustrated by the just-bathed-pure-white-open life. He invokes the New :

Oh New, come repleting
June whole sky with the crowded shape
Pervading and concealing in layers.
In clusters and in deep dark heap
Whence (you) all on a sudden
Come to hide in a moment all regions
And in your tender, black awful
In your deep darkness
Stay for a while.

The image of the New is deeply allied with the awful picture of the cloud. We are confronted with the natural phenomena specially with the dark, deep thunder and black shape of the cloud. It is a common and simple experience. But what appears to us is not the embodiment of cloud only, but along with it its devastating power, its pervasive nature. The abstract New has taken a-shape of the concrete one in its creative action, in its spreading out of the network of concealment . The image carried the mark of sensuousness and passionate experience that lies beyond the common experience and common affection because of its being distinguished as novel, audacious and unprecedented. The more crystalised form is manifested in the following consummate images. The gesticulation of the New is revealed, as it were, in the lightning under the deep secret grimace. His song comes as the roaring storm through the countless pores of the sky, his shower comes so as to strike the thirst piercing it in keen and violent swiftness; his tranquillity, as it were, bring in the sleeping, green, pervasive, deep and peaceful night. The new life, the novel world is imagined in the glaring and luminous outlook. The sensuousness, romantic atmosphere is replaced by the stern aspects of material achievement. The negative and contrasting qualities are the distinguished features to deepen the aesthetic realization of the poet. When he describes his appearances,

"This time you would n't come in,
The excitement of swing in the spring
Printing your kiss on the petal
Would no't you come in rustling
Warbling and humming
You are fortunate and blessed!
You've come like the victorious king
With the rattling chariot
Being proud and fearless
I understood or could n't understand what you uttered
In the incantation of the thunder bolt
You are victorious".

He creates an image which is presented in contradiction to Romantic emotive atmosphere. The arrival of the New is imagined as majestic and pompous arrival of the victorious monarch.

The image of the advent of 'New' marked by the majestic and pompous glory of the victorious monarch is still within the periphery of the regal and royal conception and outlook of Rabindranath although his entire outlook which is for the goodness and welfare of the people is marked by the anti-imperialistic view-point.

The image of the next stanza is audacious and striking, because of the boisterous characteristics of the advent of the New being : he addresses the New:

Oh ! turbulent oh! Ensured!

Oh New, cruel New
Simple and powerful
As the fruits emerge destroying
And casting off the withered petal
Piercing the old leaves and spreading
Out in peculiar way!
You too, are revealed with repleteness,
Have my obeisance.

The poet eulogizes the New as the tremendous, tenderly dark-coloured and unwearied, unfaded; and compares with a crown-prince and requests him to tug his bow. He compares the New with a adolescent and requests him to take the liberal war-drum and call us. The poet wants to identify himself with his activities and responds to His call.

The poet wants to forshake the bygone days and the past life which is corrupted with weariness of day-to-day life. This sort of experience has been given consummate expression by the following image : This image is created by the poet as meticulous and acute insight peeping through the back-window into the closed room which is marked by the black smut of smoke issued out of the small wick of dim candle at every night.

The poet expresses his restlessness and that is manifested in optimistic conception, not in vacuum marked with disappointment. He wants to give up the work of old ideals, worn-out conception and fatigued days. He cannot put up with the life that is divided in parts and that is wasted at every moment. The poet wants to see the almighty figure of this age of another, and requests the New to take him away from the quagmire of the day-to-day existence like the bird of pray all on a sudden and make him confronted with great and magnanimous death in the light of lightning. He wants nothing than this. He has no desire and he does not want to know whether his existence is in this world or grinded or he attains the state like the small toy which becomes the object of oblivion after the play is over. If there remains something after his cruel pilferage, he may, if he so desires, hurl the 'Ami' of the poet, on the land of forgetfulness which is the land of eternal night.

The image of the last and concluding stanza is created by the poet's optimistic outlook and keen sensuousness. Here we see even iota of dissappointment does not disturb the poet. The savour of life in the shape of shower of rain has been bestowed on the land of the sugar-cane of newly sprout uninterruptedly. The day is over through darkness of the cloud. The atmosphere is now peaceful, the earth is tender in its swelling of outburst of passion. The poet has dedicated his concluding song of the last year, that has bearing on the tranquillity of the atmosphere, and the birth of the new sprout and on the tenderly passion of the earth.

The image of the 'End of the Year' is crystalised not only in the end and concluding storm only, but in the optimistic outlook and in the birth and germination of sprout also.

"On the day of the storm" is an image itself. The impediments and obstruction caused by the rain in Autumn is the main spring from which the images are flowing out. The daring lady wants to cross the impassable path that has been inaccessible due to swelling frenzy of the storm in the corn field in Autumn. How does she recognise her way? The poet requests her not to bind the anklet round her feet and put on blue cloth, because the rain will wash out the deepness of the colour. She will not be able to show that in bashfulness.

The poetic feeling and passion and the natural atmosphere create the images in the poem on the day of the storm. The obstruction is a natural event, the poetic passion takes it in a novel and beautiful way. The impediment are of general nature, but the poet imagines that this natural obstruction will be of great uneasiness and hindrance, and requests her not to start through this calamity. The poet makes us acquainted with the fact that an impatient lady is about to start to meet some one who is a waiting her on the field that lies at the end of this crooked path and which is mixed with the cloud. The poet forbids her to go to him, who seems to have opened his door and waited for her with a burning lamp. The poet reminds her of the natural calamity for which he will not be able to light the lamp and if the flute is played on this day, the song will be drifted in the endless darkness of the Autumn. The image of the cloud along with its rumbling sound makes the readers and the sympathetic connoisseur, acquainted with the fact that the thy of the daring lady will tremble due to rumbling sound of the cloud and the question with whom lady will find fault and to whom she will inflict her anger, if her heart will shiver? At last, the poet makes some adjustment. The natural calamity he thinks is no factor, it is no impediment at all. The poet is there alone on her way to the door of his hut. The poet wants to accompany the daring lady even in the foul and clumsy weather, although the storm is at its full form, the sky is covered with clouds fully, the path becomes endless in the darkness of the night, he would not fear them at all. His heart will dance during the time of focusing of the lightning, his scarf would float in the air like the open wings and would be one with the sky and the nether world. All these images are created by the poetic sensibility arisen from a peculiar situation of rainy season and its impact on his mind. Keeping the natural phenomena intact and unblemished he has attributed to nature with human feelings and passion and creates a character to supplement his romantic consciousness. He forbids her to start for his lover, whom she thinks, will keep his door open for her and lights the lamp. At last he disappointedly asks her,

> "why do you go alone today?
> Why do you fasten the anklet
> For which reason, in this foul day
> You remember the forgotten tale of the spring?"

The poet paints a portrait of the rainy season and of a day marked with torrential rain. This material-element invokes in his mind the romantic consciousness and helps him to imagine a character who is earmarked with daring aspect. She is imagined that she will start her journey in this foul weather to meet her lover, who is waiting for her in his hut lighted by his lamp. The Image of this 'Spring' awakens the emotion laying latent in the mind of the reader. Being acquainted with this general truth, the poet brings in before the general readers the romantic outlook and perception like presentation. The common and general features of the spring which pleases the commonest feeling of the observers with her mellowing fruitfulness and flowering entity is dominant in the image of the spring. The mystery of natural processes is apprehended from different levels of perception, and the result is a rich, complex pattern. His sensible effusion is like this:

A million years ago, oh spring! on the
First appearance of Phalguna
With frenzy and curiosity
For the first time you came to this world opening
The Southern door of the Heaven.
All on a sudden you appeared at the
Courtyard of the hamlet
Wearing the yellow garment
Scattering the blossoms of Mandara
On the maddened wind
From the scarf inpatient.

The image of the spring confronts us with sensibility and peculiar aspect of his imagination. A peculiar and distinguished characteristic has been instilled in the imagination. The appearance of the spring in the common surface of nature is no new thing; but that does not mean it is presented with common vicissitude having no peculiarity and perceptibility. Rabindranath paints it attributing human qualities and animate sensation. Common men and women greet the spring. They admire the blossoming aspects of nature. But Rabindranath having kept this common experience of the human beings into in his mind depicts the reaction of their mind:

They hurried in a company opening the door of their huts with lyre and flute and being intoxicated with mad dancing hurled the pollen of the flower at one another. The poet gives expression to the feeling and passion of the men and women arisen at the sight of the first spring along with it the natural beauty. The image of the flower that has been soaked in the hot rays of the golden wine is created by the poetic passion and feeling, which seems to have been soaked in the hot rays of the golden wine is created by the poetic passion and feeling, which seems to have been identified with that of human beings who for the first time felt and enjoyed the spring. It is no fanciful occurrence on the part of the poet.

He has felt it keenly and meticulously. The Spring which comes after the chill pinch of the winter is over, with sweet sight and melodious sound is naturally greeted with full throated ease. And then what is first effect and reaction of the first appearance of the spring?

It is a natural and practical question of the common and distinguished men and women. And since then the spring has been coming to this earth with old, eternal, and endlessly aged new flowers in every year, and with that again it has adorned the bouquet. On that flowers is writ largely the forgotten message of the old days of the world. For that it's flavour bears the charming sweetness of the wearied, worn-out world and of another beyond this world. The epithet personification is aftly used by the poet with a view to establish the kinship with the past and the present. "This kinship is felt equally by the artist and the experiences, and the image is the medium through which this conviction is transferred from one mind to another."[41]

The poet observes the swelling outburst of passion in the blossomed deep bower where in the varied pangs of the endless days and nights, and tears, songs and smiles become luminous. The poet has woven the garland, which is marked by the tears of the tale of the old cravings and aspirations of nameless amorous women to dedicate to the spring.

The poet has created an image which is radiantly distinguished and luminous because of its being tinged with the sensuousness of the poet. Here we observe the poetic image is not the container of poetic feelings and passions, rather it is identical with these. In the red petal of the rose, which is newly bloomed and which is watered by the poet himself there are largely writ the marks of trembling hesitating-innumerable-kisses. The petal of the rose is vital point and it is endowed with animate throbbings of life. It resembles the hesitating and trembling mark of first love, although there are exchange of innumerable kisses and rosy blushes. This perceptibility is the guiding principle to create an image. The mode and genre of attribution of human qualities to the natural objects are the allied factors to create an image.

Then we get an image wherein the poet has expressed the amorous feeling and passion experienced in the night of the spring through exchange of secret words with his lady-love, that have been radiantly expressed through four eyes. The poet has identified himself, his feelings, even his amorous consciousness with the spring. The smiling and white-faced chamapka, bakul and restless, startled chameli (Maugolia flower) and the young bright rajanighandha, that is ernestly eager, and keenly curious, had all read the saga of his youth in the preceding years of the spring. Keeping themselves abreast with the poet they heard the lilt of the song of cravings of his heart. The complete unification with the natural phenomena is the vital point in the creation of poetic images.

In the concluding stanza the poet expresses his emotion that has been experienced coming in contact with the touch of the spring, the manifestation of which is revealed in the savour of the flowers in years to come, in the vacuum, in the waters and lands. The emotive contents being stuck in Bakul and Champaka cross the limitations and have the touch of this and another age. They will become impatient in every bower in every spring and in the warblings of the cuckoo.

The image of the immortal pangs is created by the poet by placing his emotive contents in the murmurings of the spring and by making his hot pride of youth tinged with golden rays of the evening sky of the Chaitra or April.

In the image of "Baisaka" we get different pictures and different passions. Baishaka is painted as cruel and his matted hair becomes grey coming in touch with dust and is rugged, is flying the air and is of yellowish brown. His body is hot due to austerities of ascetic practice and he calls whiffing the awful horn. All these pictures testify to the fact that the poet intends to create an atmosphere of turbulence, awfulness and terribleness, which we confront in the devastating appearance of Baishaka. The function and common activities of natural phenomena are given expression, bearing of which is coloured with poetic passion and sensibility giving rise to the poetic image. When the poet states :

You have as many as attendants, who are apparitions,
From which holes of copper-burnt-horizon

They are rushing out?
What a awful and invisible dance!
With which they become frenzied.
The silent hot
Your followers are apparitions.

The terrible atmosphere is given expression. The transferred epithet being used deepens the atmosphere. The poet creates an image of awfulness, cruelty having the abstract being concretised in the shape of perceptive natural objects.

In this connection we cite here the poetical image of Kalidasa, who is also distinguished from other Sanskrit poets in creation of living images.

With sharp shaft in blossom of
mango-tree
And shining bow string in row of
humming bee;
In hearts of passionate pain to bring
Younder comes hither the
spring.
Mango-blossom makes the pointed
shaft,
And the bow is traced in
kimsuka graft;
Row of bees maketh the gallant
string
As shining moon doth royal canopy
bring
His imperial tusker is made of
Southern wind
And bards in cuckoos please the mind.
May this bodyless love, the winner
bring
Joy to the world along with
bounteous spring.

Thus finds access to the world as envisaged by the creative artist and it is this capacity to reveal the pattern of reality that constitutes one of the salient traits of the living image.

Another characteristic feature of the successful poetical image is represented by variety. Since imagination is the instrument with which the poet explores the patterns of reality and the images are high lights by which we reveal to the reader these pattern; the more powerful the imagination of the creative artist, the more many sided is his image likely to be. A successful image comprises for its ingredients of a number of things, and this attainment of the desire and by such an image depends on the skill of the artist in combining these diverse elements into one whole.

Rabindranath also takes the same device; but what is striking in his patterns of images is the consummate and tuneful corroboration of his feelings, passions and sensibility with the modes operandi of their expression. One may be struck dumb at the sight of their staying at the same level and canvass. The typical and aesthetical expression plays the role to allow entrance to that much of opulence, grandeur and majestic propriety of the palace of poetic experience and aesthetic feeling.

The image of the fire that breathes rapidly due to absorbedly engaged in action, which is rising spirantly at a great speed with burning whirling the corn and leaves stirring in the sky the pulverized heaps of pollen, is vital and consistent with the poetic outlook and sensibility.

The poetic truth along with reality and its revelation in the form of whirling metre, rhythm touches the very sympathetic aspect of the character of the readers and the connoisseur, because of the commonness of the fact and occurrences. The readers are aware of the rugged and withered atmosphere of the nature. The rough, harsh and cruel touch of the summer season has a familiar bearing on the readers and connoisseurs. But when Rabindranath states it thus:

Oh bright eyed lean Monk
be seated on the yogic sitting
Lifting the red eyes on the forehead
On the bank of the dry river, on the
Cornless field smitten with thirst,
Oh thin Monk!
Oh indifferent and alien!
Oh bright-eyed, lean Monk!

The human feeling and passion invoked at the sight of the barrenness of nature is no new and peculiar thing, but what strikes us much is the juxtaposition of image and attribution of human feelings to inanimate things and objects. We are faced with dread-fullness of scorching sun.

The natural scene and atmosphere is carrying the terrible and dreadful aspects of it and in order to deepen the atmosphere of nature. The rest-raintful image invokes the same inflammation of rage, passion and feelings that have been experienced by the Poet.

The image of the world beyond the desolate, scorched horizon is revealed by the Poet. The Poet wants :

"Let sorrow, happiness, hope and dispairfloat in the sky like the particles of dust agitated by the whiff, and let the ardent sky be filled in with savour of the slackened flower of the bower."

The poet requests the Baisakh to lay down the border of his grey cloth on the surface of the sky covering with great stoicism, the old age, death hunger, thirst and million hearts of men and women who are exhausted and worn-out. The poet intended to go out rising from great slumber and locks beyond the din and bustle of this world. Here we are quoting G.D. Liwis a passage from "The Poetic Image" wherein he deals with poetic sympathy of dual nature, one being common to all, and another being expressed towards objects unattainable. The poet stretches his sight far beyond the scorched horizon of this world and makes us acquainted with the world be intends to observe with deep silence and reticence.

"When we speak of poetic imagination, then, we speak on the one hand of a sympathy common to all man, through in the poet specifilised, cultivated and intensified, and other hand a perpetual reaching out of this sympathy towards objects other wise unattainable, towards the past, the future, the absent, all that lies outside the compass of present experience, without which the meaning of this experience must be so much the less distinct and complete. The nature of poetic sympathy is revealed in image, and I do not know any better way of defining it them by a selection of images in which poets have embodied this sympathy or attested to it."

Rabindranath follows the same genre and mode, but what is strking in his creation of image is this that his identification with objects and facts which appeal to his senses is as simple, and beautiful, as its revelation and expression through image. The image is created as living as the first coming in contact with thc senses of the poet.

In The 'Tale' the scope of striking image is much less than that of other poems. It is like the statement of facts, or like a short story. The poet points the village situated on the bank of Churni seeming tearful in the morning dews of the autumn. The poet looks through the eyes of Rakhal, who like the Ancient Maninar observes water water everywhere. He becomes annoyed with waters that are smooth, oily, black crooked, cruel, greedy with protuberant tongue, like the malicious snake hypocritical, and full of deciats raising its millions of angs are growing, and fuming and craving the children of the earth with the carnivorous months. Side by side he has painted another picture of the mother earth- the picture of which is of affection, stability, firmness, reticence, the ancient character, the abode of pleasure and mirth, with which the aspect of all on during capability has crept in, which is as soft as greenness.

The poet has created the image making it coloured with multiform and dying, which appeals to his senses and perceptiveness. He creates an image of the greedy, agitated, cruel and boisterous waters. Side by side he paints the portrait of romantic outlook. He stretches his sight on the blue boderline of the far-off shore of the sea, swelling towards the tranquil setting of the sun in arrogant rebellion.

The poet deepens the pensive atmosphere by painting a contrasting picture. Had the portrait of the waters been insipid, merely common and of insignificant character, the whole atmosphere would be dull, and melancholy and pensive mood of this tale would resemble the mere pathetic occurrence of the day-to-day existence. So, the image has played a vital and significant role to keep the temperature of the situation intact and save it from faltering and fluctuation.

In the Repayment ("Parishodh") the poet presents the readers a romantic atmosphere in the portrait of which they are confronted with tranquil mood of nature, the waning moon, the drone-sound of the cricket, the twinkling of the decayed light. The darkness pervading under the tree shivers ceaselessly coming in touch with the drone-sound of the cricket. Putting out lamp, in front of the south window of the boat Shyma is seated alanting to the shoulder of the young with deep breathed sigh. The open scented lock of hairs fall dishevelled without restraint spreading on the region of the chest with the soft, wavy network of gloom-like deep texture of drowsiness.

The poet depicts another picture that is dyed with sensuousness. Shyama has left Bajrasena leaving behind her only one anklet. Bajrasena presses it into his breast, the sound of which begins to inflict in his breast like the thousand-mouthed arrow. In the corner there is left blue sari, loin cloth. He sinks into that and sucks the savour of beautiful body in insatiate obsession. The poet simply presents an image of atmosphere, he makes the readers confronted with the passion-contents and emotional objects, with which Bajrasena is deeply engrossed. The readers and the connoisseur feels with the poet his experience, his emotion and sensibility, that is writ large on the aesthetic expression of the Poet.

"An Appeal of Gandhari" is one of the masterpieces of Rabindranath in thought, passion, sensibility and depiction of images. Its expression and poetic thought are classically dealt and gothically imagined. The construction of the story involves no originality, no novelty, but the texture of the form, the poetic sensibility of the dramatic from of expression is striking and of much importance.

The story is of common and familiar occurrence. It has reference to the story of Mahabharata. But the form, idea, pattern of construction and depiction of characters are novel and striking. The treatment of the internal conflict between Kauraba and Pandava is made differently and distinguishingly than that as in Mahabharata. Duryadhona is not depicted as malignant and vicious character, rather the common and practical trait has been fully manifested in his character by the poet. The context is that Duryadhana by hook or by crook vanquished the pandavas. His wise father with sarcastic mood asked him whether he was happy. He became conqueror, he vanquished Pandavas, they left for the alien forest. He was then without enemy, without thorn that pricked always. He drank the savour of victory-the nectar that is radiant and burning, that is produced out of the churning of ocean of malice. He was happy they were united in the taskless, prideless, and lustreless happiness; when Pandavas gave him out of brotherly affection the portion of enjoyments that had been sucked from the mother-earth by their victory-marked hands, when he was in the affluence of the day's new enjoyments, in utter unworriedness and endless curiosity; when the peals of victory pierced through the ears of Kaurab in the form of the resounding, when the reflected image of renown illumined with its bright fingures the pale gloomy apatment of Kauraba. He was happy when they were under the canopy of the glory of Pandava. All the nimbus of glory being extinguished becomes tender and peaceful like the frogs that are in the state of inertia in Autumn. He was not happy, he was victorious.

Rabindranath creates an image that focuses the inner conflict of Duryadhana and Characterises him as a practical and common man, not of malignant nature. He makes us acquainted with the friction and affliction he suffered in his action of banishing the Pandavas his brothers, through whose veins, the stream of the same blood was flowing.

Here we feel the skill of the poet is to make out of language and the effects of language a reliable symbol of his experience to create which he utilises not only the aesthetic sensibility, but the critical intellect as well. And the symbol is understood, when the provocations of its imagery reverberates in emotions and allusions through the mind of the connoisseur in such a way that, they finally bring themselves into an imaginary experience exactly corresponding to the original experience in the poet's mind. When the poet requires both conscious thought and feeling to make up the symbol, why should not the appreciative reader require both of them to receive the symbol of poet's experience?

Rabindranath expresses his interpretation attained through thought and logical reasoning and his images revokes the emotion in the mind of the readers and enables them to understand the implication of the images introduced.

An analysis of the experience of the refined reader reveals the correctness of this statement. When the man of sound aesthetic instinct reads:

> Tossing of ripples makes
> her waist-chain jingle
> In rows of birds and
> displaying her novel
> In eddying waters, the fair
> Nirvindhya leads
> Thy course; respect her love in
> lavish waters -
> Her seeking to woo thee to her bridal
> breast
> Through gestures indeed the amorous
> maids arrest
> The torrent passed, behold the sindhu
> glide
> As though the hair-band bound
> the alender tide
> Bleached with the withered foliage
> that the breeze
> Has showered rude from
> overhanging trees;
> To thee she looks for succour
> restore
> Her lagging water, and her leafy shore.[41]

His critical intellect first of all enables him to understand the implications of the images introduced. The representation of the row of reclining birds as the waist-chain, the eddying waters as the curling navel and the lavish flow as the deep love coupled with the general expression of love introduces in his mind the picture of the loving girl out in the streets to meet her lover. When this is comprehended, the impression of love lying latent in him is called into play, as a result of which he receives the splendid experience of the poet."

Images created by him in 'An Appeal of Gandhari' are based on common and practical reason, Had it been the fact that Pandava would belong to another dynasty, he (Duryadhana) should have no perturbation and it would be similar to the fact that the Moon of the night does not hate the sun of noon; but the twin-suns cannot shine in one eastern rising mountain. All the conflicts are over, but he is alone.

The poet presents us an image that is marked with deep pensiveness. Outwardly he is haughty, arrogant, spiteful and boastful but internally at the core of his heart he is afflicted with pain, perturbation and bruised at the quick. He is the Conqueror, but he is alone on a vast end less meadow to look into himself and to count his moments. Durjadhana is like the pale emaciated orb of the moon i.e. 1/16th par of the moon that sets to-day beyond the range of the far-off forest in gloomy rays. The image ushered in make the character distinguished and marked, and prepare the ground for the readers and connoisseur with the characters and his emotion, passions and sensibilities. Through the character of Duryadhana Rabindranath presents to the readers and the connoisseurs the practical side of life where a tranquil and peaceful relation exists. But the monarchy is all-powerful. There is no parallel existence to supersede it. If there is any equipotential strength to the parallel it is great enemy to the strength. It becomes ever-obstructive, the abode of troublesome thought, and the concealment of the front, the fear of lagging behind the decaying of fame, glory and power day and night, the pilferer of the portion of riches. For this reason Pandavas are their enemy, their great foe. The monarch should not have any parallel power. They are not only brothers they are equipotential power to them. The common man of limited power makes themselves strong with the help of his friends. But monarchy becomes feeble and weak in its division. The sceptre of the monarch should be placed beyond all the powers around him. It is a fact that firm eternal crown is invisible from a far, how is his jurisdiction imposed on all? In monarchy there is no brotherhood and friendship, only these is creed of conquest. Durjadhana is gratified, he is vicious, the pinnacle of glory has waned, the barrier of estrangement is no more between Kaurabas and Pandavas.

How he is not sinful, crooked and mean, the epithet of which he heard so long. He will force them (one and all) to state that Duryadhana is a king, he cannot put up with the consure, he carries his name by himself. But the violence and viciousness of animadversion cannot stop stinging. If it is banished from the tongue it expands downwards in the deep, secret darkness of the heart stretching its deep crooked root far, keeping the mind embittered daily. On the other hand if it is allowed to go in its frivolous way, blame because worn-out and fatigued.

Rabindranath sinks deep into the bottom of animadversion and presents the psychological treatment of it. Rabindranath looks through it and makes it throbbed with living qualities. Rabindranath depicts the portrait of a blind father Dhritarastra, who is aware of his son's sin and that also is augmented and aggravated by the excessive affection and love. Still he is blamed for his heartlessness, sternness. It is manifested by following image. Duryadhana desires the mortal black kobra for the precious stone and Dhritorastra catches hold of its fang and gives it to him. He is ever blind inwardly and outwardly. He is goading Duryodhana to the ever darkness of annihilation. He is prohibited by the loud lamentation of his friends, the night faring vulture makes inauspicious cries. They are being thrusted to the wall. They shiver apprehending impending danger. Yet clasping him firmly out of boisterous affection he is running in blind swiftness on the strength of the gale into the orifice of destruction and annihilation with obsessed, frenzied laughter illumined by the meteor.

The poet makes us confronted with the image of a portrait wherein is painted the blind pursuit and running after the yawning of the annihilation; sons and father's obsseseed and frenzled passion and the total atmosphere is luminant by the meteor. The poet creates another image of the blind affection and its consequence. When they will attain consciousness,face punishment, in that critical time also there will be no ebb of fatherly affection, no apprension of that. Dhritarastra requests his son not to loose the deepn-fastened clasping of his blind affection, to pilfer all the riches with hasty hand, to be victorious, to be happy, to be king, almighty

Monarch; let the drum of victory resound, flag of conquest be hoisted. In this victorious ceremony there will be no justice, religion, friend, brother, neither Vidura Visma, nor Sanjoy. There will be no public censure, fear, shame, no fortune deity. There will be only blindfather, and blind son, and their impending lot, affection and punishment.

Rabindranath's poetic image touches even the lilt of the song. The Rabindra Sangit are not the easy statement of his emotion, perception and sensibility, (even in the statement of fact imagery finds its pertinant position). He wishes that his lady-love will pervade his heart and mind with deep and unfathomable silence and tranquility.

"Thou shall dwell in silence
in my heart
Like the full moon in the summar night
Thy sad eyes shall watch over me
in my wanderings
The shadow of thy veil shall rest
upon my heart
Thy breath like the full moon in the
Summer night shall hover about my dreams making
Them fragrant."

Rabindranath perceives the atmosphere and that is deeply marked and sensitive by his appeal to his lady-love to dwell in silence in his heart, and that resembles the calm, deep, natural, atmosphere in the summer night illumined by the full moon. He wants to express the emotional impression coming out of the dwelling of his lady love in his heart. The image of the full Moon denotes the charmness and the tranquil atmosphere. The poet creates another imagebased on the Upama instilling in it the sensuous and wandering elements. The breath of his lady-love hover about his dreams making them fragrant like the full moon in the summer night. The poet confronts us with an image that carries the calmness of deep silence in the summer night, the bright entity of the full moon in the summer night along with that the sensuous existence of his lady love. We also feel the sensuous aspects of this poem, and can state that the sensuousness and the sensibility of the poet is the dominant and vital aspect of the poetic image painted in this poem.

In another song "katha tare chiila balite" the Poet creates an images of the feeling lying hidden in this unspoken words that he thought to say to her when their eyes met in the road. The poet feels:

I thought I had something
 to say to her
When our eyes met in the road
But she passed away, and it rocks day and night -
Like an idle boat on every wave of the hours
The thing that I had to say to her.
It seems to sail in the autumn
 clouds in an endless quest
And to bloom into evening flowers
Seeking its lost words in the sunset.
It twinkles like fire-flies in my
 Heart to find
 It own meaning
In the dust of despair.
The thing that I had to say to her.

The poet had something to say to her; but she passed away, he could not avail himself of the opportunity to unlock his heart. The uneasiness due to lack of feasibility of speaking to her rocks day and night like an idle boat that rocks on every wave of the hours. If the poet simply states that he had something to say to her and he could not, and felt some uneasiness, the portrait along with the feeling and passion of the poet would become insipid and dull. The image of the rocking of idleboat is aptly introduced to pinpoint the poet's uneasiness of mind and eagerness. The poet does not stop his pen painting a single image only. Another image - "It seems to sail in the autumn cloud in an endless quest and to bloom into evening flowers seeking its lost words in the sunset, is also of permanent value and importance. The poet makes the readers and the connoisseurs aware of his-eagerness that sets out to said in the autumn in an endless quest to fish out something that he had to say to her, it identifies with the evening flowers seeking its lost words in the sunset. The image of this song is romantic. The passionate and aesthetics expression of his feeling and sensibility dominate the poetic image of this song. Identification of the something that he had to say to her with the natural objects, and for it his eagerness is the pivotal factor in creating the poetic image. When Poet states -

'It twinkles like fine flies
In my heart to bind
Its own meaning
In the dust of despair
The thing that I had to say to her.'

He pinpoints his eagerness and confronts the readers and the connoisseurs with his poetic feeling and experience and all these have created the living and consummate image in this song. These are all psychological reactions and novel treatment of natural objects and sights sounds, fragrance etc. with which the poet comes in contact. Here is the song that is the output of the oet's close union with nature.

Ceaseless in the welter of rain that
wearies the sky
Alas for the forsaken Alas for the
homeless wanderer
The shrieks of the wind die away
in sobs and sighs
what flying phantom does it pursue
across the pathless wild?
The night is hopeless like the eyes of the blind
Alas for the forsaken Alas for the
homeless wanderer!
The waves are frantic in the river
lost in the shoreless dark
The thunder growls, the lightning
flashes its teeth
The lights of the star are dead
Alas for the forsaken Alas for the
homeless wanderer!

The subject of this poem is marked by the poets deep insight into the welter of rain, that beyond the shrieks of the wind ,the sobs and sighs dominates. The language of these incantations is distinguished by its richness of phonetic, rhymical, metaphorical and alliterative effects by its weird cadences and repetitions. The assertion is couched in language that echos the ecstatic music of the dance of the frantic waves in the river, of the lightning that flashes its teeth, of the thunder that growls. All these natural phenomena have a, close and compact bearing on the poets feeling, passion and emotion. He in turn has utilised systemically and aesthetically in his creation of poetic image.

"The waves are frantic in the river lost in the shoreless dark." Here we, feel as much the nature's frantic impulse as the same that is infused and studded by the poetic thrusting and infuriation. He makes the reader see the some and feel the fury of the thunder and frantic waves. Although they will not see the scene as the poet experiences, they will feel and experience as living as anything. The image of the phenomena will flash on their inward eyes. Side by side he creates another portrait of the shrieks of the wind that die away in sobs and sighs. A melancholy atmosphere peeps through the pomp and grandeur of thunder, lightning. The night is hopeless like the eyes of the blind, Alas for the forsaken! Alas for the homeless wanderer. All these pensive mood and passion touch on the very border of circle carried by the frantic waves, growling thunder and flashing lightning. In every songs, poems we see innumerable images, that are focusing point of the poetic passion, feeling and aesthetic experience. In the following song the poet creates images that are not painted differently. The poem is the image itself.

"You have watched all night alone
your eyes are tired sweet one~
The light of the lamp has paled, it flickers
in the breeze of the dawn
Wipe away your tears, my friend
and draw up the veil over your breast
The Autumn morning is still, the smell of the soots
In in the air, the grassy path is caressingly tender
Let the wreath of the forlorn night lie
crumbled upon the bed
Come out in the world of the morning
Gather fresh flowers in your skirt
And put on new blossoms in your hair."

In the poem 'Awakening' of "Ksanika" a purposeless delight is given expression. The poet addresses himself to sing for a moment luminous by the momentary daylight. He also directs his heart to sing for those who come, and go, who smile and stare, who do not look behind their back, who run dancing ask no question, who bloom and stay for a moment. The poet wants to sing, wants to mourn in the momentary light of the day. The poet is expressing in this collection of poems 'Kshanika' absence of attachment and unconcernedness. Here, we feel a detour from which new mode of expression begins. But it is to be noted that the expression is outlined and marked by deep pensiveness, no doubt, but there is not even iota of dissapointment and stoicness. The poet is no longer engaged in the worldly activities of the same kind as the preceding. The poet in the preceding Kavya laid much stress on the texture of weaving garlands, on the creation of the tale of reminiscence. In this poem expression of simplicity in poignant ad libitum. The Poet does not want to understand what he did not realise, does not want to seek what is different and complicated. He does not satisfy the unsatiable desire, and be satisfied with which is received at hand. Let it be consumed if it ends. The image of awakening is the world the poets wants to paint for the readers and connoisseurs. Here we find no out-and-out consciousness, no realisation of aesthetic sense of the preceding valuation. The poet wants to depict the portrait of momentary happiness of purposeless delight and pleasure. The image of the purposeless delight is painted on the canvas like light runs on the surface of the waters of the river in gushes; it is symbolised in the slaken binding of the earth, in the passing, glittering life. It is crystalised in this living image.

The dew hangs touching on the fringe of sirisha flower, and the atmosphere is filled in with murmurings and song in purposeless delight. The poet is deeply engrossed with momentary pleasure and delight and that also of no purpose, no worldly happiness and grief.

In the poem 'Nababarsa' (New rainy season) Rabindranath gives experience to his passion, impulse and delight. He paints the portrait that expressed his deep pleasure coming in contact with new rains. When he speaks out his impulse:

> My heart dances like a peacock on a
> rainy day,
> Spreades its plumes tinged with
> ruptures
> And in its ecstasy seeks some
> vision in the sky
> With a longing for one whom it
> does not know
> My heart dances.

He pinpoints on the image of natural phenomena. He collects his picture from nature, and we find in the image that 'My heart like a peacock on a rainy day spreads its plumses tinged with rupturous colours of thoughts, the Poetic sensibility and emotive contents.'

In the second stanza the image is created thus:

> The cloud rumble from sky to sky
> The shower sweeps horizons
> The doves shiver in silence in their nest
> The frogs croak in the flooded fields
> And the cloud-rumble.

The picture painted in this poem pinpoints on the poetic impulse and sensibility. The reaction of the poet at the sight of the natural shower of rain is symbolised in the images. He paints the picture that is tinged with his emotion and delight.

> "Oh who is she on the king's tower
> That has loosened the braid of
> her dark hair
> Has drawn over her breasts the blue veil?
> She wildly starts and runs in the
> Sudden flashes of lightning
> And lets the dark hair dance
> on her bosom."

The atmosphere created by the shower of rain is romantic and the mere objects of nature have been attributed to with sensible and human qualities. The poet expresses his delight and rejuvanence through the images. Images of braid that is dishevelled, of the bindings of the boat by some youth on the shore of bloomed ketaki, of the shower the vakul in gushes, of the loin becoming impatient in the sky-are the world, we are being faced, that focusses the Poets' perceptibility of the natures to a rental shower, which has a common appeal to the mind specially the most susceptible mind of the poet.

The Poet expresses the outburst of joy and mirth:

"Ah my hear dances like a Peacock
The rain patters on the new leaves
of summer
The tremor of the cricket's chirp troubles
The shade of the tree,
The river overflows its bank
Washing the village meadows
My heart dances."

The poet looks into the bosom of the nature and observes the overflowing river, the pattering of the rain on the new leaves of summer. He identifies himself with outburst of joy in the shower of rain.

In the Poem 'Just place' Rabindranath seeks the just place for his songs, his poetic impulse and sensibility. He addresses his poetic impulse, his songs such as

"Where is the market for you
my songs?
it is there where the learned makes
The atmosphere thick with their snuff?
Where the dispute is never ending
whether the oil
Depends upon the cask, or the cask upon the oil
Where old manuscripts from from their yellow pages
upon thy frivolities of passings days?
My song murmurs in my ears :
"Ah, no, no, no."

The poet chides the learned for their creation of such atmosphere that is thick with their snuff and marked with never ending dispute. Through these cluster of image he presents his emotive experience and sensibility to the readers and critics.

Where is the market for you my songs?
It is there where the man of fortune sits in his marble palace,
And his books upon the shelves are numberless the books that
Are bound in leather and painted in gold, dusted by slaves,
Their virgin pages unvarished?
My songs murmur no, no, no.
Where is the market for you my Song?
Is it there where the young student
Sits with his head bent upon the books
With his mind straying in the dreamland of youth,
Where the school is too much in evidence and the poetry
Is hidden in the heart, there among the disorder of things
And you care to play hide and seek my song remains silent in hesitation.

Through these images he means to say that his songs are concerned with simplicity, easy mirth of the children, neither with complicated doctrine of the learned nor with the pressure of education on the students who sit with their heads bent on their books with their minds straying in the dreamland. When he expresses his feelings and passion.

Where is the market for you my song?
Is it there where the bride
Is busy in the house-where she runs
To her bedroom, the moment she is free and snatches
From under pillows
The book of romance so roughly handled
By the baby, so full of the faint perfume
Of her hair?
My song heaven a sigh and
trembles with desire.

Rabindranath depicts a portrait of a young woman who is always with her home works, who draws the book from her pillow, that is torn by her child, which is tinged with collyrium, marked with vermillion, and with perfume of her hair. Rabindranath chooses this place for his song who is allured to peep through closet of the lady. They shiver in temptation, but fails to go.

The concluding image focusses the poet's passion, feeling and likings as to which is the just and best place for his song.

"Where is the market for you my song?
It is there where the pair of lovers
seeks shelter from
Curious eyes, where birds notes are
Never missed, where streams bubbling finds its full
meaning,
Where all the lute strings of the world show
Thin music upon fluttering hearts?
My song bursts out and says
Yes, here is my place -

- Quoted from the *Calcutta Municipal Gazette*, Saturday, Sept. 13, 1941 by Courtesy of Nalinikanta Sarkar.

He pinpoints his poetic intention and desire on the heart of the simple, honest and opaque life of pair of lovers, who seeks shelter barring the crooked cannon of the superiors. The images of the frenzied lovers, the warbling of the birds, the bubbling sound of the streams, murmuring rhythms of flowers and the creepers, and the lute strings of the world are his best choice, and his poetic feeling passion is expressed through these cluster of images. But what is of more importance is that the image reflects the relationship between the members of the universe and thereby the experience to realise his kinship with co-members of the body: as this realisation occurs the self-love of the reader is satisfied as a result of which he experiences bliss. We quote here a beautiful illustration from the Meghaduta:

I view her now! long weeping
swells her eyes
And those dear lips are dried
Sad on her hand her pallid
check declines
And half unseen through
Trees shines
As when a darkling night the
moon enshrouds
A few faint rays break struggling
Through the clouds.

In the ordinary work the pallid check of the lady half unseen through veiling tears never imitates the charm of the moon plodding its way through the clouds in a darkling night; but the poet is eager to have a glimpse of the two shining in the glory of each other, consequently in order to bring into consummation this unsatisfied craving he moves on to the land of art and seeing the realisation of this cherished desire derives a blissful experience. The image created by him in order to transfer this blissful experience to the reader however, not only enables the appreciator to relish the beauty of the pallid check half visible through flowing tress, resplendent with the light of the struggling moon, it convinces him of his oneness with the universe, as well. The poetic image attracts the reader, because it holds reflection of his own passion and actions and thereby brings to consummation of his ego-libido."[43]

This dictum is also applicable to Rabindranath and his aesthetic expression of his feelings and poetic experiences. In the poem 'The Past' Rabindranath makes the readers and the critics acquainted with the atmosphere, the romantic nature of the time of Kalidasa.

He expresses his admiration—Had it been the fact that he would belong to the period of Kalidasa, he would crave a house surrounded with a garden situated at the secluded border of Ujjain. There would be held the meeting in the evening under the champaks (the flower of magnolia family) on the shore of the river, Reba. The poet would sing in full-throated-ease on the playing mountain. The life boat will move on in the rhythm of Mandacranta. All these happenings would occur should he be born in the time of Kalidasa. The poet diverts our attention to glorious days of the past especially in the time when Kalidasa flourished during the reign of Vikramaditya. The pictures he has painted on the supposition are like this:

He would forsake thoughts and anxieties, there would be no hastiness. He would act as if there is no death, no old age. The pangs of separation would be lonely drawn and would move with slow pace like the hot stream of tears composing prolonged saga of pity. The life would be slow-paced like the clouds of Asara and there would be no hastiness in the life.

Rabindranath being exhausted and annoyed with his contemporary life and ideal, seeks to walk on the golden pavement of the period of Kalidasa.

This desire is one of the dominant characteristics of Romanticism. The creation of the following Image reveals the poetic feeling and passion.

> The bower of Ashoke would bloom
> at the beloved's spurn
> By the Mauva of the lady-love vakul
> would be bloomed.
> The names of the lady-love would
> Utter with rhythm and metre
> Like the warbling sound of the swan
> staying at the Reba's shore.

This living and aesthetic image leads us to the romantic world of Kalidasa and realise the very essence of the aesthetic rasa Kalidasa experienced. Here through these images one aspect is revealed that is Rabindranath's identification with Kalidasa's view of life and the concept of the world. The natural phenomena is also a vital point to deepen the emotional exuberance and aesthetic sensibility. Rabindranath uses these items in comprehending the conscious thought and emotion for creation of great poetry. The characters Mandalika, Chitralekha who played a dominant role in the works of Kalidasa would also fill the heart of Rabindranath with jingling sound and rhythm. They would come to the bower in moonlit night of Chaitra month and the branches of Ashoka would be blown by the spurn of the lady-loves. They would adorn their black hair with tuft of the flower Kurubaka. The toy lotus would look beautiful at their hands. The reason is not known. They would adorn their hair with white flower (kunda flowers), wear sirisha in the ear and dangle the garland of Nabanip on the ornamental girdle. The lady would make dry her hair with the smoke of resin and smear the face with the white pollen of Ladhro flower. The deep fragrance of black sandal would stick to the clothings. Here we feel that impulse and passion of the poet is revealed through the images. The sensibility and emotion dominate the texture, and weaving of the poem. As the images is brought into being by the feeling and is adjusted according to the context of the mood, the greatness of a poetry depends to a considerable extent on it, as also on the magical phrase that unfolds figurative illustration. "Here we see two aspects on which greatness of a poetry depends, one is of feeling and passion of the poet, another is of dexterity in creative art. The following dictum is worth mentioning.

Sanskrit poetics describes a poet as surpassing any creator in point of his dexterity in creative art, and it is through the poetic figure that the poet recreates in our minds the very fact itself." When Kalidasa writes,

Should her clear current tempt
thy thirsty lip
And those inclining, bind the stream
to sip,
The form like the Indra's elephant displayed
Shall cloth the crystal waves with deepest shade,
With sacred blooms the darkening waves glide
As if at an unusual place the Jumna mixes with the tide.

It is quite a special vision of the cloud with its splendid frame reflected on the crystal waves of the Ganges that is imposed on us. The richness of the poetic figures gives a personal distinction to the image, it charges it with the Poet's singular delight."[44]

The romantic atmosphere is meant to be introduced by the poet. On the view-less wings of poesy he is soaring over the sky of Kalidasa, To depict the romantic picture, to present a consummate portrait of the time of Kalidasa and to acquaint the readers with glorious, pompous and majestic form of Capital country of Ujjain, is the Summum Bonum of Rabindranath's aim and view of this poem. The image is the vector of manifestation and revelation of this feeling and sensibility. Here he creates an image.

The breasts of the ladies would be covered with the decorative paintings of saffron. The picture of a pair of swan is painted on the border of the loin. They in the month of asara during the period of separation would wait for their lovers and court the days by the flowers of adoration.

Raising the lyre on their breast they forgot the words while singing the song, some dry hair would drop off on tearful eyes and in the night of union would ring two curved anklets. The breast would be covered with the decorative paintings of saffron.

The poetical image is designed to astound as also to give perspicuity; by doing these it seeks to work on emotions. Here Rabindranath paints a vivacious and highly decorative portrait. The readers become amazed and astounded with the living and life-like depiction of pictures. They feel as if they are amidst the ladies whose breasts are covered with decorative paintings, whose dry hairs are falling on their tearful eyes, and they hear the sweet jingling sound of their curved anklets. Side by side the readers can know the sensitive aspects of the poet, his aesthetic experience and outlook. Then he paints the same aesthetic pictures of the ladies of the time of Kalidasa. They make their pet-female-singing-black bird the beloved name and make the peacock dancing in jingling sound of the bangle. Taking the parrot on their breast they would caress them orally and feed the female stroke with the bud of the lotus.

The lady of Souresean would speak swinging the braid, rocking the lock of hairs and take to his consort clasping her shoulder "Oh my dear friend". All these images denote the same outlook i.e. the pictures painted reveal the same perception and aesthetic sensibility.

He now returns to the barren, rugged earth. He creates an image that is marked with modern outlook and sensibility. He creates an aesthetic bridge over the past and the present. Although there are no ladies to haunt the ashoke and vakul trees, the poet is not united with them. He is stricken with the pangs of separation from her, still he has got some consolation that there is bloomed living vakul flower in the tree. He feels the sweet south breeze in the month of Phalguna under the shadow of Ahoke in the slackened body and idle heart. The last stanza reveals the originality of the poet. The image of this stanza is this:

the poet is overjubilant over the fact that Kalidasa is alive in the names only, but the poet is living. Rabindranath can feel the savour of the time of Kalidasa, the amount being of much lesser portion but on the other hand Kalidasa could not get even a small particle. Rabindranath observes that before his sight the lady who fords swinging her braid is a modern pleasant looking lady, and undreamt of reputation in the imagination of the great poet, Kalidasa. Rabindranath then surpasses Kalidasa by the qualities which he achieves in craving this favour of his beloved.

Rabindranath makes the readers acquainted with the epithet 'Immodesty' in the poem 'Immodesty' the very uncommonly used epithet. Readers take the meaning of the word connate with hautiness and arrogance. But Rabindranath expounds it in a new vesture and coinage. And the foundation of image depends on this rudiments of meaning and vesture.

Oh pearless (lady) pardon me
If fickleness reveals in me today
The first day of Asara doth cometh
The woods become impatient and benumbed
An avenue of Bakul is frenzied of blossoms on the gardens
The new Kadamba (flowers) males perfumed
with besotting essence.

He enwraps the epithet of immodesty 'with romantic halo of light'. It will be felt along with lightning lighted at intervals in every side of the far-off sky and the frivolousness of the wind that haunts the inside of the room. He further creates an image of the 'Immodesty' which is painted having been allied with the bewildered melody that is put into the song. The incessant shower of rain becomes tumultous, the shores of the river get billowy, the new leaf sings murmuring sounds in the forests, the watery breeze raises in every direction the songs of rain. He begs pardon,

Oh pearless lady!
The flaw may be revealed in my conduct
today, pardon me
Today in the earth devoid of daylight
Everywhere there is flow of worklessness.
The desolate path, cowless meadow—as if
It is painted
The world is covered with
Cold darkness caused by the
severe rain

Rabindranath directs his passion of frivolousness of human nature and that is allied with natural phenomena.

Here we feel the far-flung imaginative passion and see its expression meticulous and consummate. We quote to make our dictum clear and pinpointed from Hunt's what is poetry,"[45] and want to show in the said poem the extent of his imaginative passion and its aesthetic expression.

"Poetry is imaginative passion. The quickest and subtlest test of the possession of its essence is in expression, the variety of things to be expressed shows the amount of its resources; and the continuity of the song completed the evidence of its strength and greatness. He who has thought feelings, expression, imagination, action, character and continuity, all the largest amount and highest degree is the greatest Poet." The image of the "Immodesty" has got the wide canvas of the black eyes of Nirupama (lady of matchless beauty), the shadow of the dark-blue Asara, the garland of Juthi enwrapped round the deep black curling hair, and the wicker tray of new rain placed before her forehead. Through this image we an assume that "Poetry includes whatsoever of painting can be made visible to the mind's eye, and whatsoever of music can be conveyed by sound and proportion, without singing or instrumentation .... painting in a certain apparent manner, is things themselves, music, in a certain audible manner, is their very emotion and grace. Music and painting are proud to be related to poetry, and poetry loves and is proud of them."[46]

In the poem "Quietness" the image of tranquillity is conceived. The stillness of Autumn is pervasive all over the desolate meadow in the bright noon. The open soundless stillness, devoid of movement, is felt, as if it is fatigued, spreading its horizontal golden-black wings. The thin borderline of the river signs no song, writes nothing on the surface of the sand. The countries of far-off distance, are basking in the sun with closed eyes, being idle in sleep and fatigue. What is heard through this stillness, in every herbs, dust, in his limbs and every hair, in this and another world, in the planet, the sun, the stars for eternal period is the uproar of dance raised by the atoms phere surrounding her seat in eternal warbling sound.

In the poem 'Salvation' he does not grasp the dry dogma of stoicism, rather he seeks his salvation in innumerable bindings of this earth. He seeks his salvation in the earthen pot through which the rain nectar will be showered. Like the candle the light of salvation will brighten the world of the poet in innumerable wickers. His salvation is not in restraining the senses. The poet creates an image of the tender path of the forest which is resounds delight in salvation is revealed amidst the pleasure that is manifested in sight, odour and songs. The epithet, salvation has no palpable and concrete entity. But Rabindranath has given it expression through the image that focusses his emotion and imaginative passion. In the poem 'On the Afternoon' the poet creates an image of the tender path of the forest which is resounded with murmuring and is moistened with bright dews. The poet is unmindfully laying on the shadow of the bower of the thick cluster of leaves, on the grassy bank of Tarangini hearing the warbling sound of the birds, feeling the gentle breeze. Others have gone to the temple for worship. But the poet waits for the blooming of the buds. So, we see that the poet makes us see the image that brings in the world of natural phenomena, and the imaginative passion of the poet, that looks into the warbling sound, the gentle breeze, the blooming of the buds, the resounded tender path of the forest. The painting of the portraits is presented being tinged and smeared with poetic emotion, passion and sensibility. The natural beauty, sights, sounds, fragrance of flora and fauna have been augmented by the poetic feeling, his peculiar mode of looking into bosom of the heart of it, and way of expression, that is marked by his aesthetic motion and perception.

In the poem of 'Naibedya' the poet creates an image of the depth of the immensity of a perfect unity, wherein he finds no trace of sorrow or death or separation. The poem is an image itself

> Far as I gaze at the depth of they immensity
> I find no trace there of sorrow or death or separation
> Death assumes its aspect of terror
> And sorrow, its pain
> Only when, away from Thee,
> I turn my face towards my own dark self
> Thou All perfect,
> Everything abides at Thy feet

For all time.
The bear of loss only clings to me
With its ceaseless grief,
But the shame of my penury
And my life's burden
Vanish in a moment
When I feel Thy presence
In the centre of my being.

The poet presents an image that opens a world, that is marked with a perfectness and which makes us acquainted with the existence of a perfect being. In the poem 'The Hidden' Rabindranath unlocks his heart and makes us peep through the image into his mind full of jems and pearls which preserves for his dreamland. He has got some riches. But largest portion lies in his dream, hidden dream. He then shows us an image of an entity whom he longs, to whom he appeals to come to him in deep secretness, in silent foot-stopping covering the wicker of the candle by the border of the loin. He leads us to go through the sil of the image, to look with amazement the affluence of his treasure of the dream, and of the romantic lady for whom he waits earnestly and eagerly. He entreats her to come to him not in a public thoroughfare, which becomes luminous by the severe day light.

He cannot allow her to be seen by his neighbour, although she is alien and unfamiliar to them. He only will keep her in his closest, recognize her in his ecstasy, with the wink of her tearful eyes, and will be acquainted with her observing in seclusion with great delight. He appeals to her to come under the shade of a dust, not through the light of the way, not in severe light. It may be statement –like but through this we can see and observe with exuberance of delight the opening of the petals of the bud, and this statement for which our minds have been prepared by the image of wealth available in his dream in the living stream of his emotion and imagination, passion the immutable in the midst of ever-changing gives us a point of vantage, where we may rest a moment, review the image sequence over which we have passed, and grasp its significance."

In the poem 'Recognition' Rabindranath places her on his familiar level of experience he has recognized her, and has understood her mood and expression, although she has come to him with peculiar dress. Setting the pearl on her dishevelled hair and flashing on the wink of eyes' indistinct smile she has appeared on the shore of his heart. Then he depicts the portrait of enclosure slide-glance and the clever cruel words, which focuses the sweet, beautiful atmosphere and relation between her and the poet. A libidinal and psychological relation has been manifested through the picture denoting the poetic emotion, his sensibility and aesthetic expression. All being conglomerated on single and broad-based level creates the living and perfect image.

In the poem "I am fickle" we get exciting spice to strike out the dullness of our taste. Here, we are acquainted with the fickle-minded poet, who waits unmindfully on his window in the midst of the fleeting days. He is desirous of getting the touch of the far-off being incapable of having caught hold of. That being staying at far-off distances plays the impatient flute. The poet forgets his limitation that he has no wings, and stays at a fixed location. He creates an image of the far-off being, which is manifested through the eyes of the blue sky, the dalliance of the shadow, murmurings of the trees, and through the sun-burnt idle time. The notation and desire to imbibe the romantic fragrance of the far-off being of the far-off countries is the very essence of this poem. The poignancy of the poem comes not simply from the romantic ideas of the poet, but also from certain tendencies of his age. This image pinpoints the desire of Rabindranath to flash the light of the far-off distance on the limitation of his location and his body. But what is striking is "the reverberation of sound echoing over vast regions, even into the limitless space is beyond the confidence of the world."[47]

In the poem 'One who is living abroad' the poet creates an image of an aspect of universality. The universality lies in the fact that he seeks that very Home, which is available in every place.

He wants to conquer that land in which is as his own in every land. He haunts to that as an alien in the midst of which he has got his own place. He will understand the entrance to that, he is astounded to seek him, whom he gets in every hamlet as his close relative.

The poet here relates a common and practical limitation of character. We sometimes forget that this world, this natural phenomena is a close relative to us. Yet we being forgetful of such universal bearing we are after the limited outlook. We run after the particular objects in nature, but are amazed to see that the world is our home. The poet wants to identity himself with the waters; earth and the sky, and his habitable location seems to be an alien land. He looks into his self and observes that he is pervasive and diffusive.

The poet creates an image that is tinged and smeared with tears of the bruised heart. He seeks some one in the fragrant sky of the new spring and in the auspicious moment of union. He is alien in his periphery and among his relative who involves deep pangs of separation day and night in his mind. He runs round the whole sky loosing the love of his neighbours. So, it is clear that a deep consciousness of identification with the whole world is the subject matter in predominant position of this poem. And the image is created by this imaginative passion of the poet. The poet cannot understand the passioned language of the earth delighted with the grasses. But what seems to him is that he becomes one, and an inseparable unity of herbs, waters for ages together. He does not know when he starts wandering throughout this earth. But what is striking to him is that dumb earth welters staring the poet in his face; the sky of the night stares in a peculiar way as if the stars of far-off distance are aware of his name. He cannot understand the language, with which they whisper together. What does the forgotten words of eternity remind? The friend of eternal dawn stares the poet in his face. The poet feels his identification with the earthly objects. The familiar objects reveal the eternal relation between them and the poet. On this seven-apartment house, on this homestead his whole life is bound with innumerable bindings, with countless knots. Yet, he forgets time within number and wants to setup his home in the far-off land. Is it possible for the set-up house to satisfy the desire for the home? It is regrettable to find full satisfaction on his eternal home-stead for him who takes this world as his home.

The poet pinpoints his sensibility on the pervasive identification with all the natural phenomena, flora and fauna of this earth. It is luminantly expressed in Basundhara and Samudrerprati (to the sea). The poet sings in the melody of the famous poet of England, Tennyson,

I am a part of all that I have met
Yet all experience is an arch where thro'
Gleams that untravelled world, whose margins fades
For ever and for ever when I move.[48]

An idea of pervasiveness is manifested through the image. But there is distinguished difference between Tennyson and Rabindranath. Rabindranath creates a romantic canopy over the feelings of identification, his pervasiveness, diffusion. In the image of the 'The past' Rabindranath creates an comprehensive impression on the common and practical concept. He wants to instill in the heart of the poet the throbbing of life. The past is the witness of all bygone events and happenings. It is attributed to with human feelings and habits. The poet involves in it the imaginative passion. The dead stoppage of the poet is of natural and of common place happening. But the poet tinges that with his imaginative feelings. It resembles the waveless grave reticence. The poet wants to invoke the past in his mind, and to feel the living elements of it. To him the past is not heap, or conglomeration of dead events and activities. It remains stable in the midst of fickleness in the resounded days. The image of the past is created by the poet, who has dealt the Alankara as one of the embellishments in poetry; Samasakti alankara being used instills the living element in the concept of the past. The past is a witness of all historical facts and events. The streams of all passed events get terminus in the Past. Rasa is brought to a relishable state by the Alankara. Here we see that Alankara proves itself conducive to aesthetic realisation and consequently is regarded as a benefactor to Rasa.

In the poem 'New Vesture' Rabindranath paints a romantic picture:

Oh! that day you come to my meeting. Are you?
The flute at your hand, amazed smile at your lip
That day spring became frenzied

With intoxicating sight.
Are you, that come that day in the bright dawn, in the
meeting
Of the new youth.

In this poem we see concrete sensuous form and human content. We deal that this subject can only enter into a relating with an amputee object when it confronts it sensually. Object and subject are collated in the aesthetic relationship; This object has sum for man when it is regarded not in the abstract out in all its concrete human richness; the subject terials its object by grasping it in its *coneretnun* and full human significances. A particular *eullatail* exists between subject and object (creation in accordance to this laws of beauty "or artistie assimilation of reality) in which the subject transforms the object by giving a determinants form to raw matter. The result is a new object, the atheistic object in which this human wealth of the subject is objectified or relvrad. This subject-object relationship, this aesthetic relationship, has a social character; it evokes or a socio-historical basis, in the focus of humanizing nature by means of wall, and of objectifying the human being."

Rabindranath creates an image tinged with romantic notion and perception. He creates an image that is as much marked by congruity as by audacity and freshness. He is an expert in the art of seeing Nature through the sights, sounds fragrance etc., and application of this art yields rich harvest in the shape of congruous and appropriate images. The Poem "Shibaji-Utsab" or the "Anniversary of Shibaji's is a perfect image. The poem is meant for the tribute to him, because of his thought and desire to bind the severed, split, scattered India under the dominion of one realm of justice. But his desire could not haunt the hamlet of the Bengal. At that moment Bengal like a mother spreading the soft, pure green loin on peaceful face, took the company of the innumerable drowsy rustic children to her lap in the evening. Here the poet depicts two pictures, one of Shibaji-created united India, the concept of which flashed on his inward eye, while residing at a dark cave of Maratha, another of common and beautiful aspect. He attributes to Bengal with an affectionate qualities of mother; side by side he creates a living portrait of innumerable rustic drowsy children. The Alankara Samasakti deepens the Rasa of the atmosphere. The introduction of pleasantness, softness of green loin of mother Bengal and her taming drowsy rustic children produces new and striking image. The atmosphere brings in the green, soft and delicate earth before the readers and connoisseurs. This romantic image is an object of remembrance and becomes jocund company even when the idea of Shibaji should have much worth and importance. Bengal did not pay heed to the news that came in the shape of thunder-clap. The Mughal-Dynasty tried to arrest notice of Bengal to it, she did not. Here Rabindranath propounds a praxies that informs us the consciousness and existence of man. We get acquainted with contemporary socio political consciousness. The character of so-called acting his of the counsel and the struggle for freedom.

Rabindranath here creates an image which is significant and marked with poetic evaluation of social and political happening. The image which he has created in giving expression to the change, annihilation of one form of management caused by the new tinged with dwartating aspect is an audacious and striking image. The truth is material is that the English who came to trade in Bengal as a perfect business men, but to the utter astonishment of the Bengalees they forsook the old garb and took the sceptre in their hand to govern. The epithet is aptly and beautifully used. The rank and file of the business men was turned into the sceptre of the king overnight. In this political turmoil his idea relating to united India is considered as best guide. He (Shibaji) is forgotten by everyone. His grey flag is smeared with dust, its consequence being of no significance, The history composed by the foreigner ridiculed him as a robber raising laughter. His secred efforts are deemed as nothing but a purposeless attempt of a dacoit. Rabindranath creates an image that is based on the emergence of his (Shibaji) idea which was obscure, and unravelled for a long time in the cave of the mountain. It emerged from the dark, obscure cave. It resembled the fountain of the rainy reason that awakened clearing the mountain with its full strength. The people of the world took it with amazement as to the where about of the flag, which could pervade the sky, and asked where it was kept obscure in a miniature form.

The poet instills in the dry political dogma the romantic notion, places Shibaji's greatness, genious on the natural phenomena and attributes it with local habitation and name. The poet also deals with wonder, observing the unprecedented event and exclaimed how and whence his war-drum rung on the door of the courtyard. His strength pierced through the deep darkness of three hundred years and rises in the horizon of the West spreading new rays of thought.

The poet creates an image that is various and habitual. The feelings and sensibility of the poet is crystalised in his deepest eulogy and in conveying allegiance to his genious an idea of one state. These are all dry statement of facts. But Rabindranath creates cluster of images, that reveal truth which shall be carried alive into the heart. Here we cannot but quote the famous dictum to pinpoint the image-making capability of Rabindranath as well as the factors upon which poetry's mansion is based.

"The heightened colour of words, the conscious grace, the unwonted variety and gamut in utterance by these signs we recognize poetry; but what is that touch upon the heart which, as if a master-switch had been thrown there, lights up whole roads and tenements of experience poorly mapped, functiorily visites, apprehended but dimly by us before"?[49]

This interrogation leads us to the tuneful imaginative and passionate world of images.

In the poem 'An obesiance' the poet creates an images that denotes a pervasive existence for which Arbindo dedicated his life. Rabindranath wants to make us familiar with an entity for whom the god in the form of human king is engrossed in aesthetic austerities, the poet has sung great song, great hero is on his critical journey, to whom comfort has bowed down its ashamed head, death is forgetful of. The idea of Arbinda Ghosh, the famous anarchist and also for the Alipore Bomb case is diversely painted and the tuneful image is given dominant figure and role. The following image has much importance and significance. The interrogative aspect is emphatic here.

Did God give on your right palm
with cruel caress the grief's
intense lamp?

The image of light that has been learning piecing through country-wide darkness, is dominant factor. He, poet gives us information always keeping in view that he is a poet, he gives us a wide and consummate familiarity of him. He was an out and out patriot. He (Arvinda) was punished due to his love for country. It is an event of him. The poet exclaims for the fact. He asks which king can punish him, who is the messenger of Rudra, cruelty-incarnate, and who came with lamp in hand in this world. That is to say in the time of dependence he flourished in India with Mantra, the principle 'Bande Mataram, worship mother, i.e. Mother land; He instilled in the mind of Indians the principle of Patriotism, love of country, these are all similar to light. That circumstances are over. But still we remember his genius and originality. Even today we feel his entity. He creates an atmosphere where is resounded the roaring of the sea along with hurricane, the frantic dance in blind speed of the fountain. Peal of lightning invokes the god of cruelty-all these are natural phenomena. These are all offerings which is allegiance.

The image denotes the majestic splendour of the patriot, Arabinda Ghosh.

The (Auspicious Moment' in Kheya (Ferry boat) is an image itself. The atmosphere and circumstances are peculiarly delineated. Practical events are all present to effect the total impression. But one single occurrence vivifies the total circumference. That is, the darling Prince of the king will go on the front path of the house of a young lady. This event is of much importance and significance to her. The event is the focusing point placed on the centre of the atmosphere and sequence. The poet makes us see that one young lady cannot engage herself with household works in the morning. She wants to adorn herself with new vesture, to braid her hair in a new style, to wear the garment in a new fashion. All these are in questionnaire form. The poet through the image of the lady with all her likings, activities, and reactions on the vent of the darling Princes's going on the front path of her house reveals a world where going of a young darling Prince of a king is an occurrence of much importance and significance; the valuable pearl of her heart is of no use, that is thrown on his way. Her mother is a women of common feature, practical and worldly characteristics. She takes her daughter's way of thinking and consciousness with wonder and astonishment. The poet also makes us know the fact that she the young lady knows that the king's darling Prince will not look into the bay of the window where she stands and in a moment their visits will be rung from a far off meadow in a impatient melody. The darling Prince went away on the front path of her house. His golden chariot flashed with the light of the morning. She has seen him only for a moment and thrown her necklace set with gems on the dust of the path. Her mother takes it with wonder and thinks it an affairs of frenzied person. She is taken aback that he (Prince) did not pick up the necklace which has been grinded by the wheel of the chariot. There is nothing to be left except the sign of the wheel. Her bestowals will not see the recognition of anyone rather is covered by the dust of the path. All then ingredients of this poem, the weaving of texture of the poem are peculiarly delineated. Although it has emphatic bearing on the practical side of worldly life, it has not been given predominance. We have with wonder and amazement the activities of the young lady, but we cannot but feel her passionate and loving heart, and see in the cave of her heart some uncommon, pleasant and romantic characteristics. Rabindranath creates the loving and striking image basing on this and emotive experience. In the poem 'Unnecessary' the poet shows us a world of reality where unnecessary superfluous activities are done with dominance. The poet unlocks the world of reality, that is revealed to us with the portrait that one young lady covering the lamp with her loin is going alone on the desolate shore of the river, where blooms Kasa; the poet meets her and appeals to her to keep her lamp on his dark hamlet. Raising her black two eyes before his face for a moment in the dusk says :

> "I'll cause the lamp to float
> So, after day's end I've come to the shore."

The lamp starts floating unnecessarily. The poet creates an image that focuses a world that is tinged with such human passion, which seeks something beyond the material needs and hankerings. Besides, in this poem we hear the lilt of the warbling of the streamlet. It is one of the master pieces specially in lyrical standpoint, and striking theme. The same picture is delineated in another style. The lamp is burning unnecessarily in the sky as a Akash Pradip (a light suspended from the top of a pole set up every evening by the Hindus during the month of Kartik in reverence to their deceased forefather, God) and another is adorned in the galaxy of lighted lamps.

In the poem 'Arrival' the poet delineates the picture, creates an atmosphere which is an unprecedented one. An impulse and feeling dominates the whole atmosphere of the poem. That impulse is concerned with the arrival of the Emperor, who does not come as a conqueror.

Here is a new experience. There is no preparation to greet him to adore him, then is neither light nor garland. The king, comes unsung, unhonoured. So, it is decided to greet him in the empty house with indigent hands. And it is decided to greet him with conch rung because the king of the dark has come in the deep midnight. Here is lightning, there is thunder. The king of the sad night has come with the hurricane.

The social character is manifest, along with other characteristics. Rabindranath through these poems wants to paint the human and social character of aesthetic value, in which looms long human and social relationships. We will be unable to understand aesthetic utility of these poem, if we fail to grasp the specific lease of the society, i.e. the structure of the society. We know aesthetic relating is the product of man, a historical product. Rabindranath is also a delineator of this historic occurrences. If regeneration did not occur, if social relationship did not allow revolutionary change we had seen a poet creating poems of no historical value.

The poet creates an image that reveals the world that is tinged with poetic emotion and poetic sensibility and makes us familiar with the new thought, new idea of life and consciousness.

The readers and connoisseur are shown the new world, the uncommon phenomena of reality along with it the poetic experience and impassioned imagination. The Poem 'Bestowal' the image of hardness, firmness and severity is created in contradistinction to its reverse side, softness, mildness and flexibleness. The hardness is symbolized in the feeling crystalised in the simile, such as it burns as if it is fire, it is as heavy as thunder, and softness lies with the garland that was worn in the evening.

When the poet states,

"I thought, I would crave, dared I not
The garland you wore round the neck in the dusk
I dared not long, I would not have
Thought in the morning, when you would go
Assumed the cloven garland remained in the bed
So, I came at dawn like a beggar
Yet I dared not long, I would not."

He brings in a novel phenomena of reality. This world is not strewn with soft flowers and easy ideas and thoughts; rather it is earmarked with hardness and severe experience. The garland of soft flowers does not end itself. It can emerge as a sword. It is neither a garland, nor a plate nor a basket of flavoured water; it is a awful sword, so we see the combination and contradistinction of garland and sword-the embodiment of softness and hardness. The feeling of the Poet and imaginative passion is manifested through the image of the garland, sword. And it is an expression factor that gives a pleasing transformation to the ordinary cause, as a result of which the normal becomes extra-normal-the particular becomes the universal."

Why is this so? This is due to aesthetic feasibility of the part, the aesthetic is formed only in dialectic of the subject-object relationship and therefore cannot be deduced from the properties of human consciousness or any particular structure therein, nor from the psyche or biological constitution of this subject, aesthetic consciousness, the aesthetic suwn, is not something given, innate, or biological, other, it emerges historically and socially on the basis of practical and material activities—human labour—in a relationship in which the subject exists only for this object and this object exists only for this subject. The aesthetics exists for man as a social being, independent of this individual subject, but not outside the social relationship between subject and object. It has its own reality, a human, social reality which does not exclude a certain objectivity; it is always manifested through forms that are subjective. And this spiritual content with which the subject inrasty it exists, aesthetically, only insofar as it is materialized and objectified in a concrete sensuous manner. Rabindranath expresses aesthetically the contemporary social consciousness *that way unit* cash on the historical events. The ingredients of the image of the poem (Bestowal lies in the weaving of the garland in which the easy sentiments are crept, and the emergence of the sword through the soft breast of the flowers and garland. What is true of one constituent of the poetic image holds good of the other ingredients as well, that appear in their universal aspects being presented through the medium of expression. The moods and the feelings depicted by the poet are particular since they relate to the character or the characters delineated but the words that express them being universal—they too acquire universal character, and when the appreciator experiences them they are comprehended in their generalized and impersonal aspect, enabling him to feel that the feelings relate to all members of humanity, including his own self.[50] So, we see the universal word and the universal content make the readers familiar with the imaginative passion, aesthetic experience of the poet. The poetic feeling that has been clung in the image of sword being novel and aesthetic experience that the sword is not terrible and severe only, it is a terrible ornament. It is terrible, awful but it carries the aspect of an ornament, adoration and embellishment'.

Another aspect is added to this experience that is the aspect of negative capability. To greet the beloved the lady-love would beautify her body generally. Now, she will not care for his coming to her bower. She will not beautify her body with clothings. She will not keep sitting on the dust for him alone in her room. Because the sword has adorned her fully and perfectly, so vesture is of no use to her. It is new experience, new aspect of striking expression and imaginative passion.

Here we quote a stanza from Harriet Eleanor Hamilton —Kings The Bride Reluctant,[51]

My bridegroom's bed is cold and hard
My bridegroom's kiss is ice and fire
My bridegroom's clasp is iron-barred
I am consumed in His desire
My bridegroom's touch is as a sword
That pierces every nerve and limb
"Depart from me", I mean, O lord!
All the night long I spend with him.

In this poem no contrasting picture is delineated. It is a portrait of poetic feeling and passion having no striking impression. It is a mere description of the bridegroom's two reverse feeling coolness – softness, and hardness-severity. But Rabindranath on the other hand creates an auxiliary atmosphere and environment of Rasa in order to fructily the total impression of poetic truth. When the poet states:

Oh! it is not a garland, it is your sword
If burns as the fire heavy as the thunder
As it is your sword, my lord!
The morning light spreads over her bed
Through the window
The morning bird asks with song, Oh woman!
What do you get?
It is neither a garland, nor a plate, nor a
Basket of the scented water.

It is a awful sword. The total impression of the poet is created by the poet and the poetic image becomes luminous on the production of the total impression and atmosphere.

In the poem 'The Miser' the poet gives an expression of different kind of experience and idea than that which is conceived of so long. The atmosphere and the feeling of the poet is differently and peculiarly delineated. One portrait is depicted that the poet in the form of beggar was begging from one village to another and the king was riding on his golden chariot. It seemed to be a unprecedented dream. The poet identifies himself with the happenings and phenomena of events. He thought that his day would be auspicious because of the affluence and exuberance that was allied with the name of the Maharaja, the almighty king. But to his utter astonishment and surprise he looked at the sight that the chariot stopped in front of him. He came to him with smiling face. The poet took him with all his easiness and delight and was started at the request stretching his hands, "Give me something'. It is of uncommon figure and fact, poetic experience and feelings that the king is at the door of the beggar. It resembles deception and swindle revealed peculiarly. He gave the king from his bag a particle of grain. He became astonished when he found in the midst of the alms a fine particle of gold. What he gave the king-beggar returned to him in the shape of gold. He observed in the midst of tearful eyes and concluded "why did I not give him emptying all my own."

It is marked with bizarre and queer note of things. The imaginative passion and feelings of the poet dominate the whole atmosphere of the poem and creates a perfect and striking image.

In the poem 'Waiting' the poet creates an image that shows us a galaxy of Art. The evening candle is ready for illumination, all the burdens are unloaded, the ferry boat has been found on the jetty. The person referred to as 'I' is waiting for someone who will light the candle, The Mallika (flowers) blooms in the evening, the fragrance of which delights the bower and fill the cup of the leaves of the lotus with Jasmine for the decoration of the lotus-hand of her lady-love. The image of last four lines are unique in sensuousness and sensibility.

> The relaxed body will fall
> Under the feet in sleep
> I'm waiting on the ground arranging the bed
> When will you get the time to keep.

An atmosphere of relaxation and stillness dominates the whole poem. The sensuous throbbings and meticulous insight of the poet looms large in the every portrait. The descriptive sketches, and artistic trappings all are bound together to create an consummate image. The poem 'waiting' appears before us with all the artistic painting and decorative sketches. His sensibility and imaginative passion is evinced through the portraits. So, when we read through the poem all the ingredients are resented before us not in part or division, rather in a consummate form i.e. the form of image.

In the poem 'The Pond' the poet describes the phenomena of the pond in a very common hue and paint. But the finished outcome appears to be a of uncommon colour. The cold waters in every shore are brimming bearing perfect thick deep blackness. The shadows from trees of the shore becoming deep have-fallen on the water. The last light at the end of the day has fallen on that shore of the pond. It is similar to the fact that while going the married lady looks towards her motherland with tearful eyes. He creates a perfect image that shows his shining intellect, the glow and power of his imagination he describes black water as mute, black, still solemn, gravely awful, as deep midnight that is fugitive in the cage of soil, beside her there is dusty earth the arena of activities, the abode of life.

The portrait of common hue and colour becomes uncommon coming in touch with the passion and creative capability. The cold black water of the ponds become lively and full of throbbings of life. The common factors and fresco of day-to-day existence have left their stale, insipid forms, everything that is painted in the poem appears to us as shining and effervescing. By this side the note of melancholy is felt. The poet hears in the flapping of the water of the pond the lilt of tearful songs and feels in her embrace the touch of the death that is covered in the in the scarf of the shadow. In this connection we are quoting the dictum of Dr. Nihar Ranjan Ray.

The melancholy note we find in Kheya does not express any despair. The poet feels that all his busy days of action, their excitement and their success, have not brought him any nearer to his heart's desire. The shadows of evening are heavy and dark, yet where is the boat which will carry him to the shore of a different life, the life of thought and contemplation and realization which he has been seeking?"[52] We have observed the aesthetic has a historical aspect. The melancholy note in 'Kheya' is a politic oriented aesthetic sensibility. It emanates from the notion of independent spirit. The poet wants a new word. He wants to forsake the feudal bourgeois society, this imperialist structure of India. He wants a boat which will bring him to a new world, new land and to a novel realization.

In the book of poems (*Gitanjali*) "Offering of Songs", the image created by the poet emanates from the beautiful evocations and rich feelings. The religious background adds to this wealth by giving it a deeper significance. The religious tenets are only tenets circumscribed to its own periphery. What is striking and of permanent value and vigour is the tuneful and audacious image. Here we quote the poem i.e. the fifty eighth poem of Gitanjali. "Let all the strains of joy mingle in my last song-the joy that makes the earth flow ever in the riotous excess of the grass, the joy that sets in twin brothers, life and death, dancing over the wide world, the joy that sweeps in with the tempest, shaking and waking all life with laughter, the joy that sits still with its tears on the open red lotus of pain, - and the joy that throws everything it has upon the dust, and knows not a word. "

The experience of the poet has a bearing on the common feature of human mind and thought. But the imaginative passion relating to the joy that sits still with its tears on the open red lotus of pain" is a new and novel thing. The outburst of passion of the Poet gives to the readers and connoisseurs a conception and consciousness of life. The consummation is reached in *Gitanjali,* where the new experience is celebrated in poems of extraordinary grace and beauty and freedom. But all these factors and items depend largely and luminously on the striking and metaphorical images. The images of light, world-filling light, eye-kissing light creates new outlook in the world of images. Shakespeare in the 'Romeo and Juliet' shows that light is a dominating factor in image creation. In Romeo and Juliet the beauty and ardour of young love is seen by Shakespeare as the irradiating glory of sunlight and starlight in a dark world... Each of the lovers thinks of the other as light. Romeo's overpowering impression when he first catches sight of Juliet on the fateful evening at the capulets ball is seen in his exclamation,

O, she doth teache the torches burn bright![55]

In the poem 'Sahajatri' (A lady who goes together with a man) the poet portrays an image that focuses his aim at the endless journey, his aimless flight in the midst of unlimited sea, where he wants to make his lady love alone hear the song that is similar to the Ragini bereft of the findings of language like the waves. She hears it with silent smile the poet wants to know when they will start. He thinks that it is high time to start when dusk falls on the shore of the sea, the birds of the other bounds of sea returns to their nest. He waits for the time when she will come to the ghat to let loose the knot of the boat. The boat like the fading light of the setting sun will start for the journey having no destination in the midst of the mid-night.

The atmosphere that is created by the poet and by his passions and feelings is romantic. In this context we quote the dictum of Dr. Nihar Ranjan Ray "One is admittedly their unvarnished sincerity, the absolute naivete and simplicity with which they record certain day-to-day feelings of the poet, his spiritual yearnings expressed with the least artistic trappings." We are of the same opinion, but the point on which we lay emphasis is the cornet, the consummation and the perfect images. The image instils in the mind of the readers with the idea that when a spiritual realisation is connected with an experience of nature, wonderful beauty and Poetry result, as in same of the songs of this book, and an altogether now perception is born of this union between nature and human spirit.

We are confronted with a historical outlook that the spiritual realization which symbolises in the creation image is marked as social and connected with an experience of nature. In other words, man is a natural human being, a fragment of nature that humanires itself, without breaking with nature, transmuting it in two directions; externally, by acting on the natural world to create a humanized reality, thus humanising nature and internally, by surmounting, his instinctive, purely animal, biological existence, thus transforming his own nature. The activity that makes this double transformation possible is the objectification of the human being through work; so, spiritual realization of Gitanjali is related to the contemporary social thought, to the human philosophy and renaissance, freedom movement and other regenerative outlook of the family.

The image of the following song of Gitanjali is crystalised in the light:

"Light, oh! Where is the light?

Kindle it with the burning fire of desire?

There is the lamp but never a flicker of a flame-is much thy fate, my heart'. Ah, death were better by far for thee!

Misery knock at thy door, and her message is that thy lord is wakeful and he calls thee to the love tryst through the darkness of night.

The sky is overcast with clouds and the rain is ceaseless. I know not what this is, that stirs in me, - I know not its meaning.

A moments flash of lightning drags down a deeper gloom on my sight, and my heart gropes for the path to where the music of the night calls me."

The poet creates an image of light that is the dominating factor in the poem. The image is also painted with the burning fire of desire.

"Light Oh! Where is the light! Kindle it with the burning fire of desire! It thunders and the wind rushes screaming through the void. The night is black as a black stone. Let not the hours pass by dark. Kindle the lamp of love with thy life". Here, the image of the lamp of love has played the dominant role. It is related to the contemporary social thinking. Love is not abstract. It is concretely perceived in a specific social structures. Rabindranath creates this image of this humanized reality, certainly not out of the abstract philosophical dogma. It is socially thought and accepted.

In the poem 'Bharata-Thirtha' Rabindranath paints a consummate image of India and her traditional indignity, diversity and humanized outlook. Here we quote a few lines:

Awake, my mind, gently awake
In this holy land of pilgrimage
On the shore of this vast humanity
That is India.
Here I stand with arms outstretched
To hail man-divine in his own image-
And sing to his glory in notes glad and free.

No one knows whence and at whose call
Come pouring endless inundations of men rushing
Madly along-to lose themselves
In the sea;
Aryans and non Aryans, Dravidians and Chinese,
Scythians, Huns, Pathans and mughals-all/ are mixed, merged and lost in one body.
How the door was opened to the west
And gifts in hand they beckon and they come –
They will give and take, meet and bring together
None shall be turned away
From the shore of this vast sea of humanity
That is India.

Rabindranath in the said poem maintains the same weaving of images and texture along with the same perceptibility and emotive contents. The image of Bharat Tirtha (India as a pilgrimage) is perceived in Socio-politico-historical perspective. In it looms large the vision of integrity. unity of India, the traditional thinking of development adulation civilization, struggle for freedom, outlook of nationality and above all disinclining of Indian socially comprehended by beauteous culture and philosophy.

The following poem is tinged with poet's aesthetic sensibility and emotion. Death, thy servant, is at my door. He has crossed the unknown sea and brought thy call to my home. The night is dark and my heart is fearful-yet I will take up the lamp, open my gates and bow to him my welcome. It is thy messenger who stands at my door.

I will worship him with folded hands, and with tears. I will worship him placing at his feet the treasure of my heart.

He will go back with his errand done, leaving a dark shadow on my morning and in my desolate hence only my forlorn self will remain as my last offering to thee.

We imbibe the experience of the poet that is tinged with romantic idea underling the concept of death.

In this collection of poems *Gitimalaya* (Garland of songs) we see different types of images that show different aspect of his sensibility and realization than that which proceeds it.

"I know that the flower one day shall
blossom crowning my thorns
I know my sorrow shall spread its red
rose-leaves opening its heart to the sun
The breeze of the south for which the
sky kept watch for weary days
And nights shall suddenly make
My heart quiver.
My love shall bloom in a moment; my shame shall be no
More when the flower is ripe for offering.
And with the end of the night, at the touch of my friends. It will drop at his feet and spend its last petal in joy."

The imagery in Gitamalaya appears to be more rich and varied, more highly imaginative more approachable by any other writer than that of previous works of Rabindranath. The idea and realization that "the flower one day shall blossom crowing my thorns more imaginative, subtle and complex. Similarly the imaginative, subtle and complex. Similarly the imaginative passion that 'the breeze of the south for which thy sky kept watch for weary days and nights shall suddenly make my heart quiver ' is newly and unprecedented addendum to the poetic, aesthetic realization and imagination. The image of the following poem is strung with sensuous delights.

'My heart is on fire with the
flame of the songs
It spreads and knows no bounds
It dances swinging its arms in the sky
Burning up the dead and the decaying
The silent starts watch it from across the darkness.
The drunken winds come rushing upon
It from all sides
O, this fire, like a red lotus, spreads
Its petals in the heart of the night.

The image of the 'flame' is a dominating aspect of the said poem. It is attributed with the frivolous aspect of human nature. It is imagined as dancing swinging its arms in the sky burning up the dead and the decaying. The songs in Gitali are articulations of the poet's creative spirit.'

"Thou hast come again
To me in the burst of a sudden storm
Filling my sky with the shudder of they
Shadow of clouds.
The sun is hidden, the start are lost,
The red line of the road is merged in the
Mist of the rain;
The wail of the wind comes across the water
Fitful showers, like ghastly fingers, strike
The chords of some unseen harp
Waking up the music of the dark,
Sweeping my heart with a shiver of sounds"

The image that is created by the lady love's coming to the poet in the burst of a sudden storm filling his sky with the shudder of her shadowy clouds, is new and novel one. The emergence of the new is imagined in the Kalpana. But here we see the resurgence again in a new and striking vein and colour. The image of the 'fitful showers, like ghastly fingers strike the chords of some unseen harp. Walking up the music of the dark sweeping my heart with a shiver of sounds' is novel and audacious. The consummation is reached in Gitali where the new experiences is celebrated in poems of extraordinary grace and beauty and freedom. They have above all a surpassing unity of inspiration and feeling"[55] The image of the Autumn is tinged with the sensuous aspect of poet's nature. The image is compared with a cornet of the lock of hairs wet with dews and sprawling of the lion on the path of the forest is striking on the development of poetic images of Rabindranath. The Autumn is compared with a sweet lady wearing armlet decked with gems, which do flash on the green ground. The song of the humming sound of the shade of the bower and the flapping of the scarf in a dancing style is the very ingredient of the audacious and striking images. Rabindranath represents society where social relationship has allowed a fundamental and revolutionary transformations, when feudalism hardly dominates, rather bourgeois mode of production is the determinant factor. Aesthetic feasibility emanates from this social atmosphere.

Rabindranath in creating these images express his romantic outlook, his renaissance philosophy.

> Forgive my languer, O lord
> If ever I lag behind
> Upon life's way
> For give my anguished heart
> which trembles and hesitates
> In its service.
> Forgive my fondness
> that lavishes its wealth
> Upon an unprofitable past
> Forgive these faded flowers
> in my offering
> That wilt in the fierce heat
> of panting hours.

The image that is crystalised in the poetic, sensual and subjective ejaculation is striking and novel. The image of the Balaka is tinged with flux and endless movement. "Life's central fact, as the poet sees it, is motion. Even seemingly inert matter has hidden centre of never-ceasing motion. To the poet's vision the firmly rooted tree longs to put on wings and fly away into the infinite sky, the mountain top longs to sail and vanish like a cloud the dead picture on the canvass, painted from moving life, returns to life. The universe is a universe of motion which is only reality. To insert matter, since it is a part of a dynamic universe is itself dynamic, and change is not a transformation of one form of inserted matter into another but only a moment in the internal cycle of motion which is life. He sees beauteous mysteries, possibilities of new experiences, that he had never known before when the poet emotionally apprehends an idea or truth, it embodies itself in image symbols, and thus dry abstraction is transmuted into living beauty. These images and symbols are at times of inert objects and at other times of moving objects."[56] The aforesaid theory is the guideline on which almost all the poems are based. But the point on which we hammer is not the sound and pure doctrine, rather on the very genre, the way and the modus operandi, on the beauteous expression and emphatic manifestation we direct our aim and view-point. Here we are confronted with the fruits of industrial revolution. With this introduction of railway, jute mill and cotton mill. The social structure of village civilization of India has been shattered. Capitalism created new foundation, new social infrastructure, new outlook and aesthetic sense and sensibility. Scientific outlook has been perceived. The dynamic universe is symbolized in the images in 'Balaka'. It happens because of the change of social relation, caused by the mode of production.

> The magic incandescence which
> Spring time brings
> The little hamlet flooded with the light
> The fields and meadows, bared of their harvest
> The river-side ferry boat stand,
> The meandering river's blue coast line,
> The shining sand in the distant isle,
> The birds chirp by the quiet stream.
> The mixed carols we hear
> All these sparkling pictures evergreen
> The poet has seen, many times seen,
> The light, this breeze –
> All the unexpressed melodies
> That could threat floats
> The silent shadows they throw
> Silhouetted against the sky
> Makes me happy, makes me sad
> Pensive and restive, moedy and glad
> United in pain and in pleasure
> In thunder, lightning and in rain
> My heart leaps up and seeks
> To assess and express this.

In the poem 'Sabujir Abhjan', "An expedition of the green or the new" the poet gives an idea of the advent of the new, and appeals to replace the old thought, idea and days. He makes these ideas identified with that of main outlook of Balaka i.e. life's central fact is motion, flux and endless endless movement. But the moot question is this : Whatever the grandeur and pomp the idea or doctrine has, it would become insipid and dull should it not take the form of beautiful and decorative cornet. He addresses the green as his intimate and familiar one—

Oh new, Oh my verdant
Oh green, oh my silly
Shave the half-deals
Striking a home thrust

Here he creates an image that manifests a portrait of amorous of sensuous experience. He sees beauteous mysteries, possibilities of new experiences that he had never known before, when the poet emotionally apprehends and idea or truth, it embodies itself in image and symbols, and thus dry abstraction in transmitted into living beauty."[57]

In the image of 'Sabujher Abhijan' (An expedition of The Green), the poet creates an atmosphere that signifies advent of new thing, age and thought. He wants to have the old-fashioned outlook, the traditional way of life. How does he do so? It is not the fact that he has felt in such a way. His keen perception goals him to take such a way. No, it is impossible. What happened is this : The old way of production has gone away, new mode has come with new way of life, thinking, philosophy. Rabindranath has created which is regarded as the living record of the so called going and its relationship, its aesthetic sense and sensitivity.

The image of the dawn that becomes frenzied by the nectar of the bright (red) rays manifests the very atmosphere meant for the new. He appeals to the sensuous and amorous world of us and directs our sight to the portrait of the old and the past, the ears and eyes of which are covered by the two wings, and which drowse as if they are painted on the canvass, as if they are bound in the cage in the darkness.

Side by side he creates an image of the green as a celibate and the immortal, which mopping up and the mopping out age scatters affluently the savours and fragrance of life. What are the activities of the Green, the poet assumes?

It makes the world engrossed with the green infatuation, fills the cloud of the hurricane with the lightning causes the spring to wear the impatient wreath made of Bakul of its own neck.

The motion and the flux are main tenet of image but his sensibility and emotion is given predominance.

We may hold a comparative study as to how other poets treat the advent of the green and the new; first, we quote a poem—a poem of Shakespeare

> Crabbed Age and youth
> Cannot live together
> Youth like summer morn
> Age like winter weather
> Youth is nimble, Age is lame
> Youth is hot and bold
> Age is weak and cold
> Youth is wild and Age is tame
> Age, I do abhor thee
> Youth, I do adore thee

A co-operative evaluation of the youth and age is made. Here it lacks the most evocative and artistic expression of the concept lying with them. Before looking into the rudiments of the image of the poem 'Chabi' (A portrait) we first take into account of the dictum promulgated by Dr. N.R. Roy: A portrait strikes the keynote of the volume; it is a fine poem rich in music and majesty, rich in intellectual power. This portrait of a long lost dear which the poet comes down, envokes images of á long submerged love, and the dead inert lines and paints, lights and shadows of the portrait, become endowed with life and movement, as everything else round is, restless throbbingly real and alive. Every atom of the universe is a piece of congealed motion, even particle of dust, a blade of grass and the love that lay congealed in the portrait becomes alive now in a moment. The poet may have forgotten that portrait, but does he not sometimes forget the flowers that bloom in the way side, forget the stars that shine in the sly? They exist they are alive, although the poet forgets them sometimes and so does she. "Her music, the poet says," branches in my songs; she is a poet in my poet's heart. She is not a portrait, not a mere portrait. But this is just a bold statement of the central theme; the magic of the words and evocations, this richness of the ides and vision as concentrated in moving image, are far beyond me to communicate." It is an important and valuable review of the main outlook of the poem, touching on the surface of the image. But the aesthetic experience, and the consummate form and experience on which we give much emphasis are less emphasized in the evaluation of Dr. N.R. Ray. The image of a portrait' takes new form when one entity steps its movement and another goes on and on day and night in weal and woe. The poet, as it were, identifies himself with the greater aspect of the entity. Every atom of the earth is in moving condition; the tide and ebb are agong in the light and the darkness on the ethereal sea. The host of flowers are in a flux in their silent steps in the different colours. The boisterous streamlet of life runs in a cascade ringing the armlet of death. The poet also has been going from one place to a far-lands infatuated by the lilt of the unknown and being frenzied by the delight in the wayfaring. But the another entity symbolized in the form of a ladylove of the poet did not move and remained and remained decrepit. She was off the path and remained behind this corn, this dust that star and that sun and moon. She is a portrait, only a portrait. The poet wants to catch hold of the fleeting condition of the world. He wants to portray the moving condition of the every atoms of this world, in his own poetic peculiar and fundamental genre, He attributes it with human and sexual elements. He puts it in the centre of romantic atmosphere.

"But the most evocative and artistic expression of the concept of life as perpetual change and caseless motion is to be found in the two pieces, "The Restless" and the name-poem 'Balaka'. The river's dark ceaseless role is eternal, without beginning or end, this unending invisible; swirl shakes the universe with its motion. The review made by Dr. N.R. Ray is true to the theory and concept of Balaka. But what is of permanent value is not its concept or philosophy only, but its true, life-like lively and luminous expression and revelation. In the poem' Restless' the poet creates an image of the impatient loin-cloth that rolls on the tremendous corns, on the cluster of shivering leaves in every forest- the image of flowers-Jasmine, champaks, Bakul and Parul, the fall incessantly on every path from the salver of the seasons. The concept of motionless, decrepitness is symbolized in the consummate and aesthetic image of the mute, dumb, truncated head, of the decrepit darkness, of the boisterous and corpulent hindrance. Side by side he creates another image of the flux, motion and the movement. This concept is revealed in the nature of frivolous dancing girl of the fickle beautiful nymph, invisible beauty, whose fountain eaused by her dance is impuring the universal life by exuding daily. The universal sky is manifested in the pure, blue leaving no remainder.

Rabindranath creates as tuneful image, the manifestation of which mops up the dominance of his subjective and individual element. The object and the subject of experience both are thus universalized, and when they ultimately meet for final confrontation, they give up the individualities. The universalized subject in which the sense of individuality is lulled into sleep prepares itself for a unique confrontation with the generalized character and the mood, and as this confrontation actually takes place, poetic delight is devoured: In the poem 'Balaka' a comprehensive vision is found Here we quote the famous criticism of Dr. N.R. Ray.

"In the Poem' Balaka' we shall find an even more splendid vision. As the geese fly across the sky to unknown and far away lands, they seem to him to be symbol of the restless, ever-unquenched longing of the universal life to fly away, to be lost in eternity, to seek for every the shapes and forms. that can never be found, to break all barriers and grow unchecked in infinite freedom. The poet was then living in a house boat on the Jhelum at Srinagar. The lengthening shadows of the evening darkened the river and the hills and the pines at their feet. The silence and gathering darkness seemed to throb with unspoken words, unspoken desires and passions and all the world seemed to save them. Suddenly this silence is rent asunder by the flutter of the birds' wings as they fly away across the sky into the limitless, invisible distance, and the sound sends a thrill into everything, into the pine forests, into the gloomy mountain tops, into the poet's soul also. At last a voice and symbol have been found for all the passions and all the desires that were unspoken so long, and the poet bursts into song: All things that exist murmur.

Not here, not there, but somewhere else, in some other mode of being there is fulfillment. "Even the impalpable darkness is troubled and shaken as the star quivers in the firmament. And what else is the poet's song but that never arrives: the sound of its wings has ever the same meaning. Not here, some where else".

Whatever the theory and doctrine is propounded in the said poem we see a consummate portrait. The inarticulate objects become lively and full of throbbings of life. The vision and insight of the readers and connoisseur are evidence and they can understand the voice of the stream of the Jhilon that flashes coming in contact with the red rays of the setting sun. The mountains in the darkness is given expression. It happens so, as if the cluster of unrepressed sounds and rhythms suffers from suppressed grief.

The Alankara, Same-Sakti embellishes the image of the poem and the fleeting entity, the movement of the world is deeply emphasised by the said Alankara. The role of Alankara is of much importance and significance. Here it will not be out of the tract if we in this connection take the help of the critic Dr. R.R. Mukherjee. "The question posed is: how does the Alankara help the process of Sadharanikarana-a question which deserves careful consideration. The Alankara finds out connection between his connected things and ideas abruptly and thereby excites the feeling of astonishment in the mind of the experiences: as the appreciator experiences a strong sense of wonder his mind receives a violent concussion and consequently the flow of thoughts concerning his ordinary joy and sorrow, hope and despair, gain and loss is suspended for the time being".[58]

In the poem 'Sha-Jahan' Rabindranath creates a cluster of images which reveal the poet's emotion and swelling of passion The pangs of separation due to his wife's death and sigh dominate the total atmosphere of the poem. "Let the monarchy be merged and dissolved in the dariness like the last red rays of the evening, let only one sigh make the sky pitiful being impassioned daily." This is the only longing of him. The melancholic atmosphere is given much importance and significance. The poem of gems, pearls and jewels is identical with the magical rainbow of the vacant horizon. The poet compares the grandeur of Sahajahan's kingdom with the magical rainbow of the vacant horizon. He apprehends that if it vanished from his (Sahajahan's) grasp let it vanish, but one drop of tear will remain for ever. This is symbolized in the bright and Luminant Tajmohal. The image of sorrow and pangs of separation is manifested in the cornet of tearful delight of the Autumn. The poet creates a tearful image on the canvas of which is decorated the portrait of a ladylove (Momtaj) estranged from him united with the red shadow of the morning, with the fragrance of the bodiless chameli in the full moon and that lies beyond the region of language. The wistful eyes of Shajahan comes back from its door again and again. The image of the pensiveness of the ladies of the city is crystalised in identification with the humming sound of the cricket.

We can state clearly and emphatically that Rabindra works are alive to his posterity due not only to his idea, thoughts and concepts, but the construction of his perfect and vital images also. We must agree with the dictum "One thing is certain, the poet will not become truly modern by any act of will. Modernity may be exhibited in direction, in image or in theme. We perceive, looking back over the poetry of the past, how the poet's idiom differs from that of his contemporaries and we may detect in the general poetic idiom of any given period a greater or lessor approximation to the contemporary rhythms and character of common speech. Professor Livingstone Lowes has admirably said that "poet of low vitality insensate themselves like hermit crabs, generation, in the last of shells of their predecessors. What comes through is vitality. The poet of high vitality and he alone is strong enough to live in the present to in the present to wristle with its protean nature and pin it down to an original form. He alone therefore, is truly modern; because it images the patterns that in his time are still forming, inchoate, his work also bolds good for posterity, many indeed hold mire morning for later times than for his own.

The Poetic Image-C.D. Lewis

The living images

In 'Palataka' we see new form and novel genre of expression. The common and practical habits, occurrences, and characters are the subject of these poems. Binu, Manjula, her hard-hearted father and the loving, affectionate character Pulin are men and women very known to us, and they come from our familiar hamlets and houses. But what is impressive in this poem does not lie with their characters, their habits and their behaviours; they are common, practical no doubt and that touch on our minds. It may be said unhesitatingly, but what is impressive and of much significance is the mode of expression, the manifestation; and it is curious to note that all these are manifested, crystallised in the living and vital image. In the poem 'Deception (Phenki) the poet creates an image that emanates from the poetic sensibility and romantic relation between a couple. The conversation of the newly-married couple (Binoo and her husband) which filled in their minds and unprecedented joy and mirth, although that continued for a moment only. Binoo is now worn-out lady. Natural phenomena, as it were, greets them with all their lights that fill all over the sky. The nature is imagined as a close relative in this phase. Here we quote a dictum of Dr. N. Roy for our convenience.

"In Palataka, he (Rabindranath) tells about this heaven and man-made earth. They are written in unconventional but graceful and harmonious metres, as in Balaka. But Palataka's metrical lines are of varying length, and all the sonorous splendour is shorn away, the words are the loneliness possible, simple without any vulgarity or coarseness. This bareness and familiarity shine with indescribable grace. Each of the poems tells a story. Poetry irradiates it in sudden and unexpected flashes like darts of sunlight, an image, the turn of a phrase sometimes even a word, open up limitless prospects of beauty. And the stories themselves are poetic, they modulate poetically full of the poet's ripe experience of life. They have also profundity of substance. And every where there is the reflection of the poet's love for and adoration of nature"

An Artist in Life—Dr. N.R. Ray

Although the form and nature is different from the conventional tract, they are conducive to the vital and striking images. As for example Binoo and her husband have gone out to change the climate as because Binoo is sick and the doctor advices for the same. They think, rather the poet comes them to think so that they are going out from the broken ghat of their family to the every flow of love. So long they were limited by their one location by their familiar ghat of domestic life, now they are identified with universal life. The sickly wife is bound by her limitation, her freedom was crippled by her freedom was crippled by her superiors. Now there is none to hinder to the union with husband. The poem is itself an image is tinged with pleasure, joy on the one hand, on the other, with sorrow, pangs, and pensive deception. In the poem 'Deliverance', we see the poet's sympathy with the pensive lot of the young widow to when are inflicted lot of injustices and cruelties. Manjula is one of them. She loves Pulin. Her mother likes him and gives a proposal to her husband to arrange marriage Manjula with Pulin. But the superiority, social customs, hinders him and wants to nip the bud of love nurtured in their minds. The story runs so; but the metre, the rhythm, and above all poetic perceptibility and sensibility created an image which reveals on the one hand the injustice, cruelties and portrait of the greedy father, one of the old widowers goes out to Bakherganj to marry again and the middle- aged father returns home after his remarriage and reads the letter left by his young widow daughter. She has run away with her lover, they will marry and build a home there. The father is furious and curses his daughter again and yet again. The meticulous description and multi-coloured sketches make the canvas of the image beautiful and striking. In this connection we agree with Dr. N.R. Ray.

"In Palataka the poet confirms that the men and women of this world this earthy paradise are his nearest and dearest being, that it is they who have inspired him to sing, that it is the lights and shadows of their lives that this poetry reflects. With deep gratitude the poet thanks all the men and women of the world, and the universe for all its days and nights, all its smiles and tears".

In "Purabi"* the poet shows us, the readers, and the connoisseurs the new world, new and beautiful vesture, new colour, novel form, metre and diction. The poem on Satyendranath Dutta" is a tribute of a poet to a poet, whose poems are marked with various rhythm, who plays jugglery over the diction and rhythm in Bengali Literature. In the age of Rabindranath, Satyendranath was a distinguished and most loving poet, who got much life, gratitude from Rabindranath.

---

* One of the finest systems of Indian Music, over which melancholy note is Pervasive. After his death Rabindranath, who was shocked at his death, made a poetic evaluation by dedicating his work, Purabi, named after one of the finest systems of Indian music over which melancholy is pervasive of Satyendranath Dutta. It may be said that he created a consummate image setting his canvass on the very background of nature, using the natural ink and atmosphere. His image is as tuneful as striking.

"The new cloud of the rainy season appears at the eastern door or the earth and rings thunder drum. Oh poet: will you not respond to her with your new and striking metre and rhythm? The songs of Kajali gets a new life coming in contact with the oscillation of the swing; and every leaves and every leaves and branches gets the same. In every year to this swing your words give rhythm and to the song of lightning; why does she strikes with her hand on the forehead in disappointment and welter in the dress of a widow silently on the dust? In the months of (Aswin) autumn will appear in your country and in her ceremonial dress the cornet of shephali in her beautiful and white hand every year. She used to paint every year on your forehead a holy mark of reception with sandal paste of moonlight in the lunar night. Oh poet! From today does she come to your vacant apartment and not seeing songs meant for you."

Here, Rabindranath is perfect, consummate showing his master skill in painting the images, the total picture being this that diction, although it follows the precedent, breaks through its boundary and appears being dressed in colourful and beauteous vesture, the natural phenomena adds new implication to the purport of the poem. Through the lyric of Purabi we get the poet's age-old experience and appropriate pensiveness. Age sheds a mellow, golden light over the lyricism of Purabi. The following commentary is relevant to our context. "The poet feels with a keen pang that his days in this beautiful world are coming to an end, it pains him deeply as he thinks that one day, and that day will come soon; he will no longer experience all this joy and beauty around him. Most of the poems in Purabi are full of melancholy. He remembers that his life is nearing its sunset, and images of the past of many trifling events, float back filling in him with sorrow, sorrow that trembles with tears". While eulogising the poet, Satyendranath Dutta, Rabindranath places before us a consummate portrait of sights, sounds, nature the total system of society that has been experienced by the deceased poet; and what he left us I mean his experience his creations, his sensibility, are full of abounding and overwhelming beauty warm and sensuous". We come to know the fact through the image what appears as an historical facts and figures that Satyendranath Dutta loved this beautiful earth, he fought against the social oppression, vice, the crooked, behaviour. These are all the known facts and we know that these glorify him as a man and the poet no doubt. But Rabindranath again makes us look through the pages of the read book, but does our eagerness again become arrested by fact only ? No certainly not. It is possible due to cornet, the coloured vesture and the romantic outlook and keen perceptibility of the poet, which historical fact can never grasp. The epithet of tribute is symbolized and crystalised in the following images; " You the poet come to tune up the string of the Bengali language with a unprecedented note, and that string is tuned up from to day onward in the Bengali language your own melody will be resounded sometimes in a grave sonorous voice, sometimes in a sweet- pleasant humming sound; the courtyard of Bengal, where hilarity of the rain and the spring surges out every year is painted and decorated by you with various colours. You add your note to the songs of cuckoo and to the call of the peacock; and have left a swing of delight over the leaves and flowers of the garden. In Bengal for the young adventurist who after the end of close-door night will start for with dauntless heart the expedition of a new life, face, new crux, you, the poet, have passed sleepless dark mid-night weaving the laurel of victory—left the viaticum of song filling in with the glow of fire—in the age to come too, you, my young friend, you have entwined the bindings, friendship fastened conscious knot with metres and with varied bindings. Oh worshipper of the truth."

A famous essayist can give us various and typical information, furnishes us with multicolourd interpretation and reviews of a famous poet, so that the total picture along with his distinction, characteristics his originality become revealed to us, and we can grasp it as well as essayist's scholarly nature and his penetration to the world created by the said poet with his perceptibility and keen sensibility. But here—in sphere of image the picture is of different nature. Here is also the same review, the identical aim and intention. But art of manifestation, the modus operandi are divergent. The scholarly interpretation and review touches our intellect and reasoning capability but the manifestation through the images enter into the very core of our heart, feeling and perceptibility. The total atmosphere, the poetic experience, his deep notion, his sensibility, his creative metre and rhythm, painted in the decorative canvass are made clear to us bright as anything. Above all, the atmosphere is pensive; the deep melancholy deepens the atmosphere, and heightens the limitation and closed location of the shrivelled, subjective elements deeply felt. The following image is also of the same genre, but is deeply felt.

Rabindranath alone in the dusk of sorrow and pensiveness, in the circumstances that is resounded with the flow of the river of the death puts some pertinent question that question we know, will not be answered by the poet Satyendranath himself, but the question is self-explanatory and it gives new outlook, new form, and new world of experience.

To the eyes of poet Satyendranath Dutta the daylight of the world is off but he asks whether new and beautiful Nandanlok, the world of mirth and gay is in his grip in the unblemished rays of light, where he fills his cornet with new metre, new songs of glee to adore the morning sun under the rising mountain. The melody of that song instills the lilt, that is mixed with tears in the ears of Rabindranath in the light of morning today. In that expression there lies the pangs of completion, the auspicious message of the fresh beginning, the pensive tremor of departure expressed in the Ragini, Bhairabi, the adoration of imminent union in the melody of Bhairab. The helmsmen of the ferry boat, who took the poet to the other bank of the sea in the wet shadow of Asara (July) is recognized by Rabindranath times without number he wakes from sleep by his Sarigana (the melodious song of east Bengal) and in it is writ the summons for the unknown path that strikes his heart with pain, points to the golden line beyond the setting mountain. He meets him again in the cloudy and rainy day. It is he who brings in to him the letter fragrant with pollentube fallen from Kadamba bearing the message of his last departure and the poet with the letter of answer in his hand will go on the same ferry boat, in some moonlit, peaceful, night marked with cast-off Sheuli flowers, in the morning of the spring, that is swung by the sound wind, and resounded with warbling of the birds, in the day of invitation of newly bloomed Mollika, in the evening of Shravana that is resounded deeply by the humming sound of the cricket, in the disquited midnight marked with the clamarous flood, on the veil of mist in the parting hours of the day in Autumn.

The image have come not along, but in battalion. The cluster of images are painted in deep colour and all these are made on oil-painting. The sorrow and melancholy due to passing away of the poet Satyendranath Dutta, Rabindranath expressed in his own way, in a poetic and symbolic manner.

The poem 'Breaking of Penance' according to Dr. N.R. Ray, is a superb piece and strikes a somewhat different note. Sonorous in its music, magnificent in its emotion and ides, diction and structure it is in every sense worthy of a place beside 'Urbasi' in Chitra. The God of time, Siva, destroyer and preserver, is eternal and keeps a record of every single day of man's life. Has he forgotten the poet's days of youth, days brimming over with life, with the pain of passion, the reckless daring of effort and desire? In these days the poet's hands decked out the god's space and gave him the flute and cymbal and banished his contemplation to the land of eternal snow and silence. And from an ascetic the god was transfigured by the poet's spell into the passionate and youthful lover, eager to drink in all the voluptuous that the world could offer."

An Artist in Life—Dr. N.R. Ray

Rabindranth gives new vesture, novel colour to the old portrait of Shiva. Herė the romantic state and jubilance of youth is painted in the following image:

"Oh forgetful Monk:
Have you forgotten my days
That you swelled-up coming in
  Contact with oangs of Youth?
Oh Almighty kind being unmindfully,
Filling in your water-pot, with the
Savour of intoxication of the spring
That becomes slackened due to the pressure of fragrance
Makes it dip in the hilarity of pleasantness with
  Deep idleness."

Image is created by the deep perceptibility and keen insight of the poet. The transferred epithet (Samasakti) endows with the inanimate object objects with the qualities of movement, feeling, passion, and they become lively and elegant, and decorate the image. The role of the rhetoric and adoration in this embellishment of the poem, especially of the image cannot be denied, The sensuous, meticulous and intensive, descriptive sketches would become insipid and bereft of sweetness and pleasantness, should not they play their part in the creation of total outcome.

The following image reveals the poet's concept of life which is not luminous in the hard asceticism or in the utter renunciation, rather it fructifies in the wild bacchanals of passion and delight.

I know, you oh unmindful want to rise all of a sudden with fresh zeal hearing the afflicted prayor of your ladylove again and again. You on the plea of meditation become engrossed in separation and want to cause Uma to weep inflicting her deep pangs of separation. I see varied portrait of Union after the breaking of penance in every age and play on my lyre the rage Bhairabi I am a poet of that type'. Dr.

R. Ray comments so:

"The poet (Rabindranath) cannot let the god stay hidden in his age and asceticism. He is the agent of heaven's conspiracy against all this; he knows that the god of time, siva, is only trying to deceive him by the show of a spare of withered exterior, the harsh and ungainly barks of covering his surface only. But the withered god is all the time waiting to be defeated by the poet, by the poet's beauty and youth. The poet bears enchantment in his song, and the spell will transfigure the god once again. Beautiful and young, then, the god will throw away his mighty ugly garment and wear silken robes and a garland he will return to Uma, his long forgotten bride, and as they are in one another's arm, the poet's lyre will echo the music of their union."

The nest and the sky- An Artist in life.

In Lilasangit (Sportive companion) the image of the dalliance and sweet frolicsomeness is depicted. The image depends solely on the reminiscence, of the sportive pleasure of a young man and the his Lilasangini. The poet manifests the sensuous activities and juvenile form mode, the rhythm are not unknown to the serious readers; but the vital and evocative revelation, which is predominant in the creation of the readers, the minds of the readers and the connoisseurs to the world of images solely and effectively.

"Do you remember that sportive activities, oh friend? You have opened the closed door by the jingling sound of the armlet. The signand hint floating in the air goes to my window in a round about way—sometimes in the dress of new blossom of the mange, sometimes of the gravity of the new cumulous. You have enticed me again and again momently with the fickle glance."

The image bears the testimony to the poet's keen perception and deep amotion; and leads us to the world that Shivers with throbbings of sensuous feelings and souls passion. The following images is created by the poet who is deeply engrossed in the galay of the paintings of Nature. The Romantic sense and behaviour of the Lilasangini is largely writ in the billow raised in the shore of the river by her; it is she who, coming on the path or the forest would make (the poet) indifferent smearing her body with the pollen of ketaki. All these Images reveal an allround softness and a quiet, peaceful pleasantness and these are the things of the past. The poet again wants to rejoin the broken desire of the poet to identify with the natural phenomena are the key note of the poetic image-sense. We are acquainted with the mellow pliability of the spring. The poet imagines the spring as a new bridegroom. The sexual qualities are attributed to the inanimate things. The poet desires to see him to appear before him in the dress of new bridegroom, for whom the ascetic young lady makes austere endeavours, makes her shrivelled by austic austerities, washes herself, gives up ornaments, procures fruits offerings, giving up her total possessions of the renunciation for him. The image of the spring is grasped in swelling-up murmuring sound of forest, the mirage of the horizon that is created by the vision luminous in the desolate desert of separation. The severe austerities of separation is fructified in the sweet phalguna- the flowering month of the spring. The poets create the image of the spring that pierces his appearance at the red sky hearing sound of feet, feeling the reddish fire in every petal as if auspicious oblation of fire of union is burning. The image of the glow of the colour of the grove and of the dream of crimsoned dusk in the end of the year and that of their location, and the lustre of the colour of the grove some day in the time of separation will float on the raft of crimson dusk dream, is created by the poet having deep penetration. The image manifests the poet's keen perceptibility, acute discernment and perfect hold over the phonetic and juxtaposition of portrait of words.

Now, we come to the world of "Mahua". The poem of this phase are heavy with the intoxicating fascination of the Mahua, a strong-scented spring flower. The commentary of Dr. N. R. Ray is deeply apprehended. "Mahua registers the surge of a new inspiration-spring whose approach heralds, arrives at last. The little of the book is beautifully appropriate, for the Poems in it are heavy with the intoxicating fascination of the Mahua, a strong scented spring flower. The love Poems in this book are, the most characteristic."— *An Artist in life.*

Sagarika in this phase is a most characteristic one. It reminds us of the masterpiece, *Bijoyini.* But their discrement, their artistic sense diction are different, and we think they are distinguished from each other due to their striking and vital images. The images of Sagarika, a young women residing in the island who sits on the sea shore affluent with pebbles, with dishevelled hair, bathing in the water of the sea is painted with keen sensibility and evocative power. The following images appear to us of audacious and of vital nature.

"The Slackened yellow clothing sprawls on all sides of the ground making a crooked line; on your naked breast, on the body devoid of ornaments the dawn being luminous with lustrous golden letter marks with affection; wearing the coronet having Makar as a crown on the forehead with bow and arrow in the right hand I stand in the dress of king said "I, inhabitant in a foreign land have come" Started with fear and leaving the stony seat you asked "why did you come? I said, Do not fear at all, I want to pluck flowers of worship in your garden?"

The images reveal the sensuousness of the poetic nature. The following images also constitute the soul of the poetry. Again we see that :

"When the evening star arose in the apex of the mountain, you were alone at your house. There was blue lion in your waist, the garland of Malati in your head, two armlets in your arms. While going on my way I played on the pipe, coming to your door said, I am a guest. Being frightened burning the candle with startled hand started at my

Face and said "why did you come? I said ' Do not fear' I shall decorate your thin body with my ornaments." You looked at me with smile I caused the golden garland of the half moon swing in your breast. I caused the coronet with makar-crown to put on your head rounding your braid." This image does not depend on the picture of words only but it depends on the adjustment, the juxtaposition and the total atmosphere also. The poem Sagarika is an image itself. Herein one factor is added, the factor of dramatic monologue. The poetic sensibility and emotive contents of the Poem are given movement and deepening quality, gravity and grandeur. The images inform us of the wreckage of the boat, of the arrival of the poet (young lover represented in the form 'I') with broken heart in dirty poor dress devoid of embellishment.

He comes to the door of the temple of Shiva, where he sees his beloved—silent, and with down-cast eyes. She wears his garland on her breast and he looks secretly that the rhythm of the instrument tuned by the foreign young man himself swing on her body in a wavy motion, in a billow calculated by the pleasant song. The concluding image presents that the man comes this time being destitute of everything. He had no coronet with Makar marked crown, no bow and arrow in his hand, he did not bring the cornet in the south sea, in her sea, in her garden situated at the shore of the sea. He has brought only lyre. He requests her staring at him whether the recognizes him or not. The poetic emotion, perceptibility pervade all over the circumstances. Here is no intricacy of psychological events and acute libidinal experiences, but a peaceful, quite and pleasant relation between a lover and his lady love. The total form, sketch and expression are manifested through the striking images. It is function of image. Image is effective in its idleness with poetic sensation, emotion and perception. According to I. A. Richards "images is not confined in the sight only, but it is deeply related with the memory of the total consciousness. So he says that what gives an image efficacy is less its vividness as an image than its character as a mental event connected with sensation."[59]

"The image is not an emanation from momentary object and emotion. But it comes from the whole of his sensitive life since early childhood".

In the poem 'Union'-Amorous meeting of two Entities in the courtyard of the creation "is seen and keenly felt and perceived by Rabindranath. He observes that the wind carries the letter of love, i.e.. a pollen to every blossom and asks when the time for blooming will come. For this there is glow of colour, fickleness in every ranch, there butterfly carries the metre and rhythm of the beauty in its every wing. The affluence of the swelled-up ceremony runs from one forest to another with the songs of the birds. We see that the poet creates an Image that lifts the common outlook and plane. It adds new blood to the common and day-to-day experience and embraces the quality of universal nature. It has also the same bearing on human phenomena. The sport of the creation has the same effect on human habitation, in the union of the two; and thereby un unprecedented life will evolve with multi coloured forms and figures. They (lover and the beloved) give up their works and dressed in coloured clothings are getting on the prairie, and the flute are being played on the path, and the new covering is created out of all worn-out states of the old world that is being scoured out. What is of highest value and truth and characteristics is the sport as if it is a pleasant exultation of phalguna, the flowering season, it is unhesitating it has got no paleness of the earth, it is identical with the mirth of the god.

The image of 'Union' is created by Rabindranath through employment of the appliances of simile, metaphor, parallelism, corroboration to poetic Naturalism, Emotive Embellishment and perception-like presentation.

One thing is clear from the said evaluation and commentary on the function and capacity of the image. The following dictum deserves close attention and deep consideration: (This) capacity of the image to lift the connoisseur to a higher plane by impressing on him the highly ordered design of the world reveals itself in a greater degree in images, characterised by employment of the device of corroboration. It embraces three things the meaning the particular gives to the universal, the meaning the universal lends to the particular, and the meaning which particular, and the meaning which the particular-universal relationship hears for the reader in the context of the main melody of the Poem, and thus makes transition from the individual experience to the universal experience easer."—*Alamkara and Aesthetic Realisation,* -Dr. R. R. Mukherjee, Quoted form the literary journal 'Anviksa'.

In the poem 'Sabala' Rabindranath gives a divergent and different picture. The poems of Mahua volume are mostly artistic, and poetic, they have a greater intensity and complexity of emotion. But the character portrayed in 'Sabala' channelises here emotion, her sensibility in the legitimate and pertinent right and logical and rational power. The image of the poem conforms to the same stand point. But one thing must be comprehended that dry reason and rational capability does not dominate the whole atmosphere of the poem. The following image reveals the truth.

Why deprive me, my fate
Of my woman's right
Boldly to conquer the best of life's prizes
With mine own arrogant power and
Not to keep gazing at emptiness
Waiting for some chance drifting towards
With the withered fruit of weavy days of patience?
Send me without pity to the utter risk of
My all for the treasure
Guarded behind rudely for bidding barricades.

The image of boldness, arrogance and audacity is created by the poet.

The following image pins down the poet's perceptibility and keen sensibility on woman's nature.

Never for me is to steal into the
Bridal chamber
With the timid tinkling of anklets
In a dim twilight dust
But recklessly to rush
Into the desperate danger of love
By some troubled sea,
Where its stormy vehemence would
Snatch away from my face
The veil of shrinking maidenliness
And amidst the ominous shrieks
Of sea-birds
Could be raised to my warrior
You are mine own.

Here the image of deep and intense emotion is aimed at, but that is channellised through another form. The image is marked with the item of rebellion and aspect of insurgence.

The image painting in the 'Pariseha' volume conveys the idea that the curtain was drown upon the final act of the drama of his life. Actually, the poems in 'Parishesha' heralded the beginning of a new phase of the poet's life and art, perhaps one of the richest and most significant of all the phases of his life. And this is when he was past three score and ten years. As if it were a rebirth, but with all the rich experiences of previous existences stored in the memory and consciousness of his new being."

This is the purport and main, theme of the 'Parisesha' volume. In the poem 'Pronam' i.e. act of making obeisance by lying prostrate the poet in the fag end of his life as a poet takes stock of his experiences and past days of life, the cumulous of sorrows and sufferings, exultation and mirth. Rabindranath expresses his experience of the path of his life. He collects an amusing flute of diversity marked with variegated colour on his journey. On that dawn the light and darkness become exulted and get the touch of delight in the moment of their first union under the shade of red veil. An image of the union of a couple is symbolized in the portrait of the union of a couple is symbolized in the portrait of the union of the dawn and dust. Transferred epithet being used deepens the rasa of poetry, Rabindranath assumes his life as long journey, which he takes merely as a journey. Travellers takes this for the rare and dear rising the sky-piercing-mountain, which is difficult of access, and crossing the impassable sea. He has returned touching the deepness and he has collected and accumulated nothing, only sought after the intangible. What he means to say is this that he never walks on the surface of life, the material life. The shallow mirth, joy, delight, and their combination, money, riches and fame never touch him, never catch hold of him. Rather he always wants to see the bottom to drink life to the lees. Image of this phase responds to the same outlook and phenomena. The image is created thus:

"I have filled in the flute with vitality of life only, attempted to tune up the melody of variety in the strings of mine lyre. I have invited the rhythm of pangs which arises in the core of heart of the trees in the phalguna prior to blooming of flowers in my incharted Ragini (system of music), in the modulation tremulous with eagerness. The worn-out leaves have left behind last sigh in my song. I have driven up words through the holes of this flute the silent festive sound (Uludhawni) which becomes pervaded far off, behind the grey curtain in every corn and sprout, when the sunrays peeps through the harem of the earth. The great secret years feeling which causes the figures of the night to bid the setting of beads silently in the silent prayer of hymn in the adoration of the light has been received by me alone in the tremor of my heart the flute being placed on my breast. My flute murmuring sweetly has collected in the song the suspicious pangs of the imprisoned, concealed fragrance, which is searching for a tray of altarage for worship in the heaven of dream, in the midst of the tender bud. Nataraj Shiva (the best dancer) dances in the rumbling sound of the Mridanga caused by the perturbed wave of ocean of consciousness, the dalliance of abysmal tears being units with the rearing laughter in the uproar is raising a tingling sound and the shadow and light owing in that oscillation with the incessant billow, I sitting on the shore composing my song keeping of musical time with the Rudra measure have got behind my own metre and rhythm the pangs of exultation of the endless. The feeling of the earth has created innumerable ardour in the midst of the practice of music. On the end of this path resounded with music. "oh Human Being: I have come in your temple at the end of the day, on the shore of the silent midnight at the evening of greetings a deity; I place the sportive flute of diversity at the feet of one and this is my obeisance towards Him."

The image created in the said poem is consummately and superbly imagined. Poetic sensibility and emotion are given their due weight and expression. Dr. Nihar Ranjan Ray apprehends properly in his famous book' An Artist in life' parishesha contains some poems, exaltation too, in which the story of life and beauty and youth is celebrated in tender and delightful music.

Its brevity and compression heighten the total effect. The grandeur and gravity of this poem is founding the poems of *Chitra, Manashi* volumes.

The different mode of expression and kind of image to be found in the poem Mrityunjoy, (Shiva who conquers death). The image of Shiva is created thus and its effect on the mind of the poet.

> "You seemed from afar
> Titanic in you're mysterious majesty of terror
> With palpitating heart I stood before
> Your presence,
> Your knitted brows boded ill and

Sudden came down
the blow
With a growl and a crash
My bones cracked,
With bowed head I waited
For the final fury to come.

Rabindranath creates an image of the mysterious majesty of terror conceived of Shiva, who conquers conquer the death and created another picture where Shiva the death and creates another picture where Shiva is not great, rather human being seems to be great and Titan. The image of the Shiva bereft of his power is like this:

It came
And I wondered could this be
All if the menace?
With your weapon held high in suspense
You looked mightily big.
To strike me you came down
To where I crouched low on the ground
You suddenly became small
And I stood up,
From thence there was only pain for me but no fear
Great you are as death itself,
But your victim is greater than death.

Rabindranath created this image because perhaps materialistic thought has been lulled in his mind. This image is dominated by feeling and poetic passion which is unconventional and antitraditional. In the poem (Biswoi) Rabindranath expresses his wonder and amazement. The endless wonder dominants the image of this poem.

"Once again I wake up when the light has waned
when he opens all its petals once more
And this is an endless wonder
Vast islands have sunk in the abyss unnamed,
Stars have been beggared of the last flicker of
their light,
Countless epochs have lost all their leadings
World-conquerors have vanished into
the shadow of a name

Behind dim legends
Great nations raised their towers of triumph
As mere offering to the unappeasable
Hunger of the dust.
Among this dissolving crowd of the discarded
My forehead receives the consecration of light
And this is an endless wonder
I stand for another day with the Himalayas
With constellations of stars
I am her where in the surging sea-waves
The infinite with his boisterous laughter
The centuries on which have flashed
up and foundered
Kingly crowns like bubbles
Have left their signature on the
bark of this aged tree
Where I am allowed to sit under
Its ancient shade
For one more day
And this is an endless wonder."

The image of the said poem is created out of the poetic astoundedness at the sight of the natural phenomena. Nature always appears to us in bright colour and a luminous portrait. This is no new thing. But the poet dives headlong into the fathomless savour of beauty of nature; he gives us his new outlook, he presents Nature as a novel one, an unprecedented appearance. The amazement of the poet may be grasped at by realizing the novel outlook and dominating aspect of the vital images.

The system and modes of this phase i.e. from the very last phase of the composition of the 'Parisesha' volume is different vitally and fundamentally from that of the preceding volumes. The metre, the image the rhythm and total atmosphere have changed radically and vigorously. The vital and altogether change which arrests our attraction keenly and acutely is its metre day life and in every walks of our mature and behaviour of life.

We, now, are quoting some portions of the poem 'Bansi (The flute) which manifests the very portrait of our mundane Heaven and which reveals the material outlook keeping no unreal veil therein. Each stanza of this poem is an image itself; but it is borne in mind that images created out of the seven stanzas are not distinguished and isolated; they are rather woven in a common one tuneful string that takes all the images into a consummate and perfect one.

The alley after the name kinu, the milkman
The ground floor with iron-bar of two storied
Building
is on the roadside.
Some portion of wall damaged by the damp comes off
With prominence of sand.
Some portion is marked with dampness
One single picture of god Ganesh, who grants
success Branded with coarse white fabric
Another creatures except me lives in this
House at a single rent
That is lizard
But my alienation from it
Is this only that he has got no want
of food.

What impresses us much is not only the ingredients and materials taken from the lives of the miserabile alleys Calcutta, not only for the living and vital portrait which has a fundamental bearing on the materialistic outlook and keen affinity with the people of the soil cherished in the fag end of his life, but the modes operandi, the genre of expression, the mode of manifestation also. It is the peculiarity of expression, the whole thing the total atmosphere experienced by the poet is given revelation. The passage, the mode along with the poetic aesthetic experience, the picture of decaying economy are crystallised in the image itself; it may be christened as Grecian urn, on which different portraits are depicted. The poet, Keats in his own peculiar and rudimental genre depicts different and divergent portraits. The very urn appears before us as a modus operandi- incarnate, as a embodied genre itself.

The image of the second stanza is this:

"Emoluments are twenty five rupees
(I'am) youngest clerk of the mercantile farm
I have my fooding at the house of Datta lane
Teaching their boys in turn
I go to Sealda station
To pass the evening
By that the necessity of
Burning the light is avoided
(I hear) the sharp sound of engine
And see the sound of the whistle
The hastiness of the passengers
And the repeated calling of the coolie
The clock strikes 10.30 p.m.
Coming to my room feel solitary, noiseless darkness.

The portrait of the miserable economic condition along with the atmosphere of Sealda station and his sensible adjustment are vividly depicted in the said stanza. An image reveals the poetic cravings and desire keeping his perceptibility and sensibility luminous over them.

Rabindranath was no longer engaged with the far flung imaginative sketch or with interpretation and apprehension of Jibandevata, or with making out of the voice of the lady who happened to be his lady love in his previous birth.

The image of this phase is not decorated with pompous and grandiose words and their meaning. The alonkars or the embellishment of this phase is simple, easy, inherent, and natural. Even his (poet's subjective I) –the representative of the common men having low income and education-identification with solitary, noiseless darkness strike a new meaning and thought. He gives us a meticulous portrait and thereby he seems to give us a clue and hint to some thing or some one who is liable for his (the clerk) being ill-fed and his tendency to avoid burning the light. The images does not reveal the responsibility of some one or some system that dominates his income, his tendency, his thought and everything. But the picture is depicted as vividly as anythings.

The *Bichitrita* (the variegated) volume manifests the different and multicoloured experiences, and revelation of the variously painted walks and cravings of the life of the poet. In the poem 'Pasarini', (the woman seller) Rabindranath presents an image of woman dealer before the readers, but she is of uncommon nature, who forgets to take her money and goes somewhere led by the thought. He makes us acquainted with woman who has been engaged in trafficking an every market in the morning. At the time of return to her hamlet what happens to her is not known? She sat under the shade of the tree. She left for some unknown place leaving the accumulated sums of profits in the basket. Then the poet presents the multi-coloured, multiformed natural cornet. This land, this red dust, the glossy leaves of jack-fruit brightened by rays of Agrahan (a month of winter), the breathing of the winter breeze, thrilling grass are the decorative item of the variety painted in the said poem. These items have a strong bearing on the mind of the Pasarini. The waters of the rivers stretching far that dazzles streak of light, natural phenomena that is made to bear testimony to the first remembrance of the creation are the decorative aspect of the poem. The vast open land, the inarticulate voice, the severe heat expressing emptiness, whispers in the mind of pasarini. The poet with all these decorations and embellishing aspects signifies the motionless eagerness, curiosity of stoicism. It is borne in mind that hard and dry stoicism is not aimed at by the poet. Rather he created an consummate image out of the factor and elements of natural phenomena that have been thronged with meticulous assortment leading to a perfect and tuneful assimilation and identification with the image itself.

In the poem "Biday" (farewell) Rabindranath created an image that reveals not only, departure and its pathos but the music of an unspoken love it is touched on the common and uncommon aspects of nature. It is common because departure yields sorrow, tears and pathos; it is uncommon because these aspects have created a consummate and perfect atmosphere, which is rare in the society. The following image is a perfect example.

"A veil of a thousand years
Dropped between you and me
When you turned your face and merged
in a past

Where spectre-like dwell they
Who missed love's path in a timorous
Dust of doubt.
The spectre is but narrow that
Divides us,

a tiny stream weaves in its murmur the memory of our parting moment the pathos of your passing footsteps. And all that I can offer to you is the music of an unspoken love for it to follow you and vanish.

What impresses us much is the prose form, peculiarity of contents and a radical reorientation of the poetic perspective, attitude. And whole things is expressed in striking and perfect images.

Here we are quoting a dictum, of Dr. N. R. Ray from his book *An Artist in Life* "that makes clear the profess, the technique an above all poetic, aesthetic sense and sensibility.

"From *Balaka* onwards he (Rabindranath) was steadily moving towards more and more freedom and flexibility, towards in increasing synthesis of verse and prose. This process led inevitably to what we call the prose-poems in *Punascha, Sesh Septalk, Patraput* and *Syamali,* verse form by means of which the logical and precise state ments of prose are woven into the web of verse.

Form is not something adventitious, but is the body of poetry. Its connection with the poet's imagination, experience and sensibility, is therefore, intimate. In *Balaka* the modulation of song that removes the verse to a sphere away from factual language, persists in the verse.... The verse technique of *Balaka* and *Palataka,* of *Lipika,* and *Parishesha....* proves that it has an organic history and evaluation. But a more important fact is that the poet has entered upon a new spiritual phase, and a new phase naturally carries out a distinct form and technique. The transformation is more actual and widespread. There is not only a newness of content, such as we find in *Punascha,* there is radical re-orientation of the whole sensibility, attitude and perspective.

The poet has often tried to explain the aim and significance of this new technique, and he himself has stated that underlying all this theme was a total and compulsive change of phase too. In the introduction to Punascha he says that the coyness and the excessive burden of trinkets that has so long impede the movement of poetry must be broken down; it must be given the same freedom of motion as prose has. 'The adoption of a full-hearted and unashamed prose technique will enlarge the rights and privilege of poetry, that was the faith that inspired me in this strong innovation: some of the poems have poetic notes although they are unrhymed, but even in them I have discarded all conventional poetic language".

The new technique, art and artifice, the new perspective, poetic sensibility sees its affluence in "Punascha".

In the poem Kopai (a name of the river in the District Birbhum near Santiniketan) the sketches, the forms, and colours are differently applied, peculiarly decorated. Rabindranath seems to have studied comparatively on two rivers, Padma and Kopai. The image of the poem is this: "Idly my mind follows the serious sweep of the Padma roaming under a distant sky. On the further side of her stretches the sand-bank, insensitive to the living world, defiant in its sublime in utility. It is simple sketch and outline and it is the preamble to the main story and total circumstances of the poem. On the one side crowd the bamboo, the mangotree, the patriarchal banyan; the obsolete hut in ruins; the aged jack tree of a massive trunk, the mustard field on the slope of the pond; the cane bush round the ditch by the lane; the remnant walls of an indigo plantation clinging to a silenced time, its row of casuarinas murmuring day and night in the forsaken garden."

It is similar to a multifigured and multicoloured canvas of the painter. The descriptive sketch and meticulous delineation are tinged and smeared with poetic perception and keen sensibility.

What is aimed at is to present a clear and perfect portrait of the river Padma and its surroundings, its locality and its natural phenomena.

"The colony of Rajbanshis dwell there near the rugged bank fractured into zigzags offering a scanty pastime to their goats; in the adjacent upland the corrugated roofs of the market storehouses keep staring at the sun.

The whole village stands shuddering in the constant fear of the heartless stream.

The proud river has her name in the venerable texts; through her veins runs the sacred current of the Ganges. She remains remote. The homesteads she passes by are tolerated by her, not recognised; her stately manner has a response in it to majestic silence of the mountain and the large loneliness of the sea."

The image of Padma created by the poet is the manifestation of the poet's Rasa-chetana or the capability of the appreciation. The image depends on the descriptive sketches or it is the conglomeration of different and varied pictures and portraits with jewel at the middle point i.e. the boisterous form of Padma.

He creates another image constituted of different colour, form and sensibility i.e. the image of Kopai.

"I have for my neighbour the tiny river Kopai. She lacks the distinction of ancient lineage. The primitive name of her is mixed up with the loud laughing prattle the Santal women of courtless ages.

There is no gap for discord between the land and the water in her intimacy with the villager and she easily carries the whisper of her one bank to the another. The blossoming flax field is in indulgent contact with her as the young shoots of rice.

Where the road comes to an abrupt break at the brink of her water, she graciously makes way for the passers-by across her crystal-clear garrulous stream.

Her speech is the speech of the humble home, not the language of the learned. Her rhythm has a common kinship both with the land and the water, her vagrant stream is unjealous of the green and the golden wealth of the earth. Slender is her body that glides in curves across shadows and lights clapping hands in a tripping measure."

Rabindranath creates an image of Kopai, the thin and slender bodied river, which is not marked and distinguished for her vastness, affluence of water and for her boisterousness. She becomes wild unlike Padma, her limitation illumines her character and makes her marked in her own sphere. The poet shows her so:

"In the rains her limbs become wild like those of the village girls drunk with mahua wine, yet she never even her wantonness breaks or drowns her neighbouring land; only with a jingling whirl of her skirt sweeps the banks while she runs laughing loud.

By the middle of autumn her water became limpid, her current slim, revealing the pallid glimpse of the sands underneath. Her distinction does not shame her, for her wealth is not arrogant, nor her poverty mean."

Rabindranath attributes her with human feeling and sensibilities, the artful activities of young girl. The stream, its current, its gentle sound, its stillness, sometimes boisterousness in the rainy season are viewed by the poet with his poetic perception, his tremendous imaginative vitality and integrity.

"The Kopai in her pulsation finds its semblance in the rhythm of my poet's verse, the rhythm that has formed its comradeship with the language rich in music and that which is crowded with the jarring trivialities of the work-a-day hours. Its cadence falls not the Santals boy lazily tramping along with his bow and arrows; it times itself to be lubering market cart loaded with straw; to the panting breath of the potter shouldering earthen-works in a pair of hanging baslets tied to a pole, his pet pariah dog fondly following his shadow, it makes at the pace of the weary steps of the village schoolmaster, worth three rupees a month holding an old-torn umbrella over his head."

Here we are quoting Dr. N. R. Ray for making our points clear.

Even more wonderful, however, is the clear wind bright radiance the swelling and majestic movement, the accounts rhythmic with power that we find in the best of these prose-poems along with their tremendous imaginative vitality and integrity. Most of the poems in these four volumes describe apparently trifling events or expands thoughts and imaginations that are in origin only casual. But however minute or trivial the immediate theme may seem to be, it is a part of the events and emotions of daily life; it has thus a serious and passionate background without which it is incomplete. The poet takes keen pleasure in all that happens around him and relates it to a larger significance, which is composed of the same mixture of the harsh and the sweet, the hard and the soft. There are certain poems which tell stories, and they are composed in the lament and detached mood proper to the story-telling vein. In other poems again there is an attempt to recapture in everlasting beauty and depth some sudden and flitting whim or desire. In such feeling naturally flows at a low ebb, the movement of the sensibility is undirected and uncontrolled and therefore full of sudden and unexpected turns and shifts: the attitude as a whole is somewhat indifferent, detached. Yet they have a beautiful integration of form and feeling, a firm correspondence of word and meaning and music."*

*Here are vital aspect is lacking. All these fractures and characteristics do not originate from themselves. They have

....

In this poem 'The Boy' (Cheleta) Rabindranath shows an image of the boy, that arrives, according to some critic, with a baggage of beauty and ugliness, of all sorts of wild and confusing objects and sets up a deafending turmoil of shouts and screeches and musical notes". But it is not wholly correct. Because 'The Boy', characterised by Rabindranath is a vital, vivacious and volatile character. So, if there is my ugliness, confusion, deafening turmoil, they are only items, and they are only actors to the total integrity and cohesion. The image is created thus :

The age of the boy is ten years,
Brought up at the lap of the unrelated-
As parasite that lies in the border of the broken fencing.
Gardener cares little for it.
But for it light, air, rain are ample
Insects, dusts, sands,
Sometimes goat lops it,
Cow tramples it under feet
Yet it is alive, it become strong
Stack gets thickness
Leaves are glossy green.

The image of the boy is not similar to the common place boys or our day-to-day existence. His nature is peculiarly drawn and portrayed. His peculiar and uncommon nature arrests our attention and sympathy. The poet depicts a meticulous and sympathetic biography of the boy along with his cravings, likings, ideas, his own circumference. And the poet adopts a full-hearted and unashamed prose technique to fructify his new experience and ideas of life.

The image of the boy becomes luminant by his activities, by his divergent and different cravings and likings. The image of the boy is this :

"The boy breaks his bone to pluck the palm, he swoons by eating wild, poisoned fruit. He looses his path. But nothing affects him. He comes round from his half-dead condition. He returns being lost in the midst of throng with the body smeared with clay and clothes torn. He is beaten right and left and innumerable obscene language are hurled at him. And the grip being slackened he runs again at ease."

The activities referred to are solely owned by a wicked and knotty boy, who has not been nurtured at his mother's lap. This is a common aspect and natural behaviour of the said natured boy. But what is striking and vital is not only the thorough and detailed description of his activities, but the genre, mode of exposition, and the way of manifestation also.

The following image of the natural phenomena is conducive to the Boy's mental cravings and his idea of life to plunge headlong into anything to know the thing hidden therein.

On the turn of the dried up river
Moss has accumulated abundantly
Heron remains standing on the border
The black crow sits on the branch of the Bainche tree
White kite flies in the sky,
The sailor spreads his net
Setting on the bamboo used for it
On the apex of the bamboo sits one king fisher
Ducks pick oyster by diving.
The time is soon.
He is inclined (to dive) having seen
The cursor of waters,
The mosses that remain hanging

Spreading their leaves under them;
Fishes do play.
In the deeper water he supposes the existence of
The daughter of Naga
She parts her hair with the Comb
Her zigzag shade is in the wave of water
The fancy of the boy is to plunge on that spot- that green,
Transparent water,
Like a glossy body of the snake.

The image of the Boy is comprehended deeply and peculiarly, because of its identification with natural phenomena. All the descriptive sketches and paintings aim at one and single portrait, i.e. the image of the Boy. His cravings, desires are not only peculiar, but mark unprecedented happenings and occurrences. He has a pet dog having no Pedigree, he belongs to the genealogy of the street cur. He loves him (the dog) for his nature that has a similarity to that of him. He (the boy) weeps for him, the dog, who is forced to leave this earth for attempting to eat the ready meal of his (boy's) neighbour. The image of the last stanza is vital and emphatic in direct and comprehensive expression as well as for poetic sensibility and perceptibility. The image of this: The teacher, Ambika regrets before the poet that the boy gets no interest in reading the poems meant for the study of the children written by Rabindranath-such is his dull-headedness. He cuts the leaves of the book out of his wickedness and gives a plan that the same has been mutilated by the ants—such a great monkey he is. The poet apprehends the fact and admits of his flaw and drawback. He states that

The drawback is mine
Had there been a poet of his own world
The insignificant insect would be
Evident through his metre and rhythm.
The Boy cannot neglect
Have I ever written the actual happenings of the frog
And the tragedy of that street our."

And this is evident from the Image that ' not only is the eager to write the language of ordinary of men and women, his sensibility, too, is eager to embrace the larger human consciousness. This newness of perspective comes out even more clearly in the third poem in *Punascha,* 'New Times'. So he begins new, 'in a different language from heretofore: the language of tramps, the raw accents that we hear in wayside inns."

The idea is expressed, even more clearly in a few poems in *Sesh Saptak* (Last Melodies). In one of them the poet holds his court under the sky by the dusty wayside, and he is turns over the pages of his older books, the poems seem to be supersensitive, they seem to be too subdued, too coy; indeed, they appear to be so fragile that if they leave the cool shadows of their harem and carry cut into the poem, the sunlight will at once shrivel them up. How can he present them at this court ? Here only can come those who have left home, whose clothes are dusty, who can walk steadily and sturdily even in the most difficult road, who do not have to please any one and who can shout lustily in dark forests and strange hills. It is for them and of them that the poet wants to sing his new songs. So the old poetry remains unread, and the poet goes away saying that he will 'treat difficult roads, do strenuous journey'.—*An Artist in Life,* Dr. N.R. Ray

The critic simply states the poetic idea and the sensibility, but does not tread the difficult roads which would lead him to the world of image, through which he has sung with the poet 'the harsh songs of an indifferent and sturdy soul. The image of the following poem of Sesh Saptak reveals our dictum.

I neglected to appraise your worth
Being blindly sure of my possession
The days followed each other and the rights-
Carrying your offerings to my feet
I looked at them through the corner of my eyes
As they were being sent to my store-house.
April's honey sucks added their scent to your gifts,
The full moon of the autumn night
Touched them with its glimmer.

The poetic neglect due to the poet's own possession to give value to 'your (her) worth, the use of nights and days as a conveyance to convey her gift to him, his negligence, and April's honey sucks help to her gift, and touch of the full moon of the autumn night are all common materials and object touched by the common people, who may look at the them as common and sympathetic readers and connoisseurs. They scarcely take stock of those objects at a time with sympathetic consideration. But while reading them they feel charmed and amazed at the momentum given to those common neglected objects. So, with those objects we get another set of things too, i.e. poetic emotion, poetic sensibility, his likings, his idea and valuation of his time and above all a striking and perfect form of manifestation, revelation, what we call image- in which objects, experience described by the poet do not appear, but what appears are not the things, but similitude of things and that not through the journalist's eyes and columns but through the beautiful and charming eyes of the poet. He gives another form of the image :

The poet has depicted a portrait of a man who neglects the worth of a lacy due to his pride of his possession. At last he 'Kisses the dust where who left her footprints. His pride do not remain indifferent. At last he gains her truly, for with his sorrow he has paid the price of her love'. It also emanates from the common experience and everyone feels its haughtiness, stoic indifference and at last it ends with tearful exultation, sorrow, grief bridges the gap between then. It has a bearing on the minds of the men and women. Still so, it is limited in its own supersede its boundary and four-cornerned apartments. But what we get from the said from the said poem does not only touch the cravings and sensibility of the Benglaees and Indians, the people of different countries also feel identified with the reality and poetic truth. So it is evident that something lies in the poem, which is universal and, of permanent value no doubt, but its universality and permanence does not only depend on the poetic cravings, sensibility and his imaginative faculty, but on its way presentation, its mode of manifestation and modus operandi of revelation also.

In the poem 'Panchise Baisaka' (Twenty-fifth of Baisakh) Rabindranath creates a consummate image that informs us pictures of various Tagores at various phases of life. Dr. N. R. Ray gives us a meticulous portrait of his different and divergent phases of his life. "In this forty-third poem in Sesh-saptak the poet draws pictures of himself (Tagore's) at various phases of life. After describing the phase when he reached his plenitude, the poet seventy, addressed his readers, and says: "You have come to me on this twenty-fifth Vaisakh (the first month of the Bengali calendar), amidst all the harrowing troubles and conflicts of my life. Have you known that in my self-revelation there is much that remains unfinished, much neglected, torn and scattered? In your love in your regard, in your forgiveness, you have fashioned an image of mine that is unstained by all this defeat and frustration. Let me acknowledge this as my true self on the 25th Baisakh. And I bless you. I bequeath this beautiful and pure image to be treasured in your memory all time. You will now give me leave to depart. I will retire in that nameless solitude where shadow covers all life's reflection crowed in black and white, and there at last I will learn to play all the instruments in unison with the music of the ultimate commemoration."—*An Artist in Life.*

To this dictum one thing is to be added:

"The poems he wrote on his birthdays are full of the self-analysis, but we get it in other poems too, for example, in the last there poems in *Sesh Saptak* and in numbers 5 and 12 in patraput, the last two having a deeper vision, a greater imagination range and meaning. No quotation can give any idea of the majesty and integrity, the ever-present power that informs these poems...... The self-exploration and analysis, although so complex and many sided, are nowhere foggy or confused." *Ibid.*

But one vital thing is wanting in his dictum, i. e. the beautiful integration of form, embellishment, manifestation, meaning and contemplation and imaginative faculty-that are embodied and crystalised in the perfect and striking image.

> The twenty-fifth Baisakh is carrying the succession or
> birthday
> Towards the last day.
> Sitting on that mobile seat
> Some artisans weave one garland of various Tagores
> In the periphery of insignificant birth and deaths
> (i.e. various charges)

Rabindranath gives us some intimate reflections on his personal life. An autobiographical sketch has been aimed at by the poet. But every reader and connoisseur who happens to read this poem will be charmed by its form and mode of revelation. His birthday, Pachise Baisakh seems to play a dominant role. He is not going to the dusty death, rather that day is carrying the rain of his birthdays towards deaths. Another expression is vital. Supposing a man has got different and divergent phases. One may be amazed at the identification of one portion of life with another. All these divergent aspects emanate from one and single man. It is a reality. But Rabindranath imagines that some artisan weaves one garland of various and divergent Tagores in one periphery of variances of little births and deaths. Different phases of his life are given expression in the following image.

The time is going in a chariot,
While going on foot the traveller
Brings in the pot to Him
(he) Gets some drinks;
Drinks being over he falls back in the darkness
The Broken Pot is grinded in the dust
Under the wheel.
Just behind him
he who comes running with a new pot
Gets fresh savour,
His name is the same (with the first)
but it appears to be different.

The poet wants to develop different and divergent aspects of his life showing them in assortments and secluded phases. But he presents them in a beautiful and passionate way, so that they have a beautiful integration of form and feeling, a firm correspondence of word and meaning and music.

Once I was a boy
You do not identify them
Of whose image was created
In the shape of some birthdays
Thou who knew this truth
Are no more today.
The image of that boy is neither in this own nature

Nor with the memory of some one.
He has gone away with his small world.
The reservation of smiles and tears of his those
Days does not shine with the air
The fragments of his broken toys are not seen on the dust.
On that day he was at his small window setting his
Eyes on the outward world.
His world was within the fencing of that openness.
His simple and honest, unobstructed sight was
Barred by the wall of the garden
And by the rows of the coconut trees
His evening was thick with the stories of the fairy tales
There was no sharp distinction between trust and mistrust.
The mind would easily walk in between two.
In the light and shade of the dust the shadows are
Identical with the objects;
Both belong to one family.

Through the cluster of images we get autobiographical sketches along with his thoughtful emotion and emotive thoughts, intellect, lest the materials and ingredients that have created a masterpiece would lose their sharpness and greet oblivion.

Though these portraits we are acquainted with the apex of thinking and his firmness, and his intellectual emotion-emotion devoid sentimentality and of shallowness. His birthday is not a auspicious day only, it is seen through a great change, in the dawn of phalguna and in the dimness of coloured glow. Baul of juvenile youth tuned up in his one-string instrument, and called his traceless favourite in the maddened note of uncertain pain. Hearing this maddened song Lakshmi of Baikuntha was startled and sent some lady messengers on the milky way that is saturated with colours of the forest or Palasha (Red glowers), in the morning and at afternoon that is causing to mistake the work.

They left unknowingly of the poet on the first awakened morning of twenty fifth Baisakh the garland of newly bloomed Bel flowers. The dream of the dawn was overwhelmed with that savour. The world adolescence of that birthday was contiguous to the locality of world of a fairy-tale, which is seized with the known and the non-known. There the princes was sometimes asleep in the coverage of her own dishevelled hair and sometimes awakes stricken with amazement coming in contact with the golden wand.

Those days are gone.

The coloured walls of pink-coloured twenty fifth Basisakh had broken. The path, on which the shadow started shivering due to the swing of leaves of the forest of Vakul, murmuring became obvious in the breeze, the moon became impatient in the prayer of cooing of the cuckoo separated from his lover, the bees make humming sound with their wings, that is the avenue strewn with grass, flowing with the invisible beckoning of savour of flowers arrived at the public thoroughfare paved with stone. Adolescent of that day (meaning teenaged) who practiced in his one string-instrument, adjusted it with the new string one by one.

Here we see the cluster of image revealing different and divergent aspects of his life. The simple and honest descriptions of his life have become full of vitality and vigour. Sometimes the sketches are symbolic, sometimes they are given expression tinged with poet's sensuousness and swelling of emotion. The day, insipid happenings and occurrences have become lively and luminous. It is hardly necessary to point out, in the said poem so well known and of such rich imaginative quality, how the sheer ugliness of day-to-day happenings are counteracted; superseded by the flashes of beauty in the image.

He creates another image that manifests the ups and down of the poet's life.

"On that day twenty fifth Baisakh brought me through the rugged path to the shore of the sea of people sonorous caused by the waves. In season and out of the season I spread the net weaving with the rhythm on the middle of the ocean. Someone was attracted, some one fled through the net." The poet gives meticulous description of his life. He gives his divergent and variegated experiences placing before us an image of 'various Tagores'.

We get the same perceptibility same deep emotion in the poems of Bithika volume. Here we quote a note of critic. "the poet takes keen pleasure in all that happens around him and relates it to a larger significance, a significance which is composed of the same mixture of the harsh and the sweet, the hard and the soft. There are certain poems which tell stories, and they are composed in the lambent and detached mood proper to the story- telling vein. In other poems again there is an attempt to recapture in everlasting beauty and depth some sudden and fitting whim or desire. In such poems the felling naturally flow at a low ebb, the movement of the sensibility is undirected and uncontrolled and therefore full of sudden and unexpected turns and shifts; the attitude as a whole is somewhat indifferent, detached. Yet they have a beautiful integration of form and feelings, a firm correspondence of the word and meaning and music."—Dr. N.R. Ray, *An Artist in Life.*

In the image of Santal Woman Rabindranath shows keen perception and sensibility.

"The Santal woman hurries up and down the gravelled path under
The shimool tree, a coarse grey sari closely twines her slender
Limbs, dark and compact; its red border sweeping across the air
With the flaming red magic of the palash flower. Some absent-minded
Divine designer, while fashioning a black bird with the stuff of
The July cloud and the lighting flash, must have improvised unawareness
Hidden within, nimble steps uniting in them a woman's walk and a ....

Here we see and feel Rabindranath's keen sightedness and his deep penetration into the core of objects. His lines are of an emotional rather that a visual intensity. We see in the descriptive accuracy his keen interest and passionate vision and consciousness. In the image of next stanza of this poem Rabindranath realizes the mistake of the designer. He created this Santal woman, although he wanted to design a black bird within the stuff of the July cloud and the lighting flash. But the finished product is hundred times beautiful and unexpected than that he wanted to create.

"Some absent-minded divine designer, while fashioning a black bird with the stuff of the July cloud and the lightning flash, must have improvised unawares this woman's form; her impulsive wings hidden within, her nimble steps uniting in them a woman's walk and a bird's flight.

With a few lacquer bangles on her exquisitely modelled arms and a basketful of loose earth on her head, she flits across the gravel-read path under the shimool tree." The question may be raised how far can the poet make use of ordinary objects as spice in the cauldron of the image ? "The stock answer (now a days) would run something like this: no object is inherently un-poetical, whether a poet can create an image from any object depends first upon the imaginative strength on his own response to it, and secondly upon the extent to which this object has been assimilated by the general consciousness. Now this answer needs careful examination. Let us take it, piece by piece. They are many serious-minded and puzzled people, who while admitting that in theory no object need be un-poetical, feel that in modern practice only too many objects are."*

In the district Birbhum we face everyday host of Santal girls in different, in divergent vesture, style and manner. But the image created by the poet is of permanent value and universal significance. We have never seen such smiling and beautiful Santal girl which, we are sure, has universal entity, what we face and see is detached and part of that universal figure. The image has such permanent significance and bearing." The lingering winter has finished its errand. The casual breath of the south is beginning to tease the authority of the cloud month. On the himjhury branches the leaves are taking the golden tint of a rich decay. The ripe fruits are strewn over the amlaki grove where the rowdy boys crowd to pillage them. Swarms of dead leaves and dust are capering in a ghastly whirl following sudden caprices of the wind."

Through this descriptive sketch the poet gives us a passionate background and natural hinterland, whereon he places the Santal woman. He wants to give us a consummate portrait of Santal woman along with the vastness and openness of Natural phenomena by whom she is nurtured and lulled. So, if the poet creates her image leaving aside the Nature we get only a torn portion of her, not a full bloomed young woman.

Rabindranath even in the daily activities of her sees a universal tinge.

"The building of my mud house has commenced and labourers are busy raising the walls. The distant whistle announces and the passing of the train along the railway cutting, and the ding dong of the bell is heard from the neighbouring school.

I sit on my terrace watching the young woman tailing at her task hour after hour. My heart is touched with shame when I feel that the woman's service sacredly is ordained for her loved ones, its dignity sold by the market price, should have been robbed of by me with the help of a four pieces of copper."

In the poem of the 'Patraput' volume Rabindranath manifests his affection and love for the mother earth. In 'Manashi', 'Chitra' he has painted her as a young woman with keen sensibility and sensual imagination of a young girl having teenaged child. He has felt that his days are numbered and conveys his last homage to the mother Earth, with whom he spent his sportive childhood, adolescence, and youth. At the fag end of his life he utters his faithful and obeisant tribute to her. This is the sum and substance of the poem 'Mother Earth' in the volume of Patraput. But along with it we have a beautiful, affectionate and loving revelation, without which, we are sure, a lump of insipid and dull facts would be thrusted to us. The image is alias of the said revelation, which is as follows:-

"I bow to thee O Mother Earth,
Accept this my last homage
At the alter often day that meanders and ends
Mother mine, your prowess knows no bounds,
You consort with the brave,
You are smooth, you are rough,
In you have mixed the traits of a He and a She,
You rock human life in violent struggles.
By your right hand you fill the cup

By your left hand you smash it.
Your sarcastic laughter I hear
Over the field of your chain reaction
You make a hero's life difficult and fulfilment,
A life of greatness that is his birth right.
You make more precious the values that live,
You have no mercy for those who need them.
Your trees and plants constantly register
Your every minute struggle.
They bear the cross
And their victory is assumed in flowers fruits and corns.
Your merciless battlefield
Spread over land and water
In hills, dales and fields
Life's victorious banner marches;
Through each step of Death
Civilization fulfils itself
On the basic substructure of your cruelty
You collect your toll of victory."

The poet creates an image that focuses variegated, varie-colours and variformed aspects of this earth and its creative impact on the mind of the poet. The poet stretches far his vision in the very dawn of this earth, in the very dawn of her history and gives us full-formed and comprehensive portrait of the life-story of the earth and the history of her children i.e. human beings.

The image of this train of events and facts are dominated by his keen interest perceptibility and far-fetched vision and acumen.

2

"At the dawn of your history,
In those early days
The demon rules and swayed,
He was cruel, he was inhuman
He was stupid,
His hands bore no mark of skill
With his club and his spike

In fury and foam, he ruled and roamed
And did strike
He was the monarch of all the surveyed,
In that world of Nature Primordial
He was blindly jealous of life's chatter.

5

The next era began into a new advent
The Olympian God did descend.
He chanted incantation
The demon was controlled
Matter's way wardness stopped
The Mother's groom belt spread
The dewy–dawn heralded a new day in
The Eastern horizon
And the setting of the sun a peace in the West.

Here we see and feel the poet's auditory imagination; by virtue of which critic states that 'Shakespeare excels all other English poets. What Logan Pearsale called 'the enchanted radiance' of his language is achieved by an inventiveness and daring without parallel. He plays in the great ocean of words as buoyancy as Cleopatra's dolphins.

This 'auditory imagination' Mr. T.S. Eliot has tried to define in prose and he has further described it in verse. In the use of poetry (1933) where he uses the phrase, he says it is

"the feeling for syllable and rhythm penetrating far below the conscious levels of thoughts and feeling, invigorating every word; sinking to the most primitive and forgotten, returning to the origin and bringing sometimes back, seeking the beginning and the end. It works through meanings, certainly, or not without meanings in the ordinary sense, and fuses the old and obliterated and the trite, the current and the new and surprising, the most ancient and the most civilized nationality."[62]

The readers and the connoisseurs feel with the poet his penetration, feeling and sensibility, when they read the poem 'Mother Earth' between the lines, the words and their meanings, all these factors are instruments are crystalised and manifested in one and single Prakash i.e. the luminous and juvenile expression incarnate- image.

Rabindranath gives a detailed and meticulous history of mankind and its society.

The demon was put the chains
But this age-old boar still sticks to your history
Suddenly he brings disorder in order
He slips out of his black cavern in a tortuous way
You carry this incipient intemperance
This imbalance in your pulsation:
You have the divine's chant
In your fields, forests and firmaments
Night and morn
In voice subdued and voice sublime;
Yet that mad servant whom you have half tamed
Raises his hood again
And goaded by him you strike your hapless people
Your own creation
I bow to thee, O Mother Earth
I bring the song of my storm-tossed life.
At your feet,
At the altar that is built of sound and evil
Before your mighty majesty and beauty terrifying
For the last time I touch
Search in body and mind
For a speck of life that hidden lies
And realize the deathless round of Death
Beneath the surface
The dust which covers the track of centuries
And of myriads of men.
There I bring a few handfuls of my humble own
The culminating point of all my joys and sorrows
And in the silent hour and
Still silent dust, I entomb
My name, my shape and lineage
My identity, ego and urge.
All that I prize and posses."

The poet finds his identity in the chequered and myriads human beings and the poet brings a few handfuls of his humble own, the culminating point of all his joys and sorrow and in that silent hours and still silent dust, he wants to leave behind him the last consequence of his all weals and woes.

Mother Earth, you are uncomessed in
An unmoving case
Yet you song high in the dream land of cloud
You set enthroned in the contemplation wrapped
In the serene stillness of the mountains old
You splash in hearing waves over the blue and shine
You are merciless when you have nothing and withhold
One one side your green fields and golden corn
Dance and ripple over the dewy morn
And over embers of the dying day
The sun does sing a song and say
In untold words, in accounts dear
"I am happy here.
The scene changes, you bring in Death, drought.
Desolation and famine.
A devil's dance in a mirage of sand
Strewn with skeleton all over the land. I have seen in
summer your thundery Nor'wester came
Like a storm tossed black eagle.
The whole sky rocked, shock like the mane of an
Angry lion.
Swept sunder by infuriated wind
The big trees fell helpless on the ground
The Poor man's cottage lost its mooring
Defeated and disgraced in a black turmoil.
An imprisoned robber out of his shackles;
Again in spring I have seen your south wind
Bring ambrosian night of love and laughter

As if its cup of happiness was full to the brim Sparkling like heavenly red wine in moonlit splendour. The mind of the poet was shaken and perturbed by the Turmoil and bustle of the political and national uprising.

In the thirties of the twentieth century we have seen and felt the poetic experience in the Manashi and Chitra a volume where the poet has created image that is radiant with poetic feelings and exuberance of poetic passion and emotion. Sometimes they have lost their earthly footing and douched only on the fusion of feelings and passions. But in this poem Rabindranath creates an image that is tinged with multiformed and multicoloured aspects. The poet creates this image of the Mother Earth taking the clear and proper perspective of the earth, its history and along with it the chequered history of the human beings.

The poet created an image that reveals two different and divergent aspects of nature on the same portrait.

"You are mild, you are violent,
You are the old, you are the new,
When creation was a thirst in Eternity's eon
Beyond computation in that early dawn
Around your axis and in your path
Strewn are the broken tales of History
groping in the dark
Mother, you have sustained us
In the small coteries of dissected time
With in that limit the play ends,
All reputations vanish. I have no illusions today when
I stand before you
I seek no favour
I ask for no deathless vindication For all the garlands
I have woven so many years;
In your eternal peregrination In the dawns and nights
that have come and gone
If I have been abie to give a true rendering
Of even one significant moment
If by chance I have fructified
Any portion of that life's process,
By my sorrow and tribulation,
Then put your seal of approbation
With one mud mark in my forehead
Till it fades in the supreme darkness
Of that subliminal night when every symbol
In the great cauldron of the unknown dissolved
Oh: Indifferent Earth
Till I am completely forgotten
Let my lyre be low silent inspired
At your relentless feet

My homage to thee is this.[65]

Rendered by Sudhansumohan Banerjee in
Rabindrabharati Journal No. IV 1997.

Here, if we try to look into the reaction of the mind of Rabindranath or the commotion that comes due to the waves of contemporary European movements, we see these elements are dominating factors in the images. Another aspect will have to be remembered that in 1930 Rabindranath returned from his latest world tour that included soviet Russia. He expressed his new and novel experiences in his famous book Rashiar Chithi (Lettered from Russia). "Waves of contemporary European movements in thought and literature were constantly dashing against the minds of Bengali intellectuals, forcing them into new ways of thinking and doing. Materialist thoughts, socialist and communist ideologies, social realism in art and literature, scientific humanism, psychoanalytical methods, industrial and mass psychology, Eliotian experiments in verse making images and symbols of new civilization, new techniques of expression, Joycian experiments in coming words and phrases and many other things went into this process of thought and creative expression."

The prose-poems in *Punascha, Sesh Saptak, Ratraput* and *Shyamali* bear the impress of the these experiences and impact of their movements on the mind of the poet. Still so, Rabindranath was idealistic and romantic. The fundamental change in ideology has taken shape in his own way where subjective elements are predominant. Shyamali volume bears the impression of these new and novel attitude. And images also are colourd with these panorama. The poet creates an images of subjective element that dominates the said volume.

My consciousness has coloured the emerald green
The ruby red
I opened my eyes to the heavens.
Light flamed up
In east and west
I looked at the rose and said-'Beautiful'
You will say, this is philosophy
Not a poet's words.

I will say-this is true
That is why it is poetry
This is my pride
Pride on behalf of mankind.

The creation of the creator Is on the canvas of man's proud consciousness. The philosopher repeats with each single breath

No, no, no

No you, no- I On the other side the Infinite realizes Himself

Within the limits of the human world,
Calling man 'Myself'
In the depths of that 'I' darkness met light,

Beauty appeared and sweetness. Negation suddenly became assertion as by magic

In line and colour, in joy and sorrow
Do not at this philosophy.
My heart fills with joy
When my hands lift brush and colour bowl
In the creation hall of that universal 'I'.

Rabindranath creates an image, perfect and consummate image that is tinged with subjective elements and that is as much marked by congruity as by audacity and freshness. And as the reader comprehends the implications of these images, the panorama of poetic experiences becomes luminous before him along with the objects and vies that have been grasped at by the poet.

The poetic consciousness along with the subjective valuation dominates the image in the poem ('I' Ami.) Here the poet wants to propound the superiority of consciousness to objective idea implying objective experience is preceded by consciousness. It is contradiction to the materialistic view of life. First, matter comes then consciousness of the matter follows. Still so, the intensive and audacious image attracts the mind of the readers and connoisseurs to its closet coloured and marked by poetic consciousness where subjective cravings and choices are revealed ad libitum. The next image created by the poet is this:

The Scientist says-

The old moon, his smile cruel and crafty

Comes crowing like a messenger of death
Towards the ribs of the earth
One day it will exercise its final pull on our seas and
mountains.
In the land of the mortals, in the new ledger of the god
of destruction.
One cipher will fill a whole page,
Swallowing up the daily accounts of income and expense.
His history will be besmeared with
The black ink of eternal night.

The image created by Rabindranath reminds us of the fact that: a successful poetic image shines in variety and synthesizing power, as also in the capacity to ennoble and universalize the experience. When poetry achieves perfection, it naturally becomes revelation of the ideal world..... In poetry the artist tries to give expression to his unique experience through the medium of language, but as he creates the poetic image the experience is universalised making possible the brilliant confrontation between the generalized and the universalized image, symbolising the elevated experience of the poet."—*Alankara and Aesthetic Realisation*, Dr. R. R. Mukherjee.

In this phase the poem "Africa" paves a new path, new outlook and novel idea of life. 'Patraput as a whole belong to a far higher order of poetry. There is no lyricism, one of the sudden and glancing illuminations that we associate with it, but a different quality of massive and monumental grandeur. Like Balaka, its verse form is structural, architectonic. The poems are inspired not so much by emotion as by a vision in which passion and intellect are integrated, a vision of the organic and obscure laws, difficult to realise, that eternally inform life and the world, that are the secret principles of the separate impressions and experience of life in all their variety. Whatever be the fact, the poem 'Africa' is a masterpiece or magnum opus, not only in depth of idea or ideology and thought but in expression manifestation and magnum operandi also. This poem is rich with the mature experiences of a life-time, it is the harvest of the mature time of his life. The image of the poem is dominated by the robust optimism and keen perceptibility of the struggle of humanity.

The poet gives a new and novel outlook and experience. The poet's insight has penetrated into the unfathomable darkness of Death where 'the world of prying lights was shut out' and that is congenial treading ground of the Destroyer. Here we feel and perceive the secret of originality. He has created here not only visual image, but penetrating and deeply perceptive images. If it would not be, the image would be shoddy and shallow. "Any one can vamp up a novel image; but, unless his eye is penetrating and unless his heart is in it, the image will be as shoddy" as one of those distressing 'novelties' used in the shop. Another image is this:

'Big boulders of shadows barricaded the passages of light
And created confusion-
Till they were swept away,
And the spirit of new life unbarred herself
In the luminous horizon of piece
This body of mine –
The carrier of the burden of a past-
Seemed to me like an exhausted cloud
Slipping of from the listless arm of the morning.
I felt freed from its clasp
In the heart of an incorporeal light at the furthest shore
Of evanescent things.

The poet creates an image of 'the spirit of new life that is unbarred in a luminous horizon of peace'. Here question may arise what the poet is trying to do in a poem, and them whether his image are well adapted to this purpose or not. If they are so adapted, they are I fact functional however 'decorative' in the sense of unsuggestive, shallow, ever superficial, they may appear. Once again, it would be a matter of congruity. The central theme of the poem in Senjuti (The evening Lamp, 1958) volume is life's approaching end. The title is appropriate for most of the Poems have and the mellow radiance of an evening lamp. 'Today is my Birthday' is a fine achievement like in its form and content. A new birthday has arrived, but in the celebration the poet is only a transient guest, waiting for death's signal to start on a new journey. The world has little use for him now and before casting him away altogether, it is depriving him one by one of all his physical senses.

But can this neglect really mean that the poet's life is useless now? The poet is of the human race, and to man his imperishable story the world will have to pay homage for ever. So he is reassured, strengthened in his love for the world which neglects him to day. He has always loved the world and all its rights and even in the humblest of things he has seen the radiance of immortal beauty. So mysterious was the message that the green grass spoke to his soul: only in death's land will it meaning be revealed. To the last, therefore, he will sing hymns to the earth, leaving behind him the flower that has yet to bloom, the love that has yet to be fulfilled."—*An Artist in Life.*

The image of Birthday is tinged with the soft and mellow radiance of an evening lamp.

My birthday :
With Death's passport in hand it has emerged from its
Dive into the chasm of nothingness
To breath a while on the outskirts of existence.
From the worn-out chain have dropped bends of the past years
And with this newest birthday begins the counting
Of the days of a new-born life.
The welcome offered today to me, a passer-by,
Who tries to can the signal of the moving of
An unknown star
Becoming him towards an uncharted voyage,
Is shared equally by his birthday
And the time of his death,
Who mingle their lights like those of the morning star
And of the waning moon.
And I shall sing the same chant to both,
To death and to life
Grant no, Mother Earth,
That my life's mirage born of burning thirst
May recede in the farthest horizon
And my unclean beggar's bowl empty into the dust
Its accumulated defilements

And I start my closing to the unrevealed shore
Let me never look back with longing

Those passages play their Part in the musical economy of the Poem; they represent a change of voice, change of outlook, new consciousness, a new approach to a theme, a sensuous attribution of human soft feeling and passion to the Mother earth. But they also contribute very largely to that final impression of integrity and sincerity, which is the reward of the poet's effort towards communication. All this auditory and poetic communication is crystallized in the poetic image. Rabindranath creates cluster of images that is tinged and smeared with passionate feeling and passions expressed and poured by the subjective first person of the poet towards the mother earth. He at the fag end of his life visualizes luminous and radiant entity in the midst of all those worn-out, dilapidated objects and states and creates an image pointing to the same outlook and doctrine.

Now when in this sleep-laden dusk of the day's and
The meaning is lost of the keen–bladed hunger
With which you had goaded me to drag life's chariot
You begin to withdraw your gifts from me one by one.
Slight has grown your need of me
And slight have you made me use
And set on my forehead the stamp of the discarded
I feel it all and yet I know,
All this contumely of yours
Will not reduce my worth to mouth.
Cripple me, if you will,
Shut out all light from my eyes,
Shroud me in the shadow of infirmity
Yet ancient god will remain enthroned.

Rabindranath presents an image of an entity who has capability to guide the poet in his walks of life. She can cripple him, if she desires shroud him in the shadow of infirmity. All these expressions are symbolic. Through these epigrams he means to say that this earth is not a clamp of clay, or conglomeration of inanimate and passionless objects and entities. Rather she is a mother having all feminine soft feelings and passions. She does not stand for a thing or for an idea; she is focus of relationships. The image of this Poem is dominated by the poetic keen perception and sensibility that reveals in the midst of the wreck, havoc created by the earth herself "the luminous spot of inward joy that will burn bright as ever."

The next sensuous poetic image is this :

"When I take my leave of you, Of Earth,
Take back from me, carefully reckoning
All that you had vouchsafed to me the outfit and
Provision for a life's sojourn
Yet never think that I hold your gifts but slight.
Ever grateful I am to do this clay-cast mould
Through which I have had my introduction to the formless.
Whenever I have approached your door with the mind free from
All coveting.
I have been made welcome to your heart.
I know your gifts are not for the greedy
That you withhold the nectar hidden in your earthen pot,
From the ravenous lips of those that hunger obscenely.

Here Rabindranath creates an image that is marked with magnanimity and bounteousness of Mother-Earth. Her gifts are not meant for the greedy, that 'she' withholds the nectar hidden in her earthen pot from the ravenous lips of these that hunger obscenely".

He means to attribute human and its affectionate qualities to Earth. He endows her clump of clay with motherly love, affection and eagerness, and anxiety. We see her another form of young woman with tenderly affection, anxiety portrayed in the Manashi and Chitra Volume. Now we are confronted with having the ravenous lips. So we see the image and feel the feelings and passion that the poet cherished in those days.

"You are waiting, O Earth, with your immortal gifts
To welcome the wayfarer who trends the
Arduous path of detachment.
The glutton who lust for flesh,
The traffickers in festering canyon
Have banded today in their orgies

Of violence, day and night.
Yet mockery tempts my smile, as of old
At the tyranny of the beggarly rich
At the hideous make-up of the showy
At the blasphemy that lampoons
The divine in man.
Enough of this. The bill tolls the last hour at your perch
And my heart responds to the cracking
Of the opening gates of farewell.
In this deepening gloom of the twilight
I will gather what flickering flames remain
To light my consciousness,
To offer my last worship to you. Of Earth,
Under the gaze of the Seven Rishis
And the incense of my last silent
Song will float round you.
Behind me will remain in the Nagkeshar plant
That has yet to flower,
The anguished heart of this shore
Yearning in vein for a ferry across,
And love's self-reproach at its tired memory
Vanishing behind the screen of daily task"

Here we see the necessity and use of image and express the same opinion with the following. "The word 'image' precisely because it is used to cover both metaphor and simile, can be used to point towards their fundamental identity; and if we resolutely exclude from our minds the suggestion that the image is solely or even predominantly visual, and allow the word to share in the heightened and comprehensive significance with which its derivative 'imagination' has perforce been endowed- if we conceive the image not as primary and independent, but as the most singular and potent instrument of the faculty of imagination—it is a move valuable word than those which it subserves: metaphor and simile.

The image may be visual, may be auditory, may refer back to any primary physical experience- as those hoary metaphors which described the process of thought itself as a grasping or apprehension—or it may be wholly psychological- the reference of one emotional or intellectual experience to another, as

Then felt I like some watcher of Skies
When a new planet swims into his ken.

Rabindranath through the cluster of images express his heartfelt love, affection and homage to Mother-Earth. The image in Nabajatak Volume (The newly born child) are marked with poetic reticence, restrained emotion and crystalised passion and sensibility. In the preface to the volume of Nabajatak, he admits it. "My poetry has changed its season again and again, often without my being aware of it. This change of season naturally brought about a change in my poetic technique and content again mostly unconsciously. It is the sensitive reader rather than myself who notices the change. Perhaps these (the poems in Nabajatak) are not spring flowers but the harvest of middle age, which do not care whether they are pleasant or charming. Rather, they are full of life time's mature experience, and if they were not inspiration of adult life would have been in vain."

Dr. N.R. Ray also turns up his lyre with the some melody.

"The new self or season that the poet calls Nabajatak is rooted in the heightened social consciousness, in an awareness of the dynamic life of the masses of humanity, as we have pointed out already. Yet this is not social realism either as we know it today, and the poet himself never claimed that he was a realist in the ordinary sense." I know the world of facts and objects and all its paths and bye-paths, and ever have I fulfilled all its obligations, not by words but by responding to its call, factually and objectively. Where ever there is poverty, where ever there is sections I have put off my silk robes and dressed myself in armour...." "Indeed, the poet's vision of reality is the vision of 'beauty and power going hand in hand'. The powerful and ringing poems in Navajatak, in which the poet echoes the shame and indignation of an outraged humanity, are a clear proof of this. He sees and describes the whole unmitigated shame of contemporary culture and civilization, the whole horror of the dehumanization of man in the greedy, money-grabbing civilization of today. There is nothing personal or private in the poet's passion, nothing which could not be answered back with the same intensity by the whole humanity. But where emotion does not have this mass affiliation, where it is intimate, personal and private—there is much emotion—the poet never hesitates to be romantic. We see this dualism, perhaps justifiable dualism in Navajatak".—*An Artist in Life,* Dr. N.R. Ray

This is the background and hinterground of the poetic image of Navajatak. On the one hand he creates the image of the underground gloom, lean hunger and bloated voracity, and that of aspiration after some far-off morning that is asleep in the mind.

"In the upper sky, lamped by science
The night forgets itself,
While in the underground gloom
Lean hunger and bloated voracity
Crash against each other
Till the earth begins to tremble
And the pillars of triumph
And perilously cracked
Swaying on the brink of gaping gulf.
Do not howl in fear
Or angrily judge God
Let the swelling evil brush itself in pain
And vomit out its accumulated faith.
When the victims of a carnivorous rage
And dragged by the competition of ravenous fangs
Let the hideousness of the blood-soaked blasphemy
Arouse divine anger heralding a heroic peace
Out of an awful retribution.
They throng in a church
In a primitive frenzy of faith
Made keen by fear
Which hopes to flatter their God
Into a complacent mood
Into a feebleness of leniency.
They feel half sure that peace will be brought down
Into this dominated earth
Try the mere volume of their wailing
Uttered in sacred text."

Here we feel the keen sensibility of the poet who reacts

at the sight of the voidness and emptiness of the contemporary civilization that can only exist by shaming and degrading the human spirit. In *Prantik* he creates the image that is marked with the poetic denunciation of this vileness and shame. In 'Navajatak' the poetic denunciation is fierce and speaks of no compromise. The image of this phase are dominated by poetic defiance and deep affection for the inhumanity to whom he calls to rise and to overthrow the monster that is staking the earth today, and are widely and luminously marked by his militant faith in new story and life that will be born after this nightmare of and destruction is over. So the striking image is this:

They have confidence in their indulgent God
Who may send them timely wisdom
To divert all sacrifices needed for the worship
Towards the less strong,
Leaving their own soiled hoarding undivided.
But let us hope for the sake of the dignity of moral
Justice in the world,
That god will never suffer to be cheated of his due,
By the miserly manipulation of a diplomatic piety
Carefully avoiding all cost to itself,
That a terrible penance may have
To be passed through its ultimate end,
Leaving no remnant of poison
In a very treacherously healing scar.

He is aware of the internal conflict of this civilization, he is aware that it has divided the world into two camps—that of the hungry and that often satiated, —that of the have-nots and that of the haves—and that the fight between them as bloody as it is decisive and uncompromising. He knew that best for possession alone is the governing principle of the contemporary society, that this civilization, in spite of its gorgeous façade, is really only a bottomless pit where robbers have gathered, looted and stolen the treasures.

He manifested the vileness and shaming portrait and emptiness of contemporary civilization through the images of "The hideousness of the blood-soaked blasphemy, of lean hunger and bloated voracity and through image i.e.

Let the swelling evil burst itself in pain
And vomit out its accumulated filth."

Rabindranath means to depict vividly and radiantly the black side of the civilization that has been ransacked by the overvaulting ambition of the capitalist class to suck the blood of the needy and hungry mass. So, we see in the images of this phase swelled-up emotion and passion is absent, reticence is dominant. The poet draws our sympathy and arrests notice to accumulated mass of wealth that is marked with greedy and voracious pride and haughtiness; and on the other hand is smeared with flesh, blood that has been sucked from the millions and millions of people who keep the chariot of civilization moving, who is forced to contribute to their accumulation of wealth, but they starve to death. The image of this phase is more and more crystallized, dense, pregnant; every superfluous image, every superfluous suggestion of the imagination or passion or intellect are kept away, the resultant poetry is the image itself, that is of poetic defiance of struggle, and glory and of aspiration after new life, new civilization. The same Poems of Navajatak remind us of the genre, the mode with which we have been familiar in Tagore's earlier work. Those are inspired by the vision of a secret land beyond time and human date, by the intuition of advancing death, by the dream of a sightless and formless beauty. These dreams and visions and intuitions have a background of personal life and are soaked with beloved memories of the past. This gives to these poems an intensity which is not so prominent in the earlier poems.

Now, we come to the world of images that refer to the clear transparent and immense vision which is communicated in a medium that is equally sublime and transparent in its reticent austerity. The world of his poetry in the last four volumes is beyond language and thought, but is, as it were, an extended visual image, beautiful in its stillness.

Rogusayyay (From the Sick-bed) came out towards the end of 1940 and *Arogya* (convalescence) two month later in the beginning of 1941.

A deep and stately harmony prevails in both, especially in *Rogasayyay*. Realizing death more deeply and intimately than ever before, the poet can now see into the life of things with an assured clarity, a firm faith. A powerful and invincible soul shining with a white and bright light, imparts all its sinewy strength, all its power of control to these poems which read and sound more like revealed statements uttered in deep and dignified tunes.

And this majestic distinction is present in *Janmadine* (Birthday, 1941) and in *Sesh Lekha* (The Last Writings, 1941) too there is this stillness of words and passion.

The image of the volume 'Rogsayyay' is touched with pangs, sorrows, and tears, but that do not emanate from the dumping ground of emotion and loose sentiments. Rather their importance is valued by the burning contact with the spaceless, timeless, eternal light. 'The image reveals the poetic experience that has been accumulated at the fag and of his life and that is not the conglomeration, and multitude of detached, secluded facts, and figures.

"Once you had lent to my eyes a generous portion from your limitless store of light, now at the day's end you have come to reclaim it, my master, and I know for certain that I must make good my debt."

"But why cast shadow before my evening lamp? I am but a guest for a few days in this world that has come of your light, but if out of its abundance a few fragments of that light are left behind, let them remain in careless neglect at the last trace of your chariot."

The poet feels and realizes that his days are numbered and the dreadful illness comes to him to be felt so. The image of this volume is touched with sorrow and pangs due to the parting with the earth. He feels the infinite depth of the life and its implication. He wants to repay the debt that he took in the very dawn of his life; and now prior to his departure from this world he wants pay back the debt taken from the limitless ocean of light: that the image of this poem is dominated by the light.

"Let me glean from that dust, from scattered lights and shadows, some gleam of coloured illusion with which to build my own little world as a slight remnant of your debt not worth gathering for good."

"Wonderful are the evocation of these poems, wonderful

the golden moments that are thus recalled. There is no agitation, no troubling of the soul, but there is peace, the peace that passeth all understanding. And with this sense of peace there is love and humanity. The poet cannot forget for a moment how beautiful the world is, how endless its joys."

In this Poem the poet expresses his different and divergent mood and feeling.

"On my way to recovery
When I received Nature's earliest friendly greetings
She held before my eyes her precious gift
Of endless first surprise.
And those trees and the blue sky
Bathed in morning light
Through ancient and ever-known
Revealed to me in them creation's
Everlasting first moment
And I felt that this one birth of mine
Is woven in the wave of many births
Of many changes forms
And like the sunlight composed of varied rays
Every appearance in its unity is blended with
Countless invisible other ones.

The poet has heard the death-knell and expressed his feelings and emotion. Now he comes round and feels exultation. The world which appeared before him as an clump of clay marked with disappointment, now at the time of his recovery presents itself as endless first surprise.

The reader and Connoisseurs may be struck by the creation of the image that is marked with the evocation of feelings in the minds of them. We, readers feel identified with the mood, feeling and sensibility of the poet. Common man and woman do not feel the existence of such convenience, such a precious gift of endless first surprise and may not be amazed at the sight of the new and clothings of Nature though ancient and ever-known revealed to is in them creation's everlasting first moment.

They feel with the poet that "this one birth of mine is woven in the web of many births of many changing forms and like the sunlight composed of varied rays every appearance in its unity is blended with countless invisible other ones."

Although this ideas and realization is tinged with hyperbolic expression, it points to the exultation ad libitum. Our birth and the birth of the first Amibae is inter-related and interconnected. There is no wide-marked detachment and seclusion. Rabindranath creates an image in which varied experience feelings and emotive contents are painted vividly and luminously.

In the 'Arogya' volume Rabindranath creates the cluster of images that manifest the poetic feeling, experience of illness, and post-illness-easiness and exultation. Ordinary men and women feel this easiness, and express it in a very sort-cut way, someone feel it only, but does not know to express. But Rabindranath felt it deeply and plunged in its core to the lees. He expresses in his own way, in his peculiar poetic genre.

"Blessing have I won in this life of the beautiful
In the vessel of man's affection I taste
His own divine nectar.
Sorrow, hard to bear
Has shown me the unhurt,
Unconquered soul.
On the day when I felt death's
Impending shadow,
fear's defeat has not been mine.
The great one often Earth
Have not deprived me of their touch,
Their undying words have I stored in my heart,
Grace I had from the god of life;
This memory let me leave in grateful words."

Rabindranath creates an image that has two bright items-one is the portrait of sorrow and of death's impending shadow; and another is that of man's affection and the blessings in the life of the beautiful: The portrait of sorrow and earth's impending shadow has not been painted in such a glowing and bright letters and characters. This is one side of the image. There is another important and side of it. That is the poetic emotion, imaginative passion, his sensibility and his portrait of sorrow, man's affection would be the backside of fan icon, if the striking and consummate image should not bear the responsibility to depict and explore it vividly and meticulously.

The next poem "They go on working" is characterized with materialist outlook. Rabindranath wants to paint a wide and far-flung panorama of their activities. Empire comes and go, there arrogance was heard feeble and no more. But they go on working. The chariot of civilization is being drawn by them, they become downtrodden, trampled by haughty foot; but to their utter surprise they are immortal.

He creates the image that is lively with the throbbing of their lives, activities and their country-wide nets of work,

"Floating on Time's leisurely stream
My mind moves, gaming at the empty space beyond.
Among the track of that great emptiness
Shadow-pictures form before my eyes.
Down the ages have gone processions of
People through the long Past
With conquest's Pathans have come,
And the Mughals:
Victory's Chariot-wheels
Raising patterns of dust;
Triumphant banners have flown;
At the empty path I look,
No trace of them remains today.
The blue space, at morning and eve,
Age to age
Its coloured by the light of sunrise
And sunset."

The poet presents a cornet which manifests a panoramic view of toiling masses. Here we feel with the poet the immortality of the working class and also see that history is not the heroic tale of the king, queen, princes and the empire. Empire, hungry Pathans have come, and the Mughals:

Victory's Chariot-wheels
Raising patterns of dust;
Triumphant banners have flown

The poet shows us that "at the empty path I look, no trace of them remains today", Rather "The blue space, at morning and eve, age to age is coloured by the light of Sunrise and Sunset.'

Rabindranath creates the image that shows the train of historical events and happenings. The empire of Mughal's and Pathans king being gone, the British imperialism haunts our country. The image is this:

"In that emptiness, again
Have come in bands, along iron-found rounds
In fire-breaking chariots
The powerful English
Scattering their energy.
Through their path too will flow time's current
Sweeping away the countrywide nets of empire."

Their troops, bearing merchandise will leave not a sign behind them on the empty path of the stony realm. What historians failed to sum up in his voluminous works is done by Rabindranath by creating the afore-said image. The merchant had become the ruler over-night. But being in the away of British imperialism what his vision is?

"When on this Earth I cast my eyes,
Great multitudes I see there
Moving with tumult,
Along divine path in many a group,
From age to age,
Urged by mankind's daily need in life and in death."

Rabindranath has felt the pulse of the time and its implication and in his peculiar modus operandi he visualises that in the long run the toiling masses the working class will remain in the midst of the ashes over rubbishes of the past, bygone empires and emperors.

"They, ever
Pull the oars, keep holding the helm;
They, in the fields,
Sowseeds, cut the corn.
They go on working.
The kingly sceptre breaks, the wardrums no longer
resound;

Columns of victory gape, stupidly oblivious
Of their own meaning;
Blood-stained weapons, and blood-slot
Eyes and faces
Hide their annals in children's story-books,
They go on working;
In Ango, in Bango, in Kalinga's seas
And river-ghats,
In Punjab, Bombay, and Gujrat,
The myriad horn of voices thunderous
Woven together, night and day
Makes resonant the great world's livelihood.
Sorrows and joys unceasing
Blend in chant raising the mighty hymn of life.
On the ruins of hundreds of empires
They go on working.

Rabindranath visualizes that in the country, in the city all over the land the toiling masses are engaged in their world whatever, be the sway over the land. They are ever going on working. 'The kingly sceptre breaks, the war-drums no longer resound; columns of victory gape, and blood-shot eyes and faces hide their annals in children's story-books."

Here we get a long history of ups and downs of empires and their rulers. Through these images one thing is vividly clear to us that they go on working in every centuries, when Mughals and Pathans ruled, when British was the lord, in every system of the society they were and they will be. Is it the purport of the poem? Then one thing falls short. They toiled in the past, they worked in the bygone days and they will work in future days. What is their lot? They go on working. Is there any hint or guess? That the working class is enjoying their harvest, they are happy, they are not stricken, not hard-hit by want, poverty and starving. In their sweet home there is no beggary, no unemployment, illitcracy, no obscene culture. Rabindranath looks into that fathom up to which their panoramic view is visualized. He has seen them from a remote distance, but does not enter into their hamlet that is stricken with black shadow of poverty. Their production are taken away by the parasite of the society. They are land holders. In their worn-out and torn-houses chill penury remains. He does not point to the rule of the working class.

Standing at the confluence of life and death the poems he wrote he collects under the general title, Janmadine (on birthday). These poems, though they emphasizes life are really full of a stately realization of death; in each line we hear death's footsteps. The poet, indeed, is waiting for death to appear. He has lived eighty years and he will be have to take his departure in a while and then nothing will be left of him, for he will be where life and death are one. May the distorting, disfiguring touch of death keep away from him at life's last moment, may his life set like the sun, in glory and in humanity, the east and the west shining with the same colour and looking at each other. But how can the poet, who has never deceived life and whom life has never deceived, face the great Heath empty-handed without any offering? How can the poet's instrument, once vibrant will all the chords in the earth, remain mute at such a moment? True, he will have to put off those ever now robes and those jewels in which life dressed him once, but it will be festival, never the less, light will shine, and the poet will preside, wearing a mantle of white. Across the boarder-land they are blowing conches to welcome him, and echoes are floating in the sir.

Far-reaching and penetrating are the mysterious evocations and suggestions in the poems in Janmadine. On one birthday the poet has a vision which stretches far, and losses itself infinite remoteness, where he wanders about by himself, a traveller who does not know his destiny. On another he feels he had never know himself before as he really was, for his real self was hidden behind a curtain, and he was surrounded by ignorance day and night.

The new man shall be non-attached, indifferent to material object, ever creative. It is the poet's belief that it is these non-attached, disciplined and selfless beings who are the real superman of the future, who will usher in the new creation. In this last days the poet responds his faith in them on the one hand and in nature on the other. He pays them homage again and again in his last days, for they light up life's doubtful path with the radiance of their being; to them he bows his head in reverence before he starts his journey to the land where the being and the non-being have merged into one.

The anguish of unfulfilled life is expressed in a very fine poem in Janmadine (on the birthday). It is certainly precious as poetry, but it is also valuable as an indication of a significant mood of the poet. He had known only a fragment of this vast world, and many lands and peoples, many human achievements, have remained unknown to him. He is the poet of the whole world; his instrument should, therefore, play every note that vibrates in the world. But actually there is much that was never echoed in his music. Although his poetry has covered many aspects of life, it has not touched many in obscure corner. He waits, therefore, to hear the other poets sing, who will complete the incomplete song that he has sung; he wants to hear the poet who shares the peasant's life, whose words and practice reflect one another, the poet's of the obscure and the speechless, of those whose joys and sorrows alike have no voice, whose heads are bowed down by ignorance and humiliation, who live so near us and yet so far away because we know little of their song : He creates an image that is marked with his simple and honest admittances;

"I accept my censure the rift in me
My verse, I know,
Has travelled diverse ways, but not everywhere,
And I strain to hear, the poet's voice
Who shares the peasant's life, and
Has earned true kinship,
Who touches the earth."

He creates images in context to this:

" In the vessel of my birthdays
Sacred waters from many pilgrimages
Have I gathered, this remembers,.
Once I want to the land of China,
Those whom I had not met
Put the mark of friendship on my forehead
Calling me their own.

The grab of a stranger slipped, from me unknowing,
The inner man appeared who is eternal
Revealing a joyous relationship unforeseen.
A Chinese name I took, dressed in Chinese clothes
This I know in my mind
Wherever I find my friend there
I am born anew,
Life's under he brings
In the foreign fields blossom flowers unknown,
Foreign is their name, a foreign soil
In their motherland,
Yet in soul's joyful realm their kinship
Finds unbarred welcome":

Common men and women feel in their birthdays that they crossed one year and enjoy some exultation and become satisfied by imparting some sweeps to his kith and kin that much he or she does his or her birthday. It is no universal feeling or sensibility. But when Rabindranath remembers his birthday and he feels that the grab of a stranger slipped from me unknowing. The inner man appeared who is eternal revealing a joyous relationship unforeseen. So, we feel there is a gulf of difference between the feeling and experience of the poet and that of common men and women. But when they read this poetry, feel his experience and passion; rather feel as the poet causes them to feel they are identified with his passion and sensibility. How is it so? It happens so due to the poetic peculiar passion, sensibility and feelings on the one hand, and his mode of expression, his way of manifestation, his genre of exposition on the other hand. The feelings, the passion of the poet become new thing, novel object because the poet does not convey the feelings to the reader. He first creates the atmosphere and remoulds the poetic feeling and sensibility, then he demonstrates these in a beautiful and novel cornet. All these thing and feelings are painted in one and single canvas that is called poetic image.

So we see the process how the poetic feeling is turned into fundamental and universal. As for example an accident seen and described by a ordinary person having no poetic imagination becomes pitiable no doubt, but does not attract our mind, because he narrates the happenings and the miserable condition only. But the poet creates it. He narrates the same, but his narration is not of a journalist, but of a poet. He takes it as a raw material and adds to it other ingredients and remoulds it and then gives to it a finishing touch and presents to the reader. The readers can know the happenings, its context, the pitiable condition and feel that he is identified with that person who meets an accident. The passion, feelings, expression, character are all crystallized in one poetic image. So, if we are of opinion that poetic image is the guiding principle of the poet, we do not fall in quagmire of mistakes, rather we speak the truth in toto.

The next poem of Janmadine also conveys the felicitation of the poet to the readers. Here he gives a panoramic view of nature. She also joins her hand to make his birthday festival a sweet and beautiful one. He states that

"Once again returns the day of festival
With spring's lavish honour
The branches at the poet's balcony
Fill the basket of a new birthday.
In a closed room I remain at a distance
Futile, this year, is the invention of
The flowering Palash."

In this poem Nature with her basket comes to greet him out he is not ready to accept it because the dream of impending separation gathered in his mind.

Rabindranath states that:

"My birthday, I know,
Will soon merge with one unvarying day.
And he lost in the markless sequence of Time.
This melancholy does not fill with tenderness
The shadow of flowering avenues,
Memory's pain does not sound in the
Murmur and hum of the forest.
Brushing aside, on the road, the pain of parting"

The poetic feeling is this that in his birth day he feels that the invitation of the flowering palash is futile. He feels that this melancholy does not fill with tenderness the shadow of flowering avenues, Memory's Pain does not so and in the murmur and hum of the forest. Here subjective melancholy is predominant in the fir st half of the poetry and in the second half it is driven out by the tenderness of the shadow of flowering avenues.

Now we come to the fag end of his life. Most of the poems in Sesh Lekha were composed during the last seven or eight months of his life. A few he wrote down himself, but at least two of them were dictated to his attendants from his sick-bed and later corrected, except the last one.

The poet is now past eighty, waiting for death. He is aware of the fullness that death has brought to life, a full participant in death as in life. In Sesh Lekha (Last Writing) the vision of death, complementing and rounding off life is clear and pronounced. To day after traversing sorrow's dark night, 'the path of creation entangled with variegated deceptions', after a life time of 'worship of sorrow', after having 'seen the true image of his soul drawn in blood', he has obtained in his heart the 'fearless knowledge' of the great unknown', he has known his deepest self, and has thus earned the right to deathless peace".—*An Artist of Life,* Dr. N.R. Ray

The poetic feeling of melancholy is manifested in the following Image.

> 'The sunlight blazes hot,
> This lonely mid-day
> At the empty chair I glance,
> No trace of consolation is there.
> Filling its heart
> Words of despair seem to rise in comment,
> The voice of emptiness
> Laden with compassion
> Whose inmost meaning cannot be grasped.'

Some sort of emptiness laden with compassion, of words of despair is the subject matter of the said poem. How does it attract the feelings of the readers?

'Whatever its subject' may be it must express something living in the mind from which it comes and the minds to which it goes. Wherever its body is, its soul must be here and now'.—A.C. Bradly

We are of the same opinion having added to it another

iota i.e. living image. If a Poem is to 'express something living in the mind from which it comes and the minds to which it goes; it must do so by virtue of its truth as a living image.

The image of the last stanza of the said poem of Sesh Lekha is much more impressive that other stanzas.

> More tender and more even than his pain
> Seems the voice of the chair,
> Its dumb pain of emptiness
> Pervading the room
> Bereft of the dear one.

A pensive portrait appears before us- the portrait is marked with tears of the 'dumb pain of emptiness pervading the room benefit of the dear one. The keen sensibility of the poet is perceived and the image is created in such a way that it appears as a living one and the readers feel identified with the said feelings and passions.

In the poem No. 11 of the volume 'Sesh Lekha' Rabindranath states his age-old realization. "After having worshipped sorrow for a life-time the poet has realized the sacredness of life, the sanctity of life's gifts, of woman's love and of the flowers that blossom; he has realized also that the world is no illusion, no shadow, that death has no power to shatter the vessel of life. Having seen and felt this truth the poet can listen to the bird's song with full-hearted gratitude can yearn for the touch of the loved hand as he waits in the empty sick room. The vanished dream of the past, the image of the woman whom he touched far off from his own land, came back and set up 'nets of variation' in his heart; rain washed sky seems beautiful; the friend's hand as it clasps his, speaks a deep message."

In the said poem Rabindranath speaks himself of his keen perception and poetic truth through the following image:

> On bank of Rup-Narain
> I arise, awake;
> This world I realized,
> Is not a dream.
> In words writ in blood I saw
> My being manifest,
> My own self I knew

Through repeated hurts and pain.
Heard is truth,
That hardness I loved
Never it deceives
Death-long tapasya of suffering is this life,
To win truth's terrible value
And to play all debts in death.

Rabindranath through the said image presents his realization of life. He perceives the life's truth in the suffering. The images are marked with deep, fathomless truth of poetic experience.

In the poem No. 15 of the said volume he states a teleological manifestation and implication of the Being. Although it has a metaphysical bearing it is revealed in a beautiful and consummate image. Never before have we seen such beauty and such simplicity, such renunciation and such joy, such faith, and hope and strength. No paraphrase, no translation can give any ideas of the real content of these poems.

"Sorrow's dark night, again and again
Has come to my door.
Its only weapon, I saw,
Was pain's crooked pretence;
Fear's hideous gestures
Preluding its deception in darkness.
Whenever I have believed in its mask of dread
Fruitless defeat has followed.
This game of defeat and victory is life's delusion;
From childhood, at each steps,
Clings this sceptre,
Filled with sorrow....
A moving screen of varied fears-
Death's skilful handiwork
Wrought in scattered gloom."

The image of this poem is dominated by sorrow's dark night. Rabindranath faced different types of sorrowful events in his life. The image of sorrow of this phase is not decorated or painted on a beautiful canvass. Rather it is seen through practical view. He perceives 'its only weapon.... Was pain's crooked pretence, fear's hideous gestures preluding its deception in darkness.

He looks into the life, the very core of the life with open and unbiased eyes. He states that

'This game of defeat and victory is life's delusion'.

He faces this delusion from the very childhood and opines that death's skilful handiwork is wrought in scattered gloom. He states his experience and realization of sorrow and its divergent pain. At the fag end of his life he hear the footsteps of death. He realizes everything which was very different from its previous unity. He feels the sorrow's mockery.

Now we come to the concluding phase of his life and his creation. He stretches back his sight to the far-off lands and meadows of his childhood, adolescence, youth. He feels how green was his valley? He realized the role of him in his disappointment. In *Manashi, Chitra, Chaitali, Balaka* he gives us his acquaintance. But some mysteriousness, some vagueness lies with him.

Still so, Rabindranath could not realize his familiarity and was always in a state of vagueness.

In the state of his illness he wrote this poem and expressed his admiration about his acquaintance. He creates an image that is marked with tinge of amazement.

Your creation path's you have covered
With a varied net of wiles
Thou Guileful one
False belief's snare you have
Laid with skilful hands
In simple lives.
With this deceit have you left a mark
On Greatness;
For him kept no secret night
The path that is shown to him
By your star
Is the path of his own heart
Every lucid,
Which his simple faith
Makes eternally shine,
Crooked outside yet it is straight within

In this is his pride,
Futile he is called by men.
Truth he wins
In his inner heart washed with his own light.
Noting can deceive him
The last reward he carries
To his treasure-house.
He who has easefully borne your will
Receives from your hands
The unwastering right of Peace.

"At the final stage, this deity is transformed into what the poet calls the supreme person. Yet, all the time, the attributes of formlessness, universality and infiniteness, and shall, I say, also of a sort of great mysteriousness persists. Whatever name the poet calls him in whichever shape and form he conceives, visualizes and concretizes him in different stages of his life, this Supreme Person is the guide that leads him through life and stands guard at his door-steps".—*An Artist of Life,* Dr. N.R. Ray

The idea of this Supreme Person formless, universal and infinite has nothing to do with God of theological definition or of any institutional religion. Tagore's art contains the joy and variety, the light and colours, sounds, the emotions and passions and desires in their whole tangible and sensuous naturalism of the finite world of reality. Indeed, it is only through impregnating and inseminating himself with the highest and finest possible sensuous experience that the poet at last reaches the sphere which is formless, infinite and above sense. Since the formless and the infinite has no existence apart from its many forms, to deny the reality of the latter would be a denial of the formless also.

5

Distinctive Feature of the Image Used in the Poetry of Rabindranath in Comparison with Western and Eastern, Specially in that with Bengali Poets

In this Chapter we shall lay much stress as much on the image of the Western and Eastern poets as on that of Rabindranath, and show distinctiveness and originality of Rabindranath and thereby we shall arrange a comparative and historical study of image and the imaginative passion and aesthetic realization.

We cite an example of the use of image to create an impression that without image poetry would be insipid and dull; the very essence of poetry depends on the characteristic of image, where in the originality and rudiment of poetry lies crept. We quote Sidney who preceded Shakespeare

> "Come sleep, O sleep! The certain
> Knot of peace!
> The Batting place of wit, the balm of woe,
> The poor man's wealth, the prisoner's release,
> The indifferent judge between the high and low."

Here we see the very gross output of the experience of the poet. But considering the age and time i.e. dawn of English poetry, it is of much importance and value.

Even in the dawn of English Literature, whatever be the impact and creativeness, the importance of image could not be denied. Side by side we see the capability and aesthetic sense of Rabindranath to create perfect and striking image. Here we quote a portion of Marichika (Mirage) of "Kari-o-Kamal" the early work of Rabindranath.

"Come friend, flinch not
Step down upon the hard earth
Do not gather dreams in the dusk.
Storms are brewing in the sky,
Lightning flashes are striking at our sleep.
Come down to the common life.
The web of illusion is torn,
Take shelter within walls of rough stones."

Rabindranath paints the pictures creating such impression as if the readers and connoisseurs have entered into the exhibition-gallery. They hear the storms brewing, in the sky observe through the windows of their apartment that lighting flashes are striking at their sleep, and understand the very tenet of philosophy that

"The web of illusion is torn, takes shelter within wall of rough stones: the image is striking and living. Still no, it lacks perfection as imprinted in the image of Sonar Tari, Manashi, Chitra, Balaka, his master pieces."

Sir Walter Raleigh (1552-1618) in his 'Silent lover' created images, but his images do not denote the all-rounded perfection as revealed in modern poets. But it is certain that he was aware of the role of images. They know rhetoric and its emphatic importance. They knew this art of creation and role of metre and rhythm. It is not known to them that they were creating images, the very cornerstone of the palace of poetry. All good and perfect poetry is an image itself. The imaginative passion, aesthetic realization, emotive contents and poetic experience are also included in the container of image.

When Raleigh states,

Passions are liken'd best to floods and streams:
The shallow murmur, but the deep are dumb;
So, when affection yields discourse, it seems
The bottom is but shallow, whence they come
They that are rich in words, in words discover
That they are poor in that which makes a lover.

Here the poet directs us to see his unlocked apartment to observe the pictures painted. He paints a gross and broad outline of comparison. The meticulousness and acumen is absent in the portrait.

Edmund Spenser is a master painter of the words. We observe his image creating power.

> Fresh Spring, the herald of loves
> Mighty king,
> In whose coat-armour richly are displayed
> All sorts of flowers, that which on
> Earth do spring.
> In goodly colours gloriously arrayed-
> God to my love, where she is careless lady.
> Yet in her winters bower not well awake;

He has created a romantic and sensuous image of fresh spring. The wearing of the image is striking:

He observes that the spring is the season of Love-making. Even in modern poet we see the same sensuous feelings and passion as was grossly and broadly revealed in the image of Spenser.

We quote here a portion of Prothalmian which gives expression to the discernment and perceptibility of the poet to create a weaving of sensuous images.

> "There, in a Meadow, by the river side
> A Flocke of Nymphes I chanced to espy,
> All lovely Daughters of the Flood thereby
> With goodly greenish locks, all loose untyde,
> As each had been a Bryde;
> And each one had a little wisher basket
> Made of the twigs, entrayled curiously
> In which they gathered flowers to fill their flasket.
> And with fine fingers crept full beauteously
> The tender stalkes on hye."

The whole portion of the poem is an image. The cluster of pictures has created this portrait, image. He painted a single and composite painted on a single canvass, made out of different picture i.e. portrait of a flock of Nymphs; of meadow with a river by its side, of their little wicker basket, host of flowers, varie-coloured forms and shapes. Side by side he has painted two swans of goodly hue coming softly swimming down.

Rabindranath in the very dawn of his poetic career an image that is grossly painted and that is conglomeration of sensuous and subjective ejaculations. In his collection of poems Sandhya-Sangit he creates an image that focuses and gives an outline of the acquaintance of life that is endowed with songs, dreams and the melody of Purabiraga. The image of this age is earmarked with outburst of passion, of the swelling heart, and passionate exploring.

The image of John Lyly is also of great value and prominence.

> Cupid and my Campaspe play'd
> At card of kisses- cupid paid;
> He states his quiver, bow, and arrows,
> His mother's doves and team of sparrows;
> Losses them too, then down he throws
> The coral of his lips, the rose
> Growing on's cheek (but none knows how);
> With these, the crystal of his brow,
> And then the dimple of his chin:
> All these did my Campaspe win,
> At last he set her both his eyes-
> She won, and Cupid blind did rise.
> O love! Has she done this for thee?
> What shall, alas! Become of me?

We are engaged in analogical study. The image of Chaucer, Spencer, Sidney, Langland have shown their incapability to go beyond the periphery of their bound and limitations.

So, it would be better to touch on the surface of their use of images and have an idea of image created by Chaucer only with detailed emphasis on this. Here we quote a passage from Knight's Tale:

> Ther shyveren shaftes upon sheeldes thikke....
> Up spryngen speres twenty foot on highte;
> Out goon the swerdes as the silver brighte;
> The belmes they to be win and toshrede
> Out brust the blood with stierne streams rede
> Then dtomblem streeds stronge and down gottal....

"Lightly accented by alliteration, the passage brings to eye and ear the heraldic splendour, the tall spears, the horns in mid-prance, and even the fallen warrior ('he rolleth under foot as dooth a bal') of Uceclo's great picture in the National Gallery, The Battle of San Romano, dominated by just such another figure as Duke Theseus himself"[64]

We are struck by the striking images. The passage bring to our eyes and ears the image of heraldic splendour, the tall speares, the herus in the midpranic; all is painted vividly no doubt, but-here is no varied embroidery and texture of images, variegated colours, intonation, accentuation, lilt of the music, and above all, we feel the absence of the poignant sensibility and emotive passion of the poet.

2

Now we come to the world of image created by Shakespeare. We will confront a master artist in the creation of striking and perfect images. Here we are quoting Caroline F.E. Spurgeon's 'Leading motives in the Imaginary of Shakespeare's Tragedies'..... that recurrent images play a part in raising, developing, sustaining and repeating emotion in the tragedies, which is somewhat analogous to the action of a recurrent theme or ' motif' in a musical fugue or donate, or in one of Wagner's opens. Perhaps, however, a more exact analogy to the function of Shakespeare's images is the unique work of another great artist, of the peculiar quality of which they constantly remind one, that is Blake's illustrations to his prophetic books. These are, not, for the most part, illustration in the ordinary sense of the term the translation by the artist of some incident in the narrative into a visual picture; they are rather a running accompaniment to the words in another medium, sometimes symbolically emphasizing or interpreting certain aspects of the thought, sometimes supplying frankly only decoration or atmosphere, sometimes grotesque and even repellent, vivid, strange arresting, sometime drawn with an almost unearthly beauty of form and colour. Thus, as the leaping tongues of flame which illuminate the pages of the Marriage of Heaven and

Hell show the visual form which Blake's thought evoked in his mind, and symbolize for us the purity, the beauty and the two-edged quality of life and danger in his words, so the recurrent images in Macbeth or Hamlet reveal the dominant picture or sensation- and for Shakespeare the two are identical – in terms of which he sees and feels the main problems or theme of the play thus giving us an unerring clue to the way he looked at it, as well as a direct glimpse into the working of his mind and imagination." Citing an example,

Give me my Romeo; and when he shall die
Take him and put him out in little stars
And he will make the face of heaven so fine
That all the world will be in love with night,
And pay no worship to the garish Sun.

Another is:

Her eyes in heaven
Would through the airy region stream so bright
That birds would sing and think it were not night.

In Romeo and Juliet the beauty and ardour of young love is seen by Shakespeare as the irradiating glory of Sunlight and Starlight in a dark world. The dominating image is light.

To Juliet, Romeo is day in night, to Romeo, Juliet is the sun rising from the east, and when they soar to love's ecstasy, each alike pictures the other as stars in heaven, shedding such brightness as puts to shame the heavenly bodies themselves.

We see in the said image intensity of poetic feeling and sensibility. We also can visualize the working of his mind and imagination.

More light and light: more dark
And dark our woes!
Jocund day
Stands tip-toe on the misty mountain tops,
Which forms the theme of the
Lovers' parting song; and at the last
Romeo's anguished reply to Juliet,
Pointing the contrast between the coming
Day and their own great sorrow,

More light and light more dark
And dark our woos!

And then at the end we see the darkness of the churchyard lit by the glittering torch of Paris, quickly quenched; Romeo's arrival with his torch, the swift fight and death, the dark vault which is not a grave but a lantern irradiated by Juliet's beauty, Romeo's grim jest on the lightning before death', followed immediately by the self-slaughter of the 'Star-crossed, lovers, the gathering together of the stricken mournly as the day breaks, and the 'glooming' peace of the overcast morning when

The sun for sorrow will not show his head.

Shakespeare's extraordinary susceptibility to suggestion and readiness to borrow is well exemplified in this running imagery. He took the idea from the last place we should expect from the wooden doggerel of Arthur Brooke, and the germ of it is in the sing-song line which Brooke describes the attitude of the lovers,

For each of them to other is as to the world the sun.

Shakespeare penetrates into the unfathomable depth of love and sucks image of love. Romeo's first talks to her (Juliet) is

"quick spares and glowing furious glead
......from your beauty's pleasant
eyne, Love caused to proceed
which have so set on fire each feeling
part of mine
That lo, mind doth melt away,
My outward parts do pine

which is transmuted to the delightful image of the stars which have hanged places with her eyes.

Here Sensuous aspect is predominant,
Images is tinged with poetic emotion,
Keen feelings.

But what sort of image we see in Rabindranath? Rabindranath has created varieformed images of love. They are not "quick sparks and glowing furious glead from your (Juliet's) pleasant eyre, Love caused to proceed which have so set on fire each feeling part of mine" (Romeo's), rather

Love is manifested and crystalised in passionate outburst like the fragrance of the flower that pervades the evening sky and bloomed bower (Bidal-Abhisap). The image of love created by Rabindranath is not bounded by subjective limitation, it is to be felt and perceived in the mind of natural phenomena. The passion and feeling of the lovers are to be felt along with the delightful outburst of passion in the spring. Debjani reminds kacha of the impact of the dusk, dawn, moonlight, darkness, the dark night that becomes deep due to fragrance of flower, all those mixed with his life in weal and woe-pointing to the deep love nurtured by her towards him. The poet creates, an image that is dominated by love on doubt, but love of Debjani is not a detached factor from the sub-total atmosphere. If the portrait would be marked with single emotion and libidinal experience of two lovers, then it will arrest the mind of a few to its limited closet only; so, the poet creates an image that is radiant by the halo of universal appeal and delight. The readers feel themselves identified with the characters and perceive the poetic experience and imaginative passion.

How we feel the poetic image of Ben Jonson. The poetic 'Noble Balm' is an image itself. He creates an image;

> High spirited friend,
> I send nor balms nor con'sives to your wound;
> Your fate hath found
> A gentler and more agile hand to tend
> The cure of that which is but corporal;
> And doubtful days, where were named critical,
> have made their farest flight
> And now are out of sight.
> Yet doth some whole some physic for the mind
> Wrapp'd in this paper lie
> Which in the taking if your misapply
> you are unkind.

The image is tinged with love and tenderness. It is dominated by the true valour that doth her own renown command in one full action. And emphasis has been given to' such thoughts that will make him more in love with truth.

It is wisdom, and that high
For men to use their for then recently
Even in youth.

John Donne has created much more consummate image than Ben Jonson. He creates an image that is sensuous in nature and luminous in aspect of poetic truth.

'Day break'
'Stay, o sweet, and do not rise!
The light that shines comes from thine eyes;
The day breaks not: it is my heart,
Because that you and I must part.
Stay; or else my joys will die
And perish in their infancy.

The image is dominated by love, love that is dominating entity in the poem. The passionate and sensuous image is prevalent by the light that comes from the sweetheart's eyes. The subjective 'I' of the poet will die if she will not stay. "The day breaks not; it is my heart". The sensuous and libidinal experience prevails in the image. It is not so striking and consummate image. And emotional image is created by Rabindranath.

I clasp both thine hands in mine,
And keep thine eyes prisoner with my hungry eyes;
Seeking and crying, where art thou,
Where, o, where:

The image of Donne is tinged with lover's passion and reveals a scope for the tearful atmosphere.

But in Rabindranath the image is nearly of some category. Here also the ladylove id sought. An image of sweet heart with all sorts of emotional contents are created. But beyond its limited contents there lies a universal trait or quality and that lies in the following images

"Where is the immortal flame hidden in the depth of thee!"

John Fletcher creates an image of Melancholy that is marked with sweetness, and attribution of human feelings and passions. He states in the following poetic exploration:

If men were wise to see't-

Welcome, folded arms and fixed eyes
A light that piercing mortifies
A look that a fasten'd to the ground
A tongue chain'd up without a sound.

The poet endows melancholy with embellishment.

Melancholy is attributed to with human elements. The readers feel the poetic passion and keen sensibility and acute perceptibility.

There is a most remarkable weight and unanimity of evidence, both in the verse and the critical writings of English poets, that poetry's truth comes from the perception of a unity underlying and relating all phenomena, and that poetry's task is the perpetual discovery, through its imaging, metaphor-making faculty, of new relationships within this pattern and the rediscovery and renovation of old ones". In the poem Litany to the Holy Spirit of Robert Herrick we see the subjective element is predominant; in Donne we see the preponderance of subjective element in his poetry. His cravings, his desire dominate his poetry. In Robert Herrick also we feel the same impassioned experience, the same poetic outlook along with the same poetic subjectivity. But there is divergence and difference. What Dr. Johnson wrote of Pope's genius we may quote her to appreciate the genius of Robert Herrick.

"always investigating, always aspiring, in is widest searches still longing to go forward, its highest flights still wishing to be higher, always imaging something greater then it knows."

In the hour of my distress,
When temptations me oppress,
And when I my sins confess
Sweet spirit, comfort me!
When I lie within my bed
Sick ion heart and sick in head
And with doubts discomforted
Sweet spirit, comfort me;
When the house doth sigh and weep,
And the world is drown'd in sleep,
Yet mine eyes the watch do keep,
Sweet Spirit, comfort me!

The readers look in to the poetic experience and the condition on which he falls and sees that the poet seeks comfort, he seeks solace, when the house sighs and weeps and the world is drowned in sleep i.e. when he gets no consort. The poetic passion and his sorrow touches the heart and feelings of the readers. He feels the same feelings and his mind becomes laden with grief. Rabindranath in the very dawn of his poetic career reveals the same feelings, the same melancholy. In the 'Suicide of the stars' he expresses his feelings and passions. The revelation of the feelings is not so poignant and acute. It is marked with tears and sentiments. It is novel in the sense that prior to him the special trend that is marked with subjective emotion and sentiments just begin. The famous poet Beharilal Chakraborty is the beginner of this special trend. Prior to him the Bengal literature is dominated by the age of the great epic. Rabindranath following the footsteps of Beharilal gives expression to his feelings, sentiments and sensibility, that is again marked with universality and general characteristics.

We are following the developments of poetic image. Now we come to the word of William Blake. We are quoting the poem 'To the Muses':

"Whether on Ida's shady brow
Or in the chambers of the East,
The chambers of the Sun, that now
From ancient melody have ceased;
Whether in heaven ye wander fair,
Or the green corners of the earth
Or the blue regions of the air
Where the melodious winds have birth;
Whether on crystal rocks ye rove
Beneath the bosom of the sea
Wandering in many a coral grove;
Fair Nine, forsaking poetry
How have your left the ancient love
That bards of old enjoy'd in you:
The languid strings do scarcely move,
The sound is forced, the notes are few.

The poem is an image itself. The image of the verses are marked with deeper passion and imaginative feelings of the poet. The tone and timbre of the poem moves a reader even when their full significance remains hard to define. The image of the poem becomes luminous due to its being lively on the portrait of the green corners of earth, the blue region of the air where the melodious winds have birth."

In the introduction to the songs of Experience, in the appeal of the Bard to the Earth to shake herself free from thc filters of convention and moral laws and religious taboos, there has come a new reverberant intensity:

Here the voice of the Bard:
Who Present, have heard
The Holy Word
That walk'd among the ancient trees,
Calling the laps'd soul
And weaping in evening dew;
That might control
The starry Pole
And fallen light renew:
'O Earth, o Earth, return:
Arise from out the dewy grass;
Night is worn
And the morn
Rises from the slumberous mass.
'Turn away no mire;
Why wilt than turn away?
The starry floor,
The wat'ry shore
Is given thee till the break of day'.

Rabindranath writes in almost the same vein and genre. Blake's emotion and attribution of feelings to the Earth are vividly clear and are crystalised in a striking image, there is no doubt, but his subjective element and direct involvement is much less than the romantic and modern poet. We see and feel the same sensibility in the following image created by Rabindranath but Rabindranath is distinguished and keen as his images are much more sensuous and marked with subjective elements.

"All fruitless is the cry
All vain this burning fire of desire.

The Sun goes down to his west.
There is gloom in the forest and glamour in the sky.
With downcast look and lingering steps
The evening star comes in the wake
of departing day
And the breath of the twilight is deep
With the fullness of a farewell feeling.
I clasp both thine hands in mine,
And keep thine eyes prisoner with
my hungry eyes;
Seeking and crying, where art thou
Where is the immortal flame hidden
in the depth of thee
As in the solitary star of the dark
Evening sky
The light of heaven, with its immense
Mystery, is quivering,
In thine eyes, in the depth of their darkness
There whines a soul-beam tremulous
With a wide mystery
Speechless I gaze upon it
And I plunge with all my heart
Into the deep of a fathomless longings:
I lose myself."

The poet attributes to the Natural Phenomena with poetic feelings and sensibility. The poet creates an image that is marked, tinged with poetic sorrow and melancholy. So, he sees gloom pervading all over the Nature and Earth. The departure naturally contain some sort of sorrow. He chooses the natural departing scene of the day.

"The Sun goes down to his rest.
There is gloom in the forest and
Glamour in the sky
With downcast look and lingering steps
The evening star comes in the wake
of departing day
And the breath of the twilight is
Deep with the fullness of a farewell feeling.

Here the image provokes feeling of sorrow and

melancholy in the minds of the readers. They feel the very sadness in the departing day, that lies in its heart. They see daily the rising and setting of the sun. Before reading this poem this event did never react in them. But the poet causes the readers to see and feel the natural melancholy that is manifested through the poetic Image.

5

We come to Wordsworth, who sings of truth, of grandeur beauty, love and hope, and melancholy, fear subdued by faith, of blessed consolations in distress, of moral strength and intellectual power of joy in widest commonalty spread"- Here we quote the distinguished comment of M. Arnold! We say, for brevity's sake, that he deals with life, because he deals with that in which life really consists. This is what Voltaire means to praise in the English poets,—this dealing with what is really life.

But always it is the mark of the greatest poets that they deal with it; and to say that the English poets are remarkable for dealing with it, is only another way of saying what is true, that is poetry the English genius has especially shown its powers." M. Arnold gives a review of the works of Wordsworth and sees in him that he has dealt with life and powerfully done it. But one thing is wanting. We know that the poet takes some factors of revelation to thin from Wordsworth through the medium of some portraits, pictures and above all cluster of images.

What we do see in Wordsworth's Lucy?

> Strange fits of passion have I known!
> And I will dare to tell,
> But in the Lover's ear alone,
> What once to me befell.
> Whom she I loved look'd everyday
> Fresh as a rose in June,
> I to her cottage bent my way
> Beneath an evening moon.

Here we get a portrait of a sweet, beautiful girl whom the poet loved, who looked fresh as a rose in June. An image if a girl appears before us. She appears with freshness and loveliness of a rose of June. The poet loved her but he expressed his love as

'I to her cottage bent my way
Beneath an evening moon."

He then points to the atmosphere and circumstances congenital to their love-affairs.

Upon the moon I fixed my eye,
All over the wide
With quickening pace my horse drew nigh
Those Paths so dear to me.

The poet creates an image of a sweet girl and the same congenial atmosphere, so that even paths become dear to him.

The image provokes the same feeling and sensibility in the mind of the readers and the connoisseurs. They feel with the poet and his experience and feel themselves identified with the poetic sensibility and emotive contents.

The image of Lucy is more perfect and striking when Wordsworth paints her in this fashion:

She dwelt among the untrodden ways
Beside the Springs of Dove,
A Maid whom there were none to praise
And very few to love;
A violet by a mossy stone
Half hidden from the eye!
Fair as a star, when only one
Is shining in the sky.
She lived unknown, and few could know
When Lucy caused to be;
But she is in her grave, and oh
The difference to me!

The poet creates an image that is marked with keen perceptibility and keen-edged sensuousness of the poet. He paints a portrait of sweet girl who is invisible and who is half hidden from the eye like a violet by a mosaic stone and who bids fair as a star, when only one is shining in the sky.

"She lived unknown, and few could know
When Lucy ceased to be;
But she is in her grave, and oh,

The difference to me!

Here we see that the poet is out of romantic nature. He loves the untrodden ways beside the Springs of Dove. What is not common to the conventional eyes and what is neither traditional nor of common feature attracts the romantic poet, arrests their curious insight. The romantic poets create new world, new canvass and new atmosphere and that manifests through novel, striking and consummate poetic images. The Painting of Lucy is beyond the reach of a genius even.

When Wordsworth creates the following image

Three years she grew in Sun and shower
The Nature said, "A lovelier flower
On earth was never sown;
This child I to myself will take;
She will be mine, and I will make
A lady of my own.
Myself will to my darling be
The girl, in rock and plain,
In earth and heaven, in glade and bower,
Shall feel an overseeing power-
To kindle or restrain,

The poet wants to provoke his sensibility and poetic feeling in the mind of readers. As if they are seeing the lively picture through their eyes.

Rabindranath expresses his sensibility and poetic feeling in a more perfect mode of revelation.

"I have ever loved thee in a
Hundred forms and times,
Age after age in birth following birth,
The chain of songs that my fond
Heart did weave-
Thou graciously didst take around thy neck
Age after age, in birth following birth.

The poet creates an image that is dominated by and figure wherein love-pangs are expressed. He paints

"When I listen to the tales of the
primitive past,
The love-pangs of the far distant times

The meeting and partings of the ancient ages,
I see thy from gathering light
Through the dark dimness of Eternity

Rabindranath creates an image that is marked with universality, the subjective elements is there, but never predominates.

Now we see how Coleridge meets his readers. In the poem 'Love' he creates an image that is marked with tenderness, sensuousness and intellectual beauty. Coleridge places the cornet of love in a consummate form

"All thoughts, all passions, all delights
Whatever stirs this mortal frame
All are but ministers of love
And feed his sacred flame."

Then he describes how his own dear Geneviere listened to him of the events of the knight that "wore upon his shield a furnish brand and that for ten long years he wooed "The Lady of the Land"

He creates an image of love that is crystallized and manifested in the following verses:

All impulses of soul and sense
Had thrilled my guileless Geneviere
The music and the doleful tale
The rich and balmy eve.

The poet gives a doleful description of the life story of the knight. The last four stanzas are the key portion in which the poet creates an consummate Image.

"Her bosom heaved- she stepp'd aside
As conscious of my look she stept-
Then suddenly, with timorous eye
She fled to me and wept.
She half enclosed me with her arms
She pressed me with a meek embrace
And appearing as a star ever
Fixed in the
Memory of the All."

The poet shows the readers and the connoisseurs a perfect image of love. Wordsworth paints the same image in a bit different way:

I travell'd among unknown men,
Inlands beyond the sea;
Nor, England! Did I know tell them
What love I bore to thee.
Tis past, that melancholy dream!
Now will quite thy share
A second time; for still I seen
To love thee more and more.
Among the mountain sis I feel
The joy of my desire;
And she I cherishe'd turn'd her wheel
Beside an English fire."

(Lucy)

But on the other hand Rabindranath states that

The on-rolling flood of the love eternal
Hath at last found its perfect final course
All the joys and sorrows and loving of heart,
All the memories of the moments of ecstasy
All the love –lyrics of poets of all climes
and times
Have come from the everywhere
And gathered in one single love
At the feet.
And lending back her head look'd up
And gazed upon my face
'Twas partly love, and partly fear
And partly 'twas a bashful art
That I might rather feel, than see
The swelling of her heart.
I clam'd her fears, and she was calm,
And told her love with virgin pride;
And so I won my Geneviere,
My bright and beauteous Bride".

The poet creates an image that reveals the poetic experience of love, his libidinal partakings with his lady love, his emotional effusion, and sentimental outburst.

Now side by side we quote Rabindranath's *Manas Sundari*, where he creates an image of perfect and consummate love. Here we see that the poet invokes his ladylove to embrace him with her unembellished hands devoid of ornaments so that by that sweet touch of the hands that resemble the stalk of the lotus, the heart of the poet becomes welled with extreme delight, the chest starts, trembling, eyes full of tears, charmed body if at the point of outburst, the mind only becomes brightened up the very end of the body and the binds of senses are about to tear and he requests her to cause him sit on border of the loin beside her and call him with sweet name, to say dear, dearest and to set her face marked with dishavelled hair on the chest of the poet and sing mildly and gently.

Rabindranath creates an image that is marked with the sensuous elements. The psychological treatment is dominating in the juxtaposition of the image. The image reveals the libidinal and sexual relations of the lovers, but it crosses the limited circumference of the personal relation, Rather their activities are marked with universality, because the image and the sensual happenings portrayed in it arrest the common readers and connoisseurs. It is the emotive contents, the sensibility that attracts our mind no doubt. But there is somethings beyond d it. That is the way of putting the whole thing in a peculiar diction in some good pattern. So, it is important to note that the image-patterns must in fact be patterns and not random assemblages of word pictures. What is it, for instance, that so much moves in Coleridge's image?

It ceased, yet still the sail made on
A pleasant noise till noon,
A noise like of a hidden brook
In the leafy month of June,
That to the sleeping woods all at night
Singeth a quiet tune.

It is not merely the beauty of sound and sensuous description: it is that every detail in the image corresponds with and blessedly contrasts with some part of the physical ordeal which Ancient Mariner has just passed through--the dead calm, the drought, the heat and lack of shade, the sleeplessness. Behind this, there lines the same principle that operates in all the technical features of verse—in metre, rhyme, alliteration, refrain—the principle of repetition, whereby the mind is delighted with the recognition of something familiar recurring in a new guise."

Byron creates an image that is sensuous, and widely marked with intensity of feeling.

"She walks in beauty, like the night
Of cloudless climes and starry skies;
And all that's best of dask and bright
Meet in her aspect and her eyes:
Thus mellow'd to that tender light
Which haven to gaudy day denies.
One shade the more, one ray the less,
Had half impair'd the nameless grace,
Which waves in every raven tress,
or softly lightens o'er her face,
Where thoughts serenely sweet express
How pure, how dear their dwelling peace.

Now we come to the world of images created by P.B. Shelley.

O wild west wind, thou breath of Autumn's being
Thou from whose unseen presence the leaves dead
Are driven like ghosts from an enchanter feeling,
Yellow, and black, and pale, and hectic red,
Pestilence- stricken multitudes is thou
Who chariotest to their dark wintry bed
The winged seeds, where they lie cold and low,
Each like a corpse within its grave, until
Thine azure sister of the spring shall blow
Her clarion o'er the dreaming earth, and fill
(Driving sweet buds like flocks to feed in air)
With living hues and odours plain and odours plain and hill;
Wild spirit, which art moving everywhere,
Destroyer and Preserver; hear, o hear;

We must admire the skill with which the poet has worked the idea of west wind into sensuous and striking image, so that what might have been merely an idea, a consciousness is made a full-blown image. The event that is related to the west wind is natural and practical. But this natural phenomena is given expression in such a way, in such a genre that it touches our feelings, our emotive contents, and sensibility. The "West Wind" drives all the worn-out, all the dilapidated rubbishes, all the fallen and ripened white leaves of the trees. Shelley creates the following image of the dead leaves.

> "Yellow, and black, and pale, and hectic red
> Pestilence-stricken multitudes."

The wild west wind is attributed to with the power of the creator and destroyer. He drives out everything on the one hand, and creates on the heaps of the dead the new life, new objects on the other hand.

Shelley creates an image in which we feel 'the emotional apprehension of thought, and we understand the fusion of thought with feelings, the perception of thought in terms of thought.

So, we see in the following image, the suggestive and decorative aspects of imagery.

> 'Thou an whole stream, 'mid the steep
> sh's commotion
> Loose clouds like earth's decaying leaves are shed,
> Shook from the tangled boughs of heaven
> and ocean,
> Angels of rain, and lightning: there are spread
> On the blue surface of thine airy surge,
> Like the bright hair uplifted from the head
> of some fierce Macnad, even from the dim verse
> of the horizon to the zeneth's height
> The locks of the approaching storm. Thou verse
> of the dying year, to which this closing night
> Will be the dome of a vast Sepulchre,
> Vaulted will all thy congregated might
> of vapours, from whose solid atmosphere
> Black rain, and fire, and hail
> Will burst: o hear:

Here, what is striking to us and what is luminous in the said cluster of images is the poetic attribution of human feelings and intellect and the application of intellectual emotive, contents, and the emotional congruity and adaptability. The images must be congruous with each other. Whatever be the pitch or scale on which the images are turned up there must be congruousness. "We must ask ourselves first what the poet is trying to do in a poem, and then whether his images are well adapted to this purpose or not. If they are so adapted, they are in fact functional however 'decorative' in the sense of unsuggestive, shallow, ever superficial they may appear. Once again, it is a matter of congruity. The Augustans and imagery are congruous with the purpose and pattern of their Poems, whether these were said, mock-heroic or contemplative; and therefore their images, though often flat, are at least congruous with each other". *Ibid.*

So, it is clear to us that all the cluster of images being painted on one and single canvas reveals only one portrait, only one striking image. The ingredient- ' the tangled boughs of heaven and ocean', ' the blue surface of thine airy surge', 'like the bright hair uplifted from the head', 'the dim verge of the horizon to the zenith's Height', 'the lock of the approaching storm', 'the dome of a vast sepulchre', 'black rain, and fire, and hail"—are all decorative aspects of one single Image. These, if detached from the consummate form and shape, appear to us meaningless and inconsistent and, if these appear in a multitude with inherent meaning with congruity, we will see a luminous image bearing with inherent meaning with congruity, we will see is luminous image bearing with it poetic emotion, sensibility and the testimony of his unique and peculiar experience. In the last stanza Shelley wants his age-old and worn-out ideas of life be driven out with the departure of the year; with the advent of the New Year let new ideas and ideals come to his life as the new foliage comes to the leafless plants and trees in the new year.

> Make me thy lyre, even as the forest is:
> What if my leaves are falling
> like its own?
> The tumult of thy mighty harmonies
> Will take from both a deep autumnal tone,
> Sweet.though in sadness Be then,
> spirit fierce,
> My spirit: Be thou me impetuous one!
> Drive my dead thoughts over the universe,
> Like wither'd leaves, to quicken a new birth;
> And, by the incantation of this verse,

Scatter, as from an unextinghish'd hearth
Ashes and sparks, my words among making;
Be through my lips to unawaken'd earth
The trumpet of a prophecy! O Wind
If winter comes, can Spring be far behind?

The poet identifies himself with the natural phenomena and banks a new implication out of it and that new thought, novel idea of life is crystalised in the said striking image. The Romantic image is a mode of exploring reality, by which the poet is in effect asking imagery to reveal to him the meaning of his own experience. With the Romantic poet, the image seeking faculty is unleashed and wanders at large, whereas with the classical it is tethered to a thought to a thought, a meaning, a poetic purpose already clarified, and its radius of action is thus far limited:

Keats creates images that manifest poetic experience and his peculiar approach to the readers and the connoisseurs. The other romantic poets like Wordsworth, Shelley, Byron have traded their poetic Path in their own way, by which they are acquainted, they are familiar.

Keats images are peculiarly marked with sensuousness and intense feeling. He does not haunt the readers with a basket of ideas and philosophy. He presents his experience, his feelings, his sensibility and perceptive capability. He gives descriptive sketches, panorama of facts and sentiments. Taking an example

"O for a draught of vintage! that hath been
Cooll'd a long age in the deep-delvb'd earth,
Tasting of Flora and the country-green,
Dance, and Provincial song, and Sunburnt mirth!
O for a beaker full of the warm south!
Full of the true, the blushful Hippocrene
With beaded bubbles winking at the brim
And purple-stained month;
That I might drink, and leave the world unseen,
And with thee fade away into the forest dim:"

Every image is marked with sensuousness, and intense poetic feeling. As if Keats through the striking images makes the readers see in their own eyes "the beaded bubbles winning at the brim, 'and purple-stained month; and' tasking of Flora and the country-green, dance, and subburnt mirth."

What he means to say is not the be-all and end-all of his poetic theory and reality: how does he portray or depict his poetic experience is the summum bonum of his poetic genius? A great critic having him in mind makes a comprehensive dictum in a more succinct from: "The Nightingle is the most passionate strain of song. "In the very genre of expression, in the very revelation of poetic experience Keats pins down on the very ornaments and decorative aspects of image:

"Where palsy shakes a few, sad, last grey hairs,
Where youth grown pale, and spectre- thin and dies,
Where but to think is to be full of sorrow
And laden-eyed despairs."
"Clustered around by all her starry eyes
But here there is no light.
Save what from heaven is with the breezes ways.

We in every-form of expression, in every image, in every shape poetic manifestation feel a different savour of poetic experience and poetic emotive contents. Keats in a different distinguished genre has expressed his poetic reality, which is not concluded fact, rather it is obvious from the face of the verbiage, from the coinage of the words and from sensuous portraits of objects and feelings. Following the same principle as the aforesaid:

"I cannot see what flowers are at my feet
Nor what soft incense hangs upon the boughs
But, embalmed darkness, guess each sweet
Where with the seasonable month endows
The grass, and the pastoral' eglantine,
Fast-fading violets cover'd up in leaves,
And mid-May's eldest child,
The coming musk-rose, full of dewy wine,
The numerous haunt off his on summer eves.

So, we see that whatever be the poetic truth, or poetic reality we are first struck by the striking verbiage and beautiful coinage—and their peculiar and universal implication. 'Verdurous glooms and winding mossy ways', 'embalmed darkness', the pastoral eglantine, and 'murmurous haunt on flies or summer eves" are no new words, but they are striking and bear the charming impression due to some amount of intellectual emotion's attribution and juxtaposition of the images. The poet expresses his emotion through his peculiar genre of expression, and that is crystalised and revealed through the poetic image.

Through the image we are acquainted with poetic passion, his emotive intellect and intellectual emotion. All these qualities are given expression and we can know along with the images. In the image of Rabindranath we feel his passion, his poetic experience, his sensibility different and more acute and pungent than that of Keats. In the poem 'Basundhara—The Earth' Rabindranath creates an images that focuses his passionate, sensuous nature. He states that "in your heart what sort of flow of the savour of life is current day and night, the buds and flowers are impatient on which blind delight on the beautiful foliage, the plants, grass, bush on which deep delight on which charmed exultation are glad and satiated like the children who are tired after drinking their mother's milk, and with smiling face due to happy dream". Here we see his passionate nature and sensuousness. The poet feels delight in the sunrays that fall on the apex of ripened golden field, the impatience on the recapitulation of his being identified with waters, soils, with the foliages of the forest and blueness of the sky. He wants to see and feel the palpable portrait of this sky, this earth, and the while, quiet and asleep moon rays.

So, it is quite clear that" what comes through is vitality. The poet of high vitality, and he alone, is strong enough to live in the present and pin it down to an original form. He along, therefore, is truly modern; and because it images the patterns that in his time are still forming still inchoate."

We quote here the comment of a critic for our guidance:

"Autumn is surely the most perfect, or one of the most perfect poems in the language, with its wonderful double evolution, the rising of the passionate movement in the second stanza marked by the transition from concrete description to transfiguring personification, and that followed in the final stanza by the return to the calmer rendering of objective details:

Hedge-crickets sing; and now with treble soft
The red-breast whistles from a garden croft,
gathering tuitter in the skies and emotion as well as her
peculiarly.
And with this emotional rise and fall
Goes the passing of the season from
Autumn at the close of summer:
And still more, later flowers for the bees,
Until they think warm days will never cease.
For summer has o'ver-brimm'd their clammy cells.

We come to the Victorian age which is marked with intellectual romanticism and scientific emotive contents. The poets of this age are romantic unlike the romantic poets. Elisabeth Barrett Borwing is one of the poets of Victorian period. The image she created is actually tinged and marked with keen sensibility and imaginative passion. Through the images she marks her acumen and genius. Even in the age of the great poets Tennyson and Browning her poems bear the testimony of the great genius and her distinction. In the following poem the poet gives a vivid expression of this:

"I tell you, hopeless grief is passionless;
That only men incredulous of despair
Half-taught in anguish, through the midnight air
Best upward to God's throne in loud access
of shrinking and reproach. Full desertness,
In souls as countries with silent-leave
under the blanching, vertical eye-glare
of the absolute Heavens. Deep hearted man, express
Grief for they Dead in silence like to Death-
Most like a monumental stature set
In everlasting watch and moveless woe
Till itself crumble to the dust beneath.
Touch it; the marble eye lids are not wet:
If it could weep, it could arise and go."
-Grief.

What is marked and dominating is the poetic sensibility own expression. Through these images she is content to record her own inner life and feelings. Even in these, as in her poems on larger themes, Mrs. Browning stands a little on tiptoe, does not lose her self-consciousness in the single passion.

She is always conscious of herself as a women and a poet, a frail woman one whom has been laid the burden of a poet and a champion of her sex. This dual consciousness found expression in one immortal lyric, a jet of song that flows from first to last without a check, in a manner that recalls Shelley great lyric the "Hymn of Pan; and Mrs. Browning's concern is also with Pan:

> What was he doing, the great god Pan,
> Down in the roads by the river?
> Spreading ruin and scattering ban
> Splashing and Paddling with hoofs of a goat,
> And breaking the golden lilies afloat
> With the dragon-fly on the river.

Now we come to the world of images, the galaxy of painting-the world of Lord Tennyson. Here we see that the poet paints with words not with idea.

> When he says:
> On either side the river lie
> Longfields of barley and of rye
> And thro'th field the road runs by
> To many-towered Camelot;
> And up and down the people go,
> Gazing where the lilies blow
> Round an island there below,
> The is land of Shallot".

The poet gives a vivid description and a panorama of the atmosphere and invokes in the mind of the readers the poetic experience. He creates an image that focuses his sensibility and emotive contents. He depicts the mysterious atmosphere in such a decorative and majestic way that even the mind of readers of scientific and modern idea and thought is arrested to it.

When he gives a descriptive sketch:

> Willows whiten, aspens quiver,
> Little breezes dusk and shiver
> Thro' the wave that runs for ever
> By the island in the river
> Flowing down to camelot.
> Four grey walls and four grey towers

Overlook a apace of flowers
And the silent isle imbowers
The Lady of Shallott.

He simply gives vivid and meticulous description of the atmosphere. He wants to lead the reader to the mysterious place of Lady Shallot. Prior to that he gives ample scope and materials to prepare our mind to confront the Lady, the beautiful and mysterious Lady. She does not resemble the Lady portrayed by Coleridge. The supernatural entity is absent in this poem. Tennyson in the last phase of this Poem stamps his poem bears his immortal genius:

"Who is this? And what is here?
And in the lighted place near
Did the sound of royal cheer;
And they cross'd themselves for fear
All the knights at Camelot:
But Lancelot mused a little space;
He said, "she has a lovely face;
God in His mercy lend her grace,
The Lady of Shallot!

This image, he suggests, awakens in us a sense that we feel her mystic love and her pangs. It reminds us of a certain experience, and by its style it awakens a certain faculty for that experience. We are told of a thing; we are made to feel as if that thing was possible to us; and we are so made to feel it- whatever the thing may be, joy or despair or what not-that such knowledge is an intense satisfaction to us.

Robert Browning gives his valuable and marked money to the development of images. His images are marked with his restrained emotion, with constrained sensibility. He endows the emotive contents with poignant sharpness and boisterous movement.

When he creates an image in The Last Ride Together

"I said-Then, dearest, since 'tis so
Since now at length my fate I know,
Since nothing all my love avails,
Since this was written and needs must be-
My whole heart rises up to bless
Your name in pride and thankfulness;

Take back the hope your gave,- I claim
Only a memory of the dame,
-And this beside, if you will not blame;
Your leave for one more last ride with me."

The poet creates an image that is marked with love, emotion and poetic sensibility. There is frustration in love but that is no dominating factor. Rather there is an ample scope for reconcilement. He creates an atmosphere over-swelled by love. The over is given by his lady love, who is no more with him, the last chance to ride together. The lover is overwhelmed with joy. His frustration in love is no more, although he knows it(love) will last for a while. The poet creates an image that focuses that portrait of love and poetic emotion:

"Hush! If you saw some western cloud
All billony-bosom'd over-bow'd
By many benedictions- sun's
And hours and evening star's at once
And so, you, your passion drew
cloud, sunset, moon rise star-shine too."
Down on you, near and yet more near,
Till flesh must fade for heaven was here!
Thus leant she and linger'd- joy and fear
Thus lay she a moment on my breast."

The said image gives a vivid and meticulous description of love and its romantic atmosphere. The lover has forgotten the fact that his lady love will forshake him after the last ride that also will continue only for a while. The poet holds the joy for a few hours or few moments in an immortal cornet. The emotion and passion of the lover, who has been frustrated in love is crystalised in the following Image:

"My Soul
Smoth'd itself out, a long-cramp'd scroll
Freshening and fluttering in the wind.
Past hopes already lay behind."

Then the poet enters into the very core of the immortal joy that the lover enjoyes in the Last Ride together. He gives the comprehensive review of the workings and their gains, benefits of this world. The tenure of love-making is extremely limited. The lover will not be allowed to love his beloved for the indefinite period. But he asks who succeeds after striking hard. So, if he fails in love, if he is frustrated in love there is consolation, there is solace that no one in this world succeeds leaving 'Petty-done, the undone vast.' The poet speaks of the predominant passion of the lover. His lady-love allows him to ride with her. This is more than a boon; because

"Where had I been now if the worst befell?"

The passionate flow of poetry is focused and manifested in the following Image:

"Fail I alone, in words and deeds?
Why, all men strive and whew succeeds?
We rode; it seem'd my spirit flew,
Saw other regions, cities new.
As the world rushed by on our side.
I thought all labour, yet no less
Bear up beneath their unsuccess.
Look at the end of work, contrast-
The petty done, the undone vast,
This present of theirs with the hopeful past!
I hoped she would love me; here we ride."

"What strikes us first of all in Browning is his superabundant energy. Since the main haunt and region of his song was the soul, his energies are chiefly mental, he does not brood and meditate, but darts on his pry in every direction, like a spider that" feels in each thread and lives along the line." It is the same with his descriptions of physical objects and actions; he loves bold, jagged outlines: it is the leaping from rock up to rock that yields David the wild joy of living. What he adores in Nature is not beauty or sublimity, but life, the pressure of life in plant, insect, bird and beast when spring returns and God renews His ancient rapture."

All these aspects and items that isolately and detachedly impart and subscribe to sum total poetic experience and passionate outflow of emotion are all painted in the single canvass of image. The readers view them all in multitude, not singly and detachedly.

In the following image the poetic truth and his optimistic outlook is focused and crystalised:

And yet-she has not spoke so long:
What if heaven be that, fair and strong
At life's best, with our eyes up turn'd
Whither life's flower is first discern'd
We, fixed so, ever should go abide?
What if we still ride on, we two
With life for ever old yet new,
Changed not in kind but in degree,
The instant made eternity-
And heaven just prove that I and she
Ride, ride together, for ever ride?

Rabindranath in his poem 'Purposeless Journey' gives and descriptive journey of a lover, with a mysterious Lady-love. He does not know to which destination she leads him. He seems to be rather at her mercy. But she exerts no influence on him. She smiles only when he presses or urges to say something about their journey and the destiny for which they are crossing the impatient ocean. He creates an image that is marked with romantic sense and sensibility. The poet in the character of lover asks the lady whether that place, where the day's pyre burns in the evening, the waters seem to be liquid fire, as if the sky is melting, the deity of the surging ocean and in the foot of the sky- kissing setting mountain? The lady smiles telling nothing to him. Browning appraises the lady in the following epithets:

My mistress bent that brow of hers
Those deep dark eyes where pride demurs.

Here is an image that is dominated by the qualities of a lady who is very much sympathetic to consider his case to ride for the last time with the man whom she loved once. But in Rabindranath the case and history is different. We find here that one mysterious lady is leading a golden boat, where her lover gets a chance to it to go with her in such mysterious and long journey. He puts several questions and gives probable hints and suggestions, but to every question and hint she smiles sweetly speaking noting to him. We find some mysteriousness in Tennyson's Lady of shallot. She is in her abode alone and,

There she weaves by night and day

A magic web with colours gay.
She has heard a whisper say,
A curse is on her if she stay
To look down to Camelot.
She knows not what the curse may be
And so she weareth steadily,
And little other care hath she,
The Lady of Shalott."

Here also we feel her desire to break and pierce through the network that covers her life and her view and thought. She wants to come down from the palace, when

"Sometimes a troop of damsels glad,
An abbot on an ambling pad,
Sometimes a curly shepherd lad,
Or long-havied page in crimson clad;
But in her web she still delights
To weave the mirror's magic sights,
A funeral, with plumes and lights
And music, went to Camelot:
or when the moon was overhead,
came two young lovers lately wed.
"I am half sick of shadows: said
The lady of Shallot.

Here we find the earnest desire and cravings of her to see the material world; she rather identifies herself with the love and desire of the two young lovers lately wed. But Rabindranath creates an image of a young lady that focuses a mysteriousness, but that mystery did not cross the periphery of material world. The lover gets the fragrance of her hairs, hears the surging waves of the ocean, he feels that sweet touch of her dishavelled hairs." Rabindranath creates an aesthetic and consummate image that is distinguished from the images created by Browning and Tennyson.

Then we come to the worlds of Mathew Arnold. He creates an image that is tinged with tears of pangs of separation. He presents to the readers and to the connoisseurs a consummate crystal of image. Arnold states:

Yes: in the sea of life enisled

With echoing straits between us thrown,
Dotting the shoreless watery wild,
We mortal millions live alone
The islands feel the unelasping flow
And then are swept by balms of spring,
And in their glens, on starry nights,
The nightingales divinely sing;
And lovely notes, from shore to shore,
Across the sounds and channels pour;

What the poet means to say is this that this life resembles the vastness and depth of the sea with echoing straits between human beings. There is pangs of separation between everyman and woman. He visualized this earth is stricken with pages of separation and despair. He creates an image

"O then a longing like despair
Is to their farthest caverns sent:
For surely once, they feel, we were
Parts of a single continent.
Now round us spreads the watery plain-
O might our surges meet again!
Who order'd that their longing's fire
Should be, as soon as kindled, cool'd?
Who renders vain their deep desire?
A God, a God their severance rul'd,
And bade betwixt their shares to be
The unplumb'd salt, estranging sea.

Rabindranath in the Poem Meghdut (The cloud as Messenger) creates the same image as Mathew Arnold. But his modus operandi is different, his aesthetic sense and sensibility is distinguished. The poet experiences this that he has got the Heaven of Separation, where his lady-love has been passing day and night in the midst of eternal beauty alone in the world. This poet creates the image that reveals the poetic experience and his aesthetic sense. Arnold finds in the life the unplumb'd salt, entrancing sea! But on the other had Rabindranath in the ceaseless outpour of rains visualizes separation, and exclaims who there is to inflict imprecation, why unsatiated desire becomes fruitless and tinged with tears! Rabindranath enters into the very core of pangs, separation and, having this perspective he creates the following image:

"The day is over. The time has come to take leave.
Come, o woman, with your vessel full of tears
Let your sad eyes shed tender glow on the farewell
Path and the touch of thy trembling hand make
the parting hour full.
Come, sad woman, with your
Vessel of tears."

The image of sorrow bears the testimony of a master artist. Pensiveness is attributed to with human qualities. It is not only a quality, but it is treated as lively and living entity. Arnold speaks of an eternal separation, but does not characterize it as Rabindranath does. Rabindranath creates such a consummate and striking image, so that the readers and connoisseurs identify with the poetic experience and his aesthetic sense.

Now we come to the world of modern poets, where we see the cluster of images marked with dappled and variegated colours and fragrance; and a new taste comes through the image/. The modern period of English Literature becomes more acute, more critical and more sensitive than that of the preceding periods. So, its mark and testimony characterizes the modern images. In this period we see that image manifests not only the problem and crux of human beings, but their form, their shape, their movement show much restraint and perfection in expression and demonstration. They try to avoid some kind of looseness, slackness in forms and feature. The modern poet following the lilt of the previous poets praises God, but his expression, his modus operandi is much more restrained having no such shamble and dilatoriness.

G.M. Hopkins is marked with the said characteristics. He presents a consummate picture of natural objects rather panorama of Nature, along with tribute to God.

Glory be to God for dappled things-
For skies of couple-colour as brinded cow;
For rose-moles all in stipple
upon trout that swim;
Fresh-fire coal plotted chestnut-falls;
Finches' wings;

Landscape plotted and pierced-fold, fallow
And plough;
And all trades, their gear and tackle and trim
All things counter, original's spare, strange;
Whatever is fickle, freckled (who knows how):
With swift, slow; sweet, sour, dazzle dim;
He fathers- forth whose beauty is past change:
Praise him.

But in the image of God Rabindranath creates the different and divergent thing. He does not describe the beauty in his creation, rather he enters into the core of His circumference.

'O Man divine, sanctify our efforts
With the light of thy sacred touch,
Dwell in our hearts,
Hold before us the image of thy greatness.
Forgive our transgression,
Teach us to forgive.
Guide us into serene fortitude
Through all joys and sorrows,
Inspire us with love
Overcoming pride of self,
And let our devotion for thee
Banish all enmity.

Rabindranath crates an image of the Almighty Power. He submits his cravings and desires, he beseeches His guidance into 'Serene fortitude through all joys and sorrows. Through this image he wants to create another i.e. the image of a great and magnificent human beings who is widely marked with serene fortitude, and who bears the testimony to His greatness.

The famous poet Robert Bridges has created an image of love of two lovers in the poem; My delight and Thy delight'. This image is deeply and core-heartedly tinged with sensual love and libidinal experience of the lovers, but the everlasting strife in the mystery of life has not been avoided; rather it has a vital role contiguous to the love- affairs.

The image of the said poem is as follows

"My delight and thy delight

Walking, like two angles white,
In the gardens of the night;
My desire and thy desire
Twining to a tongue of fire
Leaping live and laughing higher;
Thro' the everlasting strife
Love, from whom the world begun
Hath the secret of the sun.

The poet creates an image of love characterizing it with a vital force and an internal power that because of it each atom knows its own, and the million stars wore strewn, and due to it, inspite of woe and death gay is life, and sweet is breath. He means to say is this that love has a great and magnificent role to play in the creation and in the material life. Love is synchronizing factor between human beings and natural phonemena.

The concept and idea of love is manifested in the following crystalised image.

"This he taught us, this we know,
Happy in his science true;
Hand in hand as we stood
'Neath the shadows of the wood,
Heart to heart as we lay
In the dawning of the day.

Here we see a universal portrait of love. In the said image poet did not mention the name of love, but he creates a congenial atmosphere of love.

That is to state that the poet creates an image of immortal and eternal love that guides over psychological and sexual life

Rabindranath with the same coin of love gives us divergent and different harvest. He gives us new experiences, new outlook and novel idea. According to Bridges Love is the dominating factor of life and specially of lovers. But with the same view of love Rabindranath gives now taste and new feelings i.e.

"Love thou hast made great my life with death's magnificence and hast tinted all my thoughts and dreams with radiant hues of thy farewell rays.

The tear-washed limpid light reveals at life's last sunset-point the hints of Paradise, where descending flame of kiss from starry sphere of love lights the sorrows of our earth to splendour of their end, in one blazing ecstasy of uttermost extinction. Love, thou hast made one vast wonder Life and Death for me."

Bridges places love in the midst of everlasting strife and tastes it in the mystery of life also. But Rabindranath gives to it new outlook, new vesture. He endows it with death's magnificence and with radiant hues of tearful farewell rays.

W.B. Yeats is a master- artist in the field of images. His poems are an images themselves. His simple connotation and symbolic expression dominate the poetic image.

Even the trifling happening of day-to-day existence would become striking and objects of interest and delight. And the following poem bears the testimony to this fact.

> "When you are old and gray
> And full of sleep
> And nodding by the fire, take down this book
> And slowly read, and dream of the soft look
> Your eyes had one, and of their shadows deep;
> How many love your moments of glad grace,
> And loved your beauty with love false or true;
> But one man loved the pilgrim soul in you,
> And loved the sorrows of your changing face;
> And bending down beside the glowing loves
> Murmur, a little sadly, how love fled
> And paced upon the mountains over head,
> And hid his face amid a crowd of stars.

The poet recapitulates the loving moments of cheerful grace of the lady whom he loved her beauty not with sensual feelings and passion. He loved her having the pilgrim soul in her and loved the sorrows of her changing face. That is to say, that their love were not reciprocal. This image is tinged and smeared with sighs and tears. But the images is given ample scope to provoke the feelings and passion in the minds of the readers and connoisseurs.

Rabindranath on the other hand gives us different outlook and panorama of love. Yeats in the portrait of frustration and disappointment in love causes the readers to feel the perfectness and consummateness of love and its incarnation. Rabindranath shows us directly the full-bloomed flower of love.

The image of it is as follows:-

'Thou art a glimmer of gold
From the dawn on my life's shore,
A dew-drop on the first white flower of autumn.
Thou are a rainbow from the distant sky
Bending o'er the dust,
A dream of this crescent morn touched with a white curd
Thou are a secret of paradise
Revealed by change to the earth".

These are the sensual overflow of poetic emotion and passion made in recognition of special qualities of the lady-love.

Walter De La Mare is a distinguished name in the world of images. He makes an image that is tinged with farewell tears and sorrows. The image makes us confronted with circumstances and association of environment which someone faces when he bids farewell to the world and its phenomena. The image is this:

When I lie where shades of darkness
Shall no more assail mine eyes,
Nor the rain make lamentation
When the wind sighs;
How will fare the world whose wonder
Was the every proof of me?
Memory fades, must the remember'd
Perishing be?

But Rabindranath in the same text gives different and divergent outlook and poetic sensibility. Farewell to him contains neither sigh nor lamentation. It is neither destruction, death nor any fear of separation. It is only completion. It is some sort of transition-from happiness to sweet memory, from pain to music, from boat to the shore- from the playing to tiredness, from desire to tranquillity and from the endless sky to the nest. It is the plain statement arising out of the farewell.

Now the poet creates crystalised form of images

"Let the soft touch of the hand of the day's end fall on the head and sleep on the eyes. Let the flowers of the night bloom secretly in the cup made of leaves of the heart, let the full consequence come down at the blow of the conch during the time of greeting a deity. Now it is not the time of smile; tears, but it is the extensive rest full of lofty stoicism.

Rabindranath attributes human quality to the abstract form of pensiveness, melancholy. He addresses it as 'oh! The great beautiful consequence', oh motionless Farewell oh, unruffled Melancholy provoking in the mind of the readers that it has got some quality to instill movement.

He requests this attributed quality to stand before him steadfastly and to bless him wiping his tears and again requests it so that he bend his head on its feet on its journey and greets it silently with the motionless candle in the calm and tranquil world.

So, we see that the image of Farewell is a new experience with new and novel outlook and its presentation through the focusing implements is unique and exploration of the genius of a master artist. Walter-De La Mare's expression is unique no doubt. But his outlook is quite natural having no new item to add to the poetic experience. But Rabindranath's is striking and epoch-making. The modus operandi is congenial to the idea, outlook and the purport of the poem.

Among the modern poets T.S. Eliot paves a new way and his new way is manifested through the striking and consummate image.

> "Let us go then, you and I
> When the evening is spread out
> Like a patient etherized upon a table;
> Let us go, through certain half-deserted streets,
> The muttering nights in one-night cheap hotels
> And sawdust restaurants with oyster-shells:
> Streets the follow lime a tedious argument
> Of insidious intent
> To lead you to an overwhelming question
> Oh, do not ask, "what is it?"
> Let us and make our visit".

The poet presents us an image of sensual reaction that it imagined, and its environment and allied association of ideas and occurrences. But what is said is said through the poetic images. The images themselves are not pure; they are mixed with' grosser elements's emotion sensuousness, and prose meaning, etc. the sensuous associations of its images pitch the poem at a certain emotional key, and all feel a mood; the emotional progress of the images follows an invisible but unbroken thread, and we feel a meaning; this thread is invisible only because the images are strong along it contagiously, but it is there none-the-less and it is a thread of argument, of Prose meaning".

In the Poem 'Grention' T.S. Eliot gives a comprehensive outlook of old age and its condition, feelings and association of ideas.

> Here I am, an old man in a dry month
> Being read to by a boy, waiting for rain
> I was neither at the hot gates
> Now fought in the warm rain
> Now knee deep in the salt marsh having
> a cut lass,
> Bitten by flies, fought.
> My house is a decayed house,
> And the jew squats on the window sill,
> The owner.
> Spawned in some estaminent of Antwerp,
> Blistered in Brussels, patched
> and puled in London.
> The goat caught at night in the
> field overhead;
> Rock, moss, stonecrop, iron, merds.
> The woman keeps the kitchen, makes tea
> Sneeres at evening, poking the purish gutter.
> I am old man,
> A dull head among windy spaces.

T.S. Eliot creates image that is as much marked by congruity as by audacity and freshness. We also bear in mind that the capacity of the poetic image to lift the connoisseur to a higher plane by impressing on him the highly ordered design of the world reveals itself in a greater degree in images, characterised by employment of the device of corroboration. It embraces three things- the meaning the particular gives to the universal, the meaning the universal lends to the particular, and the meaning which the particular- universal relationship bears for the reader in the context of the main melody of the poem, and thus makes transition from the individual experience both universal experience easier."*Anviksha-Alamkara and Aesthetic Realisation*-Dr. R.R. Mukherjee.

Rabindranath's outlook and impression of old age differs from that of T. S. Eliot. When he states the end of a man:

"The end, proud man, is one with
The end of the cattle that graze no more;
For when thy life's wine is spilt
To its last drop,
The cup is flung away in final unconcern.
I cry in answer:
Mine is not merely the life that pays its
bed and board
With its bankrupt bones, and is made destitute."

We feel his distinction, his keen sensibility and deep feelings. Apart from it "his matter, as it existed in the general imagination, was already highly poetical. A world not of bodiless thoughts and emotions, but of scenes, figures, actions and events. For the most part he lived in unity with it; it appealed to his own religious and moral feelings and beliefs.—*The Poetic Image,* C.D. Lewis.

We end this with the quotation of a famous poem of the Rabindranath, which is an image itself. Even in his fag end of his poetic career he could not forget his craftsmanship and skillness in embellishment and in adding new beauty to his poetry. He addresses the creator or his Jibandevata as a Helmsman and requests him to launch his boat.

"In front lies the ocean of peace.
Launch the boat, Helmsman.
You will be the comrade ever,
Take O take him in your Lap
In the path of the Infinite
Will shine the Dhruva-Tara, etc.

He seeks his wealth inexhaustible in his eternal journey and that is manifested in the striking and perfect image.

Now we come to the world of images created by the modern Bengali poets and place the images of Rabindranath and arrange a comparative study giving rise to the distinction of Rabindranath. In the poem of Budhadev Bose, "Adoration of the Prisoner" we get an application of itinerant images, for example, burnt-out, grudge, a flame of fire, cruel inauspicious, curse, robber, beast, insect, binding, incapable, feeble, pauper, brittle, lameness the tarnished water of mud.

> I am a worn-out nightfarer
> My throne lies in the darkness,
> I am ferocious, terrible bestial.
> -Fallen by curse
> Burnt day; bitter poison; on the very verse
> of the ocean of weeping
> The Time (Mahakala) becomes tinged with the
> passionate kiss of fire;
> Paleness of Death; the silent movement of the goblin;

All these depiction and exploration and true picture; they are clear and consummate portrait no doubt. Attribution of qualities to inanimate objects is sometimes beyond the reach of common readers. As for example in the Poem Amitar Prem (Love of Amita) the poet presents to the readers and connoisseurs a very uncommon experience that is marked with imaginative passion of the poet.

"I am ugly, and abominable, my eyes are sickly; I am ill-shaped, all the stigmas belong to me; all the stains are mine; the paleness of the mind; the mud as bed; like the insects; like the worm; the mean-souled." The poet has created an image of the state, that is widely and squarely marked with all sorts of abominable objects and pictures. The subjective element is here predominant.

Yet one thing is lacking. That is perfect juxtaposition. The ingredients of the image have individual distinction no doubt; but they belong to one single state and poetic experience. They are portraits, revelation and exploration of an idea, thought and view no doubt. But the overall synthesis and synchronization has a dummy show. The individual element, the subjective predominance prevails the image of Budhadeva

Bose. The image of the poet reveals the sense and sensibility of his youth. His youthful feelings and emotion does not take shape in the application of one and single application or image, rather it has given rise to one far-reaching and everchanging images and that creates an environment. The readers may enter into that orbit through the passage of images. The knowledge of the abominableness and hatefulness and commotion due to that are revealed in the image. The emotion. Through the knowledge and experience of the sum-total image we fan arrive at the orbit of feelings and poetic reality.

If we take an example from Rabindranath we see the images that reveal a consummate and striking environment in which images are no single factor, they are contiguous factors and congenial aspects of the total poetic experience and emotive contents.

> Little songs and little things come to
> my mind this morning.
> I seem to be floating on stream in a boat, passing
> by the world on both banks.
> Every little scene gives a sigh and
> Says, "I go".
> World's pleasure and pain, like brother and sister,
> lift their pathetic eyes upon my face
> from afar.

Homely love peeps form her cottage corner to give me her passing glance. With eager eyes I gaze from my heart's window on to the heart of the world. And feel that with all its good and bad it is lovable."

Rabindranath creates an image tinging it with the savour of his feelings and passion. He creates an environment to which the readers may enter through the images. The images of the said poem is crystalised in the feeling and sensibility that is manifested in a symbolic genre:

"I seem to be floating on a stream in a boat, passing by the world on both banks.

Every little scene gives a sigh and says, "I go."

The image of Jibanananda has a string phenomena. He is distinguished permanent in his own environment. Among tis Pots who are distinguished and have a prominence beyond the influence of the amount genius of Rabindranath; Jibanananda is a eminent name.

He creates an image that is marked with libidinal experience of the poet.

> You come straight
> You will come all
> To the shadow and dream
> Inquest of allaying as much desires
> The heart has.
> Forget that pain, obstruction in reality.
> All the time those whom
> Dream- only dream prevails on
> Clasping the hands each other
> Besides the lovely waves,
> In this hazy sky of the dusk;
> And whose desires are born and dies all
> Do not hear the hue and cry
> Of the night and day of this earth.
> Leaving aside the bright path of the day
> Going far to the grey dreamland
> If your get satisfied raising waves
> In the river of desires of heart
> If satisfied in raising waves
> If satisfied in raising the waves
> Do not dare write in inarticulate characters-
> The bidding of your heart.
> (one day) The bright luminous day becomes off
> The span of life comes to an end.
> That old way of the world wipes out its imprint
> But the world of dream remains for ever.

What he impresses much is his way of exploration, genre of putting the vital problem in a very cryptic mode, in a symbolic way. The poet in this poem creates an image of an escapist. He has lifted his feet from the material world and entered into the dreamland. The poet does not prefer the material world to that of dreams. But side by side he holds another portrait. The image of the vague sky of dusk, the lonely waves, the land of the grey dream, the river of desires of the heart are all decorated paintings giving rise to the uncommon feelings and emotion of the readers and connoisseurs.

Samar Sen presents a different kind of images, the savour, fragrance, colour, manifestation of which are different, distinguished from that of other modern poets. We place the images of Rabindranath in the midst of the modern images, and arrange a comparative study. First we cite an example of the poetic images of the modern poet Samar Sen.

> And how much red loin and soft breast,
> and smooth man of parted hair,
> And the smell of Good Flake in the air
> O Great city : The citizen."

In these lines the word 'And' is used frequently giving rise to the association of ideas. The red loin, the soft breast, the parted-haired smooth man and The Great City which creates an association is easily grasped at.

In the poem of Bisnu Day we get the same association, and environment of poetic experience and sensibility.

Taking an example from the Poem 'Tappa-Tumri' (The Special demonstration of the Indian Classical Music)

> In the shore of Barabazar strewn with Pebbles
> The turbulent flow of the mass are fomenting
> And the smoke of the Biri, and of Cigarette, and of the fire place and of the Mill.
> And the spittle of the betel
> And the sigh
> In the scolding of the office master
> (And that) In the hint winked at the tawny eyes of the big boss
> In the tired possibility of the union of the couple
> And in the repentance of the excess of the children."

We face the same association of ideas and circumstances. But what impresses us much is its method of operation and manifestation?

Sukanto Bhattacharjee gives his divergent and different view and outlook than the other idealist poets. His images are tinged with problems that face everyman and woman. His image focuses the materialistic idea of life. His images are resonant with daring courage, optimistic idea, hatred for pilferage and sucking of blood by the rich. His image resembles nithrs that of the poets that preceded him nor that follows him.

"Today I am the guard in the front.
Crossing so many blood-stained paths
Today coming here I stopped suddenly
At the border of my motherland.
From the gray Tunicia to tender Italy
From tender Italy I rushed to revolutionary France
Like the destiny regulated by the stars,
With the unchecked and unvanquished Riphel in hand.
From 'France to the neighbour land Burma too,
Today in my body the well armour
of the soldier
still I own turbulent Riphel.

He creates this image and changes some sot of taste in literature by furnishing the new item in poetic experience. But when he creates the following image

"I fought many a battle for the other.
This time I fight for you and myself.
If you ask what I got fighting so many battle?
The answer to this is:-
In Tunicia I've got conquest
In Italy friendship of the mass-
In France the resolve for liberation
And in troubleless Burma I've got
the urge to return home.
I, as it were, am, the lamp-kindlier
Who in this evening kindles the evening kindles the
lamps in the street.
But poverty for bids him to light in his herusi
In his own house is coagulated
The unbearable darkness."
he touches the very problem
that faces us daily, with his
keen sensibility and acute emotion.

Sudhindranath Dutta is a distinguished figure and name. His poem 'Hell' is an assemblage of images. Through interpretative hurdle of images the reality and truth of his poem will be grasped. His image is like this:

"In the darkness no trace is found.
The night is long:
Like the age-old harlots
Who, On the path of unaccessible place of pilgrimage
Being companionless fell on sleep
An if they are beside the unknown hospitality
In rigid practice."

The poet arrests our insight into the very core of his poetic experience. He causes us understand how he comprehends the poetic Reality or Truth through the cluster of images. We have some conception of the Hell. But it is half-truth, when we come to know:

"The formless desire and smile,
The incorporeal shame and discontent,
Futile unrealizable desire and pride, abortive malice
Whispers together stealthily."

We are faced with that all these images are distinguished and striking no doubt; they are the very broadway leading to the poetic imagination. The modern poetic outlook and their comprehensive grip of life and its ideal are all manifested through the poetic image is deemed as touchstone by means of which poetic genius is judged; it may be said in this way also that the poetic genius depends solely on the poetic image, the only modus operandi of expression or demonstration.

The different movement in poetry is held and comprehended through poetic images. If we analyse the different movements and have comparative study i.e. of the romantic revival to modern movement of classical movement to romantic, we see their characteristic, their colour, their fragrance, and their distinction depends solely on the striking and consummate images.

The early Romantics were in search of a faith to revive or replace the Christianity which for Pope was an accepted social fact, for Cowper a deep personal resonance. This search extended their field of subject-matter because it carried their imaginations farther into the world of nature than their predecessors had needed to explore, farther also into the human heart. Pope's the proper study of mankind is Man' became for Wordsworth.

Not chaos, not
The darkest Pit of lowest Ere bus
Nor autht of blinder vacancy, scooped out
By help of dream, can breed such fear and awe
As fall upon us when we look
Into our Minds, into the Mind of Man,
My haunt, and the main region of my song.

These lines are indeed the enunciation of modern poetry. Whatever be the trend and thought in modern poetry, it is striking and bears the testimony of aesthetic experience of the poet and arrests our mind because of the audacious, consummate, striking images that come to the readers and connoisseurs with the emotional apprehension of thought, feelings and sensibility for the poet.

Rabindranath in this sense, is a master-artist. Hie poetic theory or reality is distinguished and more perfect than the poet's that preceeded him and the poets who followed him. This perfectness and consummateness depends solely and widely on the striking perfect and audacious images and that is market with congruousness and integrity.

6

The Co-relation between the Analytical Estimate of the Poetic Image and the Art of Criticism

In the previous chapters we have discussed the nature and radical features of poetry alongwith other ingredients and come to the conclusion making our melody tuned up to that of poet-critic T.S. Eliot that a poetry is not a turning loose of emotion, but an escape from personality. "We also taking the same coin in our hand have propounded that poetry cannot emanate from the dumping ground of emotion. But it is mistaken to interpret that emotion is untouchable in the sphere of criticism or evaluation of poetry. Rather emotion along with intellect, reason, restraint and above all poetic sensibility is of absolute necessity.

In this chapter we shall discuss the co-relation and the reciprocal dealings between poetic image and art of criticism. We have discussed vividly and widely the function and art of poetic image. Now, first, we shall take stock-position of criticisms and see distinguished existence of it placing the same by the side of the glamorous and majestic form of the poetic image. So, we are quoting the dictum of Herbert Read so that we perceive the nature and role of criticism. "I believe that criticism must concern itself, not only with the work or art in itself, but also with the process of writing, and with the writer's state of mind when inspired—that is to say, critic must concern himself, not only with the finished work of art, but also with the workman, his mental activity and his tools!"

We shall define criticism and point to the varied and expanded world of criticism. Criticism is not mere appreciation of work or sheer evaluation of an art. The good and creative criticism bears the testimony of skillness wherein appreciation and review are based on facts and reason. It is widely marked with intellectual discipline. There is no scope or room for the swelling of baseless outburst of passion in good and consummate criticism. The spontaneous appreciation as a bearing on criticism no doubt, but intellectual appreciation of works differs from the same widely and squarely. Why, this difference and distinction? Creation may be spontaneous and bears the marks of inborn qualities. These identities may not attract the readers, rather has different and divergent appeal to the different readers. So, it is of absolute pity to have a general and perfect genre of appreciation of the works of the writers, so that one general and perfect genre of appreciation, which does not depend on personal likings and evaluation rather on the consciousness of multitude and intellectual discipline will be formed. As criticism is a great skilful creative art, so its art, greatness, and appreciative perceptibility largely depend on its own modus operandi, on its own genre.

Perfect criticism is largely related to the linguistics and history of language. Language is the conveyance of literature and criticism. So, the first and foremost task of the critic is to take stock of the words and to look deep into their core of the expression. is the output of deep and keen appreciation. Language is always flowing. It sees divergent detours, changes. It is given new blood in the shape of new words. Insipid words die away. All these divergences and changes have mark and bearing on the literature.

2

Now, we give conventional definition of criticism. T.S. Eliot opines 'the commentation of works of art by means of written words'. His another comment is this that 'criticism must always profess an end in view, which roughly speaking, appears to be the elucidation of works of art and the correction of taste." Arnold states that (criticism) is a disinterested endeavour to learn and propagate the best that is known and thought in the world." He states further:

"Its business is, simply to know the best that is known and thought in the world, and by in its turn making this known, to create a current of true and fresh ideas." "Criticism, as I understand it, is the endeavour to discriminate between experience and to evaluate them", it is the comment of Richards.

Henry Lewis Menken states that" The function of a genuine critic of the arts is to provoke a reaction between the work of art and the spectator, the spectator, untutored stands unmoved; he sees the work of art, but it fails to make any intellegible impression on him; if he were spontaneously sensitive to it, there would be no need for criticism."

Ezra Pound gives his distinguished money to it. "Excernment- the general ordering and weeding art of what was actually been performed, the ordering of knowledge so that the next man (or generation) can most readily find the live part of it, and waste the least possible time among obsolete issues."

According to Dr. Lewis "The critic's aim is first, to realize as sensitively and completely as possible this or that which claims his attention and certain valuing is implicit in the realizing. A philosophic training might possible, ideally would make a critic surer and more penetrating in the perception of significance and relation and in judgement of value. The business of the literary critic is to attain a peculiar completeness of response and to observe a peculiarly strict relevance in developing his response into commentary; he must be on guard against abstracting improperly from what is in front of him and against any premature or irrelevant generalising.

3

From the above commentaries one thing becomes obvious that there is a coherent similarity between the analytical study of the image along with the estimate of the poetic image, and the harvest of the genuine criticism. We know, 'The function of a genuine critic of the arts is to provoke a reaction between the work of art and the spectator; the spectator, untutored, stands unmoved; he sees the work of art, but it fails to make any intelligible impression on him; if he were spontaneously sensitive to it, there would be no need for criticism!

Then we see that the critic brings into our notice the poetic experience, his passion, his imaginative feelings and even to the unfathomable source lying in the mind of the poet, his reaction on the main trends of the contemporary age and culture. The main function of the critic is to take a comprehensive stock of the harvest of the poet and to bring the readers in to the warehouse. So, it is clear to us that it is identical with the analytical estimate of the poetic image. The image manifests the poetic feelings, his sensibility, his imaginative passion, his mode of thinking, his peculiar genre of expression and his modus operandi, diction, rhythm, lilt and melody. The contents of the poetic image are largely and squarely similar to the purport of the poem. If we analyse an image, if we see its stock piecemeal, if we assort the contents in clear and meticulous parts and division, we are confronted with the aforesaid ingredients of the poem. The analytical estimate of the poetic image draws us near, very near to what the critic seeks to give to the readers, to what he wants to dip his insight into the poet's own emotional contents, his sensitive subjects, and his created environment and atmosphere. Here, to make our point and subject clear we are quoting a distinguished commentary on Burns and on his poems—

"He wrote fresh songs to old airs very often starting from an existent chorus, as in 'Duncan Gray' from a chorus in Herd's manuscript. It is still difficult to say of many of Burn's songs that this is entirely Burns's work.

Taking it then as it stands what is the peculiar quality, the special excellence of Burn's but with a difference. In the John recast by Shakespeare the old play to Shakespeare, but with a difference. In the recast by Shakespeare the old play say the troublesome reign of king practically disappears. All that is dramatic and poetic is due to Shakespeare. It is not quite so with Burns's song. The old note of folk-song is audible through the new song, is indeed a quality—its simplicity, for example humour, pathos—which the poet is fain to preserve. He does not always succeed, for Burns too at times succumbs to the taste of the day for elegance and decoration. Burns's wandering willice has not the perfect, the poignant simplicity of the original as preserved by Herd. Let us cite the original, as it will serve a double purpose:

Here awa, there awa, hand awa willice,
Here awa, there awa, hand awa hame;
Long have I sought thee, dear
Have I brought thee.
Now I have gotten my Willice again
Thro' the long muir I have followed my Willice,
Thro' the long muir I have followed him home
Whate'er betide us, nought shall divide us;
Love now rewards all my sorrow and pain.
Here awa, there awa, hand awa hame...
Come love, believe me, nothing can grieeve me
Like thing pleases while's at hame.

There is the essential simplicity of the folk-song whether its theme be sentiment or bawdry. The poet goes straight to the heart of the matter with sentiment or bawdry. The poet goes straight to the heart of the matter with no embroidery, metaphysical or decorative. Burns adds a little of both:

Come to my bosom, my aim only dearie
And tell me thou bright me my Willice the same.

Quoted from the Book "A critical History of English Poetry.", Hurbert Grierson and J.C. Smith.

It is clear that the art of criticism is to a greater extent related to the analytical estimate of the poetic image.

Now our task is to go through the different trends of criticism and analyse it vividly to have a clear view of it and to show its relation to the Estimation of poetic image.

4

Schlegel attempts to describe what is needed in good criticism.

"(1) a kind of geography of a world of art;

(2) a spiritual and aesthetic architectories of the work, its nature, its tone, and finally

(3) its psychological genesis, its motivation by laws and conditions of human nature."

He speaks constantly of the whole: the spirit, the tone, the general impression. Mostly he thinks of criticism as a 'reconstructive' process. The critic must' reconstruct, perceive, and characterize the more subtle peculiarities of a whole..... one can say that one has understood a work and a mind only if one can reconstruct its course and structure. This profound understanding, if expressed in definite words, is called characterization and is the actual business and inner essence of criticism."—*A History of Modern Criticism*, Rene' Wellek.

Side by side we study the function and form of poetic image.

"In its simplest terms, it is a picture made out of words. An epithet, a metaphor, a simile may create an image; or an image may be presented to us in a phrase or passage on the face of it purely descriptive, but everything to our imagination something more than the accurate reflection of an external reality. Every poetic image, therefore, is to some degree metaphorical. It looks out from a mirror in which life perceives not so much its face as some truth about its face.....The commonest type of image is a visual one, and many more images which may seem un-sensuous, have still in fact some faint visual association adhering to them. But obviously an image may derive from and appeal to other senses then that of sight, Clare appeals to hearing as well as sight when he clarifies the events.

"Cracking their jarring melancholy cry
Through the long journey of the cheerless sky.
Jonson appeals to our sense of touch in:
"Have you felt the wool of bearer
Or Swan's down ever?"

Tennyson to the senses of smell and hearing in:

"And many a rose- carnation feed
With summer spice the humming air."

Yet each of the last two images holds a certain visual significance for us beneath its evocation of the feeling or sound or smell of things. It can be argued, I think, that every image-even the most purely emotional or intellectual one- has some trace of the sensuous in it.

> Finish, good lady, the bright day is done
> And we are for the dark.

That is a great cry and climax of emotion: but although it presents no picture to the eye, it speaks in the language of sight

Have we, then, perfected the definition if we say that the poetic image is a acute in words touched with some sensuous quality?—*The Poetic Image,* C. Day Lewis.

So it is obvious from the above statement of facts and definition that the study of image, or analytical estimate of the poetic image reveals the very function of criticism. In the analytical study of images we look into the poetic emotion, poetic sensibility, his experience, imaginative passion. The poet creates an image; rather, it may be said, he presents an image or a portrait in which lies his distinction, his verbiage, selection of words, his passion, and idea etc, so, it is clear to us that by study of poetic image we reach the poet's own worlds, his mental capability, his peculiar sensibility etc. Now, we may opine or come to the conclusion that there is a close affinity or reciprocal relation between the analytical study of poetic image, and function and art of criticism.

Now, we give a meticulous and detailed description of both the studies.

"The Literary criticism of William Wordsworth is usually considered the manifesto of the English romantic movement, the signal for the break with the age of neoclassicism. All the emphasis is out on Wordsworth's rejection of the 18th century diction, on his identification of the 'language of prose." With that of metrical composition and of the language of poetry with the language spoken by the 'middle and lower classes of society'. This plea for a kind of magnetism- is seen as combined with' emotionalism', the view that poetry is Wordsworth's famous phrase is the spontaneous overflow of powerful feelings:"

These ideas do appear in wordsworth's theory and they proved historically most important, but if we examine the whole range of Wordsworth's literary criticism- prefaces of 1800, and 1815, the Appendix of 1802 the supplementary Essay of 1815, the three essays upon epitaphs and the correspondence—we must come to the conclusion that Wordsworth modified these ideas considerably and that they actually need reinterpretation as elements of a inherent body of thought with very different assumptions. The disapproval of poetic diction, the idea of imitating rustic speech, the concept of poetry as the overflow of feelings do not particularly appeal to our time and cannot be reconciled with a rational concept of literary theory.

Another dictum is that "Poetry to Wordswoerth is primarily a manipulation of human feelings". A great poet ought to rectify men's feelings, to give permanent, in short, more consonant to nature, that is the external nature, and permanent, in short, more consonant to nature., that is the external nature, and the great moving spirit of things." Quoted from *A History of Modern Criticism*.

Here we see that critic evaluates the poetic feelings, his sensibilities, his emotive contents. The readers cannot make out the implication of poetry. They are often unaware of the poetic aesthetic sense. The critics help them in understanding and realizing the poetic reality, his (poet's) contents, his reaction to contemporary trends that is manifested in his creation. The readers fail to enter his snout into that. So, it is obvious that the function of the critic is to present to the readers a clear view of the works and provoke the emotion in the mind of the readers, that lies in the mind of the poet or author; and that lies in his creation sometimes in symbolic form, sometimes in a cryptic shape.

So, it is vividly clear to us that analytical estimate of the image is to a greater extent similar to the aim and function of the Art of criticism, we cite an example:

> The sea of faith
> Was once, too, at the full and round
> Earth's shore
> Lay like the folds of a bright girdle furl'd
> But now I only hear

Its melancholy, long with drawing roar
Retreating to the breath
Of the night-wind down the vast edges drear.
And naked shingles of the world."

The language there is romantic. The romantic image is a mode of exploring reality, by which the poet is in effect asking imagery to reveal to him the meaning of his own experience. The poet creates an image to reveal to him the meaning of his own experience. The poet crates an image of the sea of faith that lay like to folds of a bright girdle furl'd and that at present it causes the poet hear its melancholy, long, withdrawing roar, retreating to the breath

Of the night-wind down the vast edges....
And naked shingles of the world.

If we sit for studying the said image or analyse it vividly and meticulously, we receive the cornet of poetic sensibility the poetic experience and emotive contents, the poet's reaction to the contemporary age, his poetic response to the same. What the critic does is to comprehend the poetic's implication of his poetic truth, his peculiar sensibility, and his distinction from his previous and contemporary one and he gives a wide and comprehensive panorama of poetic feelings and emotion of his contemporary and preceding ages.

What Coleridge speaks of this problem we are to see?

"Poetry must be passion, Coleridge draws, not always clearly, a distinction between a 'state of excitement expressed immediately and crudely and the role of excitement in stimulating the two main techniques of poetry, figurative language and metre on this point Coleridge, curiously enough. "Strong passions command figurative language".

"Figures of speech are originally the off-spring of passion." Strong passion "has a language more measured than is employed in common speaking". Metre itself implies passion, Coleridge even speaks of "nature of the poet" alluded to the passionate speech of distressed mothers, and uses, Deborah's song as an example of lyrical; repetitions and sublime tautology. On occasions he seems to accept the historical scheme of primitivism: he reflects on "the ever-increasing sameness of human life" which has led to the decay of strong emotions and the disuse of forceful language."

He gives a historical dictum that "Passion was the true parent of every word in existence in every languages, and hence the "elder languages are fitter for poetry." Here one iota is missing i.e. prior to passion there was something. Primitive people first saw the objects and then expressed their passion, their feelings, in between them some energy had been spent to feel the objects and express their feelings. That is labour power. Following it there grew consciousness.

"But Coleridge tried to define poetry with very traditional terminology: as pleasure for the reader and passion in the author during composition. But he also wanted to differentiate between poetry and verse and thus to recognize poetry outside of metrical compositions. He argues that there is poetry of the highest kind without meter, and he quoted Plato, Jeremy Taylor, Burnet, and Isaiah as examples."—*Ibid.*

From the above commentary it is quite natural to come to the conclusion that what Coleridge draws as a definition of poetry or the fundamental nomenclature of poetic theory is to a greater extent identical with the analytical approach to the poetic image. Coleridge pays his great head to the poetic passion, feelings and sensibility. While analyzing the poetic image we also have to lay much stress on the predominating factor of images. Critic gives a guideline, he gives a figurative and descriptive acquaintance of the poet and his poetry; he also goes upto the very source of imaginative faculty. But one who sits for analysing the pattern of images its form, shape, of a critic, but his function, the aim of analytical approach is different from the art and function of criticism.

The critic, as it has been said already, gives a wide and farflung guideline. He dives headlong into the unfathomable depth of his passion and poetic experience. By the image we are also acquainted with the poetic passion, his experience, his mode of expression, his cravings and idea. But it is not so far-flung. It is engaged with an estimate only; it gives no guideline. It reveals the poetic distinction, his strikingness, his universality. It is the quality and qualification of the poet. It differs from poet to poet, as the paintings of Raphel differs from that of Leonardo de Vinci. But it is obvious that through the painting of the artist we come to know the peculiar genre of expression, his consciousness, his peculiar faculty, his creative imagination. All these qualities are to be known from the peculiar way of his adornation, his embellishment. This is true to the image also. Image is the path leading to imagination. It is an expression itself.

"Lamb's formal reviews, such as that of Wordsworth's Excursion and of Keats's Lamia volume, are largely strings of extracts with pronouncements of preferences. The much admired review of Keats, which selects fine passages from a poet then quite unrecognized, still comes to the false conclusion that Isabella is better than Lamia, The Eve of St. Agnes and the Odeson the ground that "an ounce of feeling is worth a pound of fancy", this and many other judgements show Lamb's emotional romanticism, the view that passion is "the all in all in poetry". Lamb, of course, wanted to point out fine passage and convey his own enthusiasm to his readers. He knew that he was no theorist and not even a regular critic; with his usual modesty he speaks of his "inability of reviewing, of giving account of a book in any methodical way". "I can vehemently applaud, or perversely stickler, at parts: but I can to grasp at a whole." At the same time he recognized the deficiencies of all selections, all snippets: "how beggarly and how bold even Shakespeare's princely pieces look when thus violently divorced from connection or circumstances......... Everything in heaven, and earth, in man and in story, in books and in fancy, acts by confederacy, by juxtaposition, by circumstances and place'. Lamb also understood Wordsworth's and Coleridge's theory of the imagination of which he said (earlier than any of their extensive discussion is in print) that it "draws all things into one.... Makes things animate and inanimate, brings with their attributes, subjects and their accessories, take one colour, and serve to one effect.

Some of Lamb's 'Obiter dicta', scattered over the essays and letters, may seem to us mistaken, but his dislike of Shelley and Byron, his description of Goethe's Faust as "a disagreeable canting tale of seduction", his approval of Wordsworth's opinion about the dullness of Voltaire's Candida cannot surprise if we know the political and social context. Nevertheless we must agree with him when he praises the

Ancient Mariner or chides Wordsworth for his overt didacticism and for" continually putting a sing post up to show where you art to feel. Lamb's most" creative "criticism is his most indirect. His pastiches and imitations of Burton and Sir Thomas Browne's "Beautiful obliquities" show that he had a true feeling for their style even though he was unwilling or unable to define or analyse it intellectually".—*A History of Modern Criticism*.

Lamb conveys his romantic emotionalism, and his enthusiasm to the readers and connoisseurs that passion" is the all in all in poetry". That is to say, the critic first grasps at the very feelings and passion of the poet. When common readers fail to understand. The critic, who has comprehensive knowledge of the preceding tradition of the poetry and who knows the contemporary trends has dominated the poets, conveys his reaction, his emotional impression to the readers.

Here, we give another picture seen from the analytical approach research of the images. "Mr. Auden's images are often thus symbolic, just as his human figures, like the typed in a Morality Play, crude, yet vivacious and forceful. Above all, they are modern. In spite of (or perhaps because of) his genuine historical sense, this poet is positively obsessed by the contemporary sense, the modern predicament in its variations. And reading his work, we realize how new sense-data-engines, aeroplanes, factories, and so on-are only one source of material for novel images: these are also new ideas, without which indeed new sense data may prove intractable to the poet." —*The Poetic Image,* C.D. Lewis

It is obvious that analytical study of the images gives to the readers and connoisseurs a comprehensive knowledge of the poet and his poetry, his distinction from other poets and his proper place in the literatures. The critic analyses the works of the poet, dramatist, novelist etc, clearly and meticulously, judges it from the traditional point of view, placing on the contemporary context and conveys his (critic's) impression, his enthusiasm. He judges the work in its full significance, in its consummate form. Thus is the aim and function of the literary criticism. But what does the image give up? Prior to the answer of this question we are quoting A.C. Bradly who helps us in this regard.

"If a poem is to be anything like a great it must, in one sense be concerned with the present. Whatever its subject may be it must express something living in the mind from which it comes and the mind to which it goes. Wherever its body is, its soul must be here and now."

What is something living in the mind from which it comes and the mid to which it goes is manifested and painted in the living and consummate image. If the said image is reviewed and commented; and poet's emotion and sensibility is touched; if the readers are informed of the nature of the same, then a critical and artistic work on the image is to be made. It is nearly the same function as of the critic. We feel a close affinity between the art of literary criticism and the analytical study of the image.

In the history of criticism Keats is distinguished name.

"The best known and most striking passages in Keats' letters are those in the impersonality, the "negative capability" means to Keats something quite specific, the capability of "being in uncertainties, mysterious doubts, without any irritable reaching after fact and reason". By this standard the poet (and Keats always has Shakespeare as a model for himself in mind) should not be committed, should not be like Coleridge, a philosopher" incapable of remaining content with half knowledge." Negative capability is thus a phrase which is not the same as the intellectual or the didactic. Keats condemns the variety didactic many times. "We hate", we do not want to be bullied into a certain philosophy. Shelley seems to Keats too much of a propagandist in verse: in the only letter he wrote him he advised him to "curb his magnanimity" and the mire of an artist and "to load every rift of his subject with one. "But this recognition of the special workings of poetry does not mean the later 19th century aestheticism, the view that the poet is a maker of merely beautiful and useless decorative things. It means that Keats "never wrote a single line of poetry with the least shadow of public thought, "that poetry should come (as Keats felt that it did to him in his best moments) as "naturally as the leaves of a tree."

The "genius of poetry must work out its own salvation in a man: it cannot be matured by law and precept, but by sensation and watchfulness in itself. "That which is creative must create itself." Thus poetry is to Keats mainly self-expression and an expression of feeling rather than of ideas or moral precepts."—*A History of Modern Criticism.*

He does not want to say the last word in poetry. The readers and connoisseurs are there to grasp the meaning and impression emanating from his poetry. Keats, speaking of the reader of poetry, said, that "The rise, the progress, the setting of imagery should like the due fame natural to him-shine over him and set soberly although in magnificence, leaving him in luxury of twilight."

We should agree that images be they never so surprising at first sight, should finally leave the reader with the impression that they are the natural language of their theme. But this does not imply they will have come easily, or naturally to the poet. Keats's corrections on the opening lines of Hyperion are very much to the point here; and, though they have become a locus classical of criticism, they will bear examination once again. Here is the final version:

> Deep in the shady sadness of a vale
> Far-sunken from the healthy breath of morn,
> Far from the fiery noon, and eve's quiet as a stone,
> Still as the silence round about his hair
> Forest on forest hung about his head
> Like cloud on could. No stir of air was there
> Not so much life as on a summer's day
> Robs not one light seed form the feather'd grass
> But where the dead leaf full,
> there dud it rest.

The readers are given a consummate picture, an image of "Shady Sadness". The poet does not haunt the readers with an epitaph of certitude or certainty, he does not tease their judgement. Rather he gives all the materials, his poetic experience and poetic reality to be seen and to be appreciated by the readers and connoisseurs. So, it is obvious that the critic-Keats's criticism gives the same panorama as the analytical approach of the image. What, according to Keats, is the inspiration of poetry or what kind of passion lies in the poetry?

"The truth is that" the yearing passion for the beautiful, "which was Keats, as he himself truly says, the master-passion, is not a passion of the sensuous or sentimental man, is not a passion of the sensuous or sentimental poet. It is an intellectual and spiritual passion. It is "connected and made one". As Keats declares that in his case it was, "with the ambition of the intellect". "It is", as he again says, "the mighty abstract idea of beauty in all things." And in his last days Keats wrote: "If I should die, I have left no immortal work behind me nothing to make my friends proud of my memory; but I have loved the principle of beauty in all things, and if I had had time I would have made myself remembered. "He has made himself remembered, and remembered as no merely sensuous poet could be; and he had done it by having "loved the principle of beauty in all things."—*Essays in Criticism*-John Keats- M. Arnold:

If we analyse his poems and sonnets we will feel his poetic experience, his poetic truth and guiding principle that it is not sensuous passion that dominates his poetry, it is not loose emotions and sentiments passion and sentiment that are crystalised in his creation of image.

> "Beauty is truth, truth beauty, that is all
> Ye know on earth, and all ye need to know".

The image of Beauty and image of Truth is identical and this is the only principle of this world to know. So, it is clear to us that the Critic-Keats's dictum and criticism creates nearly the same figure and picture as created by the poet Keats.

"The most original insights of the "Defence of Poetry" are historical. In Shelley the platonic vision is at the centre of argument. It is asserted without misgivings, eloquently, even stridently. Shelley draws from Plato, directly or indirectly, the view of poetry as the creative principle in man. Poets are "not only the authors of language and of music, of the dance, and architecture, and statuary, and painting; they are the institutors of laws, "the teachers of religion. "The poets are "men of the most spotless virtue, the most consummate prudence, the most fortunate of men." Poets are also "philosophers of the very loftiest power", and poetry is" the centre and circumference of knowledge", that which comprehends all science." The historical rose of poetry is exalted to that of the primary civilizing factor in the dim past, in the present age, and in the future. In the concluding words of the Defence of poetry, "poets are the unacknowledged legislators of the world"—*Ibid*.

According to Shelley, "a great poem is a fountain for ever overflowing with the waters of wisdom and delight; and after one person and one age has exhausted all its divine affluence which their peculiar relations enable them to share, another and yet another succeeds and new relations are over developed, the source of an unforeseen and an unconceived delight."—*A History of Modern Criticism,* Rene Wellek

It would not be out of track if we cite here an example and look into the poetic experience and the profile of the poetic image

The Moon

I

And, like a dying lady lean and pale
Who totters forth, wrapped in a gaudy veil,
Out of her chamber, led by the in sane
And feeble wanderings of her fading brain
The moon arose up in the musky east
A white and shapeless mass.

II

Art thou pale for weariness
of climbing heaven and gazing on the earth
wandering companionless
Among the stars that have as different birth
And ever changing, a joyless eye
That finds no object worth its constancy?

What does it present? The poet gives this reaction having seen the Moon, her beauty and shape. If he paints her portrait as common man is habituated to see it, nothing strikes to mark some demarcation between the common man and the poet. He reacts like this:

"Like a dying lady lean and pale
Who totters forth, wrapp'd in a gaudy veil.

The moon is attributed to first with human qualities, some animate feelings, secondly with some peculiar and uncommon feelings. If she would resemble a beautiful sweet sixteen if she would appear having exquisite forms and colours, the moon could not strike some much, impress so much as she has done being like a 'dying lady lean and pale'. So, we can opine that this intellectual attribution of emotion and imaginative passion make this poem more beautiful and consummate than that which is commonly built whatever be its purport and truth crept there. So, it is obvious that the poet created an image of the Moon that is tinged and marked leanness, feebleness. The poet paints the portrait of the Moon attributing her with the qualities of a dying lady lean and pale who totters forth, wrapp'd in a gauzy veil; the Moon does not appear with all her brightness and luminosity. Rather the moon appears with the 'feeble wanderings of her fading brain! It is striking and novel; it bears the mark of originality and the vector of universality. Because it gives a new and a novel experience on the one hand, and it depicts the true profile of the Moon along-with some attributory and complimentary qualities and acumen, so that readers of different tastes are likings and thronged together to imbibe its savour and be satisfied.

This evaluation emanates from the analytical approach of the image. What is the critic's dictum or judgement? "a great poem is a foundation for ever overflowing with the waters of wisdom and delight."

The analytical approach of the image gives us the merely the same picture. The poet-critic Shelley defines poetry and points to its originality and fundamental qualities of poetry. Thus critic stated further that, ... after one person and one age has exhausted all its divine influence which their peculiar relations enable them to share an unforeseen and unconceived delight."

The critic pinpoints on the ever developing qualities of the poem.

So, the literary criticism is to a great extent related to the analytical approach or analytical estimate of the poetic image.

5

Now, we come to the final portion of evaluating images, we have seen the close relationship between the function of criticism and the analytical approach and estimate of the images although they have got their different way of approach, dealings and estimate.

Here we shall analyse the dictum and criticism of the poet-critic Rabindranath and see a close propinquity between the world of images and that of art of criticism.

Prior to this we quote some jottings regarding the analysis of the poem.

"The qualification of a good critic are three. He must be an adept at experiencing, without eccentricities, the state of mind relevant to the work of art he is judging. Secondly, he must be able to distinguish experiences from one another as regards their less superficial features. Thirdly, he must be a sound judge of values.

Upon all these matters psychology even in its present conjectural state, has a direct bearing. The critic is, throughout, judging of experience, of state of in but too often he is needlessly ignorant of the general psychological form of the experiences with which he is concerned. He has no clear ideas as to the elements present or as to their relative importance. Thus, an outline or scheme of the mental events which make up the experience of" looking at" a picture or' reading' a poem, can be of great assistance. At the very least an understanding of the probable structures of these experiences can remove certain misconceptions which tend to make the opinions of individuals of less service to their individuals that need be.

Two instances will show this.

There are certain broad features in which all agree a poem of Swinburne is unlike a poem of Hardy. The use of words by the poets is different. Their methods are dissimilar and the proper approach for a reader correspondingly. An attempt to read them in the same way, is unfair to one of the poets to both and leads inevitably to defects in criticism which a little reflection would remove. It is absurd to read Pope as though he were Shelley, but the essential difference cannot be clearly marked out unless such an outline of the general form of a poetic experience, as is here attempted has been provided. The psychological means employed by these poets are demonstrably different. Whether the effects are also dissimilar is a further question for which the same kind of analysis is equally required."

From the above analysis we come to know the distinction between the poets. The critic tries to define it; he wants to reveal the source, the outlet, the stream and overall phenomena of the mental and psychological environment of the poet. He penetrates into the core of the poetic heart and poetic experiences. He manifests the peculiar method of expression and modus operandi. In the analytical approach of the image we face the same fashion and the same outlook. When we take the stock of the poetic images, we try to fish out the poetic experiences, the distinguished experiences from one another and poetic values crept in the images.

Now, we come to the world of criticism of Rabindranath where we shall see that he is a distinguished master artist, and his interpretation reveals new outlook and novel idea. He states that criticism is tinged with emotion of worship and the critic is the worshipper-priest. Interpretation of facts, subject is these but the manifestation of emotive-contents dominate the total atmosphere and environment of criticism. He lays much stress and emphasis on the keenness of feelings and its depth and spontaneity of emotion on the one hand and on the other he is much known for his skill hand and acumen in creative criticism. Still so, he establishes greatest importance of intelligence and cognition in the sphere of criticism. According to him criticism is not a attributed or ascribed conception. There is a close and deep relationship and affinity between work of literature, its mode of expression and art of criticism. The following dictum is of much importance and consistence to this context.

"To know a work of literature is to know the soul of the man who created it, and who created it in order that his soul should be known." And "the function of criticism is primarily the function of literature itself, to provide a means of self-expression for the critic."

Middleton Murry rightly asserts:

The principles and rudiments that are kept radiant in his critical essays' old Literature, Modern Literature and Folk Literature are not at all the characteristics of the common literary criticism. Rabindranath did not pave the same way that bears testimony of the foot prints of the previous critics. His criticism is interpretative; it is not aimed at the finding fault with the works or giving any final verdict to it. It follows the works with the mind of worship and emotion of adoration. The aim of criticism, according to Ranbindranath cannot culminate with the interpretation only, but with provocation of feelings and passion in the minds of the readers, and with the giving clear picture of the works art and its creator. If it would be the fact, then the art of criticism, the work of criticism will end with or vanish with the exit of the literary works. So, we see that criticism holds the character of the parasite. It is not fully correct. The poetics of Aristotle, the Natya Sastra of Bharata still attracts the minds of the readers and connoisseurs by the principle of literary criticism. So, it is proved that criticism has a fundamental and rudimental aspects that are independent of the works of literature. Rabindranath in his critical essays on Sakuntala, Kumar Sambhava, the portrait of Kadambari follows the greatest literary artist Kalidasa, but never imitated him, never ended his work with appraisal and adoration only. He never appeared before the greatest play-write with bended knees. He interprets in a new creative way. His criticism forsakes the old vesture and costume and appears before us as a new and novel creation.

In the essay "Meghduta" Rabindranath presents to us a creation independent of the original Meghduta. In the form it is not formal interpretation.

We come to the fag end of our thesis. We are engaged here to hold a comparative study of the art of criticism and analytical estimate of the poetic images Rabindranath in his art of criticism gives us a new world, wherein we see critical interpretation not always in the expression of the pursuance of the original work. His view of criticism differs from that of the previous one. Now we will see wherein the two ends meet—one end of criticism and another of analytical approach of the poetic images.

We have traversed, a long way to see the development of images. Here we see a close and deep relationship and affinity between the critical approach of the poetic images and art of criticism, and specially in the art of criticism of Rabindranath and his poetic images.

Now, we take only one poem of Rabindranath and show his creative and striking images, and hold a analytical estimate of the said image. We therefore will see how the analytical estimate comes very near to the domain of literary criticism.

We are quoting the poem "To the Sea" one of the masterpieces of Rabindranath and see its striking and consummate images.

> O primal Mother surging without rest
> Earth, your child, clutching to your rest
> On weaves of hopes and fears forever cast,
> In solemn tones communing with the vast,
> Vigilant, you watch with sleepless eyes,
> While from your inmost heart rapt
> prayers arise
> And to the calm, heavens without surcease
> you raise
> Your deep resounding voice in songs of praise
> Her silence deep, her sparkling radiant speech
> Her tears, how copious split upon the beach,
> Till her swollen paps, too full of milk she rushes,
> And in her arms the frightened earth she crushes,
> Earth trembles caught in her tremendous grasp,
> Trying to be free from her titanic clasp
> Mad mother with love insatiable a-thirst
> That would her very life -strings snap and burst,
> Next moment guiltily she likes quite still
> Beside the beach, silent gazing her fill
> The tranquil dawn upon her casts her light
> Evening friendly passes into night
> A sharp pang of repentance the heart of ocean tears
> Deeply she groans, might her moaning hearts.

Rabindranath through the images of the sea shows us a consummate portrait of a young, affectionate mother, who is always anxious about her child, who watches with sleepless eyes for her child, only child, the earth, and who is primal Mother of the creatures. His image makes us confronted with the emotive contents and attributed motherly affection, love of inanimate objects. We feel the poetic outlook, his keen sensibility and feelings. His images are so lively and radiant that we, the readers feel identified with the poetic feeling and sensibility and see through our eyes the primal Mother surging without rest clutching her child to her breast on waves of hopes and fears forever last in solemn tones communing with the vast being vigilant watches with sleepless eyes, and feel the very feeling and emotions of the poet:

> Child of your earth I sit upon your strand
> Listening to your music, majestic grand
> Me seems your worlds I' understand your mood
> As by signs the words of the dumb are understood
> Me seems my surging blood in its ebb and flow
> The feeling of your music pure must know.
> When formless, one wit the embryonic earth
> In your vast womb I stayed without a birth
> That beat eternal enwombed can still impart
> Its music in each vein felt ever more
> As with lowered eyes I sit upon yours shore
> That ancient music echoed earth to sky
> From age to age in vacuum high

When the poet presents the aforesaid immortal images we see just before our eyes the portrait of Mother tinged with halo of light, radiant with motherly affection and brightness, gayful with grand and majestic passion and lofty with deep eager love.

> O primal Mother, unfathomed, deep your
> heart imparts
> To your child some word of comfort
> Words tender with love and cool as July rain
> Your pure maternal hand on her brow insane
> With fevered thought, o lay and in rhythmic glow
> Kiss her again and again bending low.
> And say, my child, peace, deep peace in there
> Hush they anxious thought in sleep divine.

If we analyse the images of the aforesaid poem, we get a comprehensive stock of poetic thought, idea, feelings principles, outlook and his distinction from other poets, his keen and sharp-edged sensibility and above all, his experiences.

The whole poem is an image itself. The tendency of a purer poetry, we are discussing, is to substitute images (though by no means always sensuous images) for the abstract idea, that is for the statement of this idea in poetic but non-pictorial terms. As a result, the reader sees nothing but a succession of pictures, cannot see the theme behind them: and the more personal and arbitrary these images are, the less the whole picture, the poem itself has reference to general human experience, for the poet has discarded those non-pictorial passages by which the images could be related to and a theme made explicit.

Another dictum is to be comprehended in this connection.

"Verses are not as people imagine simply feelings (we have these seen enough): they are experiences. In order to write a single verse, one must see many cities, and men and things; one must get to know animals and the flight of birds and the gestures that the little flowers make when they open out to the morning. One must be able to return in thought to roads in unknown regions, to unexpected encounters, and to partings that had been long foreseen; to days of childhood that are still indistinct, and to parents whom one hand to hurt when they sought to give one same pleasure which one did not understand. There must be memories of many nights of love, each one unlike the others, of the screams of women in labour, and of women in child-bed light and blanched and steeping, shutting themselves in. But one must also have been beside the dying, must have sit beside the dead in a room with open windows and fitful noises. And still it is not yet enough to have memories. One must be able to forget them when they are many and one must have the immense patience to wait until they come again. For it is the memories themselves that matter only when they have turned to blood within us, to be distinguished from ourselves only then can it happen that in a most rare hour the first word of a poem arises in their midst and goes forth from them".

From all these comments and dictums what come clearly to us is an impression that analytical approach of the image or estimate of the image draws us very near to the pompous and majestic world of literary criticism. Even if we analyse the poetic image of Rabindranath by radical principles of criticism, we see that worshipping faculty of criticism is to a greater extent identical with the analytical approach or estimate of the poetic image. We, therefore conclude with the maxim that analytical approach or estimate of the poetic image is closely related to the art of literary criticism. We must bear in mind, that a poem is not an abstract idea or a bare isolated fact, but an assemblage of figures, scenes, actions and events, above all a consummate and lively image, which already appeal to emotional imagination; and it is already in some degree organized and formed.

All these have a strong bearing on the poetic image and art of criticism.

Notes and References

1. *The Lyric,* J. Drinkwater
2. *History of Indian Poetics—The Origin and Growth of Poetics,* P.V. Kane.
3. *On the Poetry of Pope,* G. Tillotson, p. 92.
4. *Imagery in Poetry—An Indian Approach,* Dr. R.R. Mukherjee
5. *Ode on a Grecian Urn.* Keats
6. *The Design of the Image,* Dr. R.R. Mukherjee
7. *Ibid.*
8. *Ibid.*
9. *Ibid.*
10. *Ibid.*
11. *A Study of Wordsworth* –J.C. Smith.
12. *Image and Experience* –Greham Hough
13. *Indian Aesthetics and Science of Language,* Tarapada Chakraborty
14. Quotation taken from the Book *Poetic Image* –C.D. Lewis
15. *Poetic Image* – C.D. Lewis
16. *Sensitive Plant-* P.B. Shelley
17. "Alankara and Aesthetic Realisation", In the Journal- *Anviksa* – by Dr. R.R. Mukherjee, Vol VI- 1972
18. *Poetic Image* –C.D.Lewis
19. *Ibid.*
20. *Alankara and Aesthetic Realisation-* Dr. R.R. Mukherjee in *Anviksha,* Vol VI -1972
21. 'Invocation'- Francis Brett Young.
22. *Ullysis,* Tennyson
23. *Poetic Image,* C.D. Lewis.
24. *Don Juan* –Lord Byron
25. *Imagery in Poetry- An Indian Apprroach,* Dr. R.R. Mukherjee.

26. *Ibid.*
27. *The Language of Renaissance Poetry* –A.C.Partridge
28. *Imagery in Poetry,* Dr. S. Bhattacharjee
29. *Imagery in Mahabharata,* Dr. S. Bhattacharjee
30. *Beauty Bathing-* Anthony Munday
31. *Poems-* Rabindranath Tagore No. 11 English Verson (Visva-Bharati)
32. *Points of View* – p.38- T.S.Eliot
33. *Romeo and Juliet* –Shakespeare
34. *Poetic Image*-C.D.Lewis
35. *Ibid.*
36. *Ibid.*
37. *Ibid.*
38. *Imagery in Poetry,* Dr. R.R. Mukherjee
39. *Meghduta- Purbamegha,* Quotation for the book *Imagery in Poetry,* Dr. R.R. Mukherjee
40. *Ibid.*
41. *Ibid.*
42. *What is Poetry?* – L. Hunt
43. *Ibid.*
44. *Imagery of Shakespeare's Tragedies-* C.F.E. Spurgion.
46. *Ibid.*
47. *Poetic Image* – C.D. Lewis.
48. *Poetry* – Dr. R.R. Mukherjee
49. *King's The Bride Reluctant* – Harriet Eleanor Hamilton.
50. *An Artist in Life* — Dr. Niharranjan Ray
51. Leading Motive in Imagery of Shakespeare's Tragedies – C.F.E. Spurgeon.
52. *An Artist in Life* – Dr. N.R. Ray
53. Imagery in Poetry – Dr. R.R. Mukherjee
54. *Principles of Literary Criticism* – I.A. Richards
55. *The Use of poetry and the use of Criticism* – T. S. Eliot.
56. The Art of T. S. Eliot – Helen Gardner.
57. *Rabindra Bharati Journal* – No. IV 1971 – Rendered in English by Sudhansu Mohan Banerjee.
58. *The poet Choucer – Tales and Tellers* – Nevill Coghill
59. *Essays in Criticism* – M. Arnold Second Series.
60. *A Critical History of English Poetry* – H. Grierson and G.C. Smith
61 *Notebook of Multi Laurids Bridge* – Rilke.
62. *A History of Modern Criticism* – Rene Wellek
63. *Sanchayita* (Selected poems of Rabindranath).
64. *Art and Society : Essays in Marxist Aesthetics by:* Adolfo Sanchez Vasquez Translated by Maro Riofrancos.

A Bibliography of Tagore's Works

A
Atmasakti
Achalayatan
Adhunik Sahitya
Ashramer Swarup o Bikash
Atma Parichaya

B
Bichitra Prabandha
Banaphul
Bouthakuranir hat
Bisarsjan
Baikunther Khata
Balaka
Bhagna Hridaya
Bharatbarsha
Bansuri
Banabani
Basanta
Bithika
Byango Koutuk
Bangla Bhasa Parichay
Bichitrita
Brahmacharya Ashram

C
Chandalika
Chitra
Chitrangada
Chaitali
Chrokumar Sabha
Chaturanga
Chabi O Gan
Char Adhyay
Chara
Chanda
Christa
Chelebela

D
Dui Bon

E
Europe Prabasir Patra
Europe Prabasir Diary

F
Falguni

G
Gitanjali
Gitimalya
Gitali
Gora
Guru
Galpa Salpa
Galpa Guchcha
Ghare Baire

H
Hasya Koutuk

J
Jibandebata
Jibansmriti

K
Karuna
Kabikahini
Kalpana
Kanika
Kahini
Katha
Khapchara
Kalmrigaya

L
Letters
Lok Sahitya

M
Mayar Khela
Malini
Mukut
Muktadhara
Malancha
Mahuya
Muktir Upaya
Mahatma Gandhi

N
Noukadubi
Nalina
Nabin
Nabajatak
Naibedya

P
Prithiraj Parajaya
Prabhat Sangit
Prajapatir Nirbandha
Prayaschitya
Prakitir Pratisodh
Prahasini
Patraput
Parashye
Punascha
Palataka
Purabi
Parishesha
Paritran

R
Rajapraja
Raja
Rajarashi
Religion
Rakta Karabi
Russiar Chithi
Rudra Chanda
Rog Sayaya
River

S
Sandhya Sangit
Sonartari
Swadesh
Sishu Sahitya
Sahityer Pathe
Sodhbodh
Seser Kabita
Saisab Sangit
Samabainiti

T
Tapati
Tinsangi

U
Utsanga

V
Vanusingher Padabali
Valimiki Pratibha

Y
Yogajog

Index